The Antifederalists

The Antifederalists

Men of Great Faith and Forbearance

David J. Siemers

A Madison House Book

ROWMAN & LITTLEFIELD PUBLISHERS, INC.
Lanham • Boulder • New York • Oxford

ROWMAN & LITTLEFIELD PUBLISHERS, INC.

Published in the United States of America
by Rowman & Littlefield Publishers, Inc.
A wholly owned subsidiary of The Rowman & Littlefield Publishing Group, Inc.
4501 Forbes Boulevard, Suite 200, Lanham, Maryland 20706
www.rowmanlittlefield.com

PO Box 317
Oxford
OX2 9RU, UK

British Library Cataloguing in Publication Information Available

Library of Congress Cataloging-in-Publication Data

Siemers, David J.
  The Antifederalists: Men of Great Faith and Forbearance / David J.
Siemers.
     p. cm.
Includes bibliographical references and index.
  ISBN 0-7425-2259-8 (alk. paper)—ISBN 0-7425-2260-1 (pbk.: alk.
paper)
  1. United States—Politics and government—1783–1789. 2.
Constitutional history—United States. I. Title.
  JK116.S53 2003
  320.473′049′09033–dc21

                                                    2003004360

Printed in the United States of America.

∞™ The paper used in this publication meets the minimum requirements
of American National Standard for Information Sciences—Permanence of
Paper for Printed Library Materials, ANSI/NISO Z39.48-1992.

Contents

Preface

The first phrase in the Constitution is "We the People of the United States." This opening is logical, but critics of the Constitution disliked it. What was the problem with those seven seemingly innocuous words? To these critics, the phrase threatened the fundamental accomplishment of the American Revolution. To most of these "Antifederalists," the greatest benefit of the recently completed war was that it took power from a distant, centralized government ruling over a vast area, the British Empire, and resituated it in much smaller political communities, the individual states. Each state was distinctive, possessing its own political culture. For instance, the interests of Massachusetts, with its Puritan heritage and its thriving manufacturing and trading economy, were far different from Virginia's tobacco plantation culture. Only if each individual state were able to make its own laws, reflecting its particular interests and values, could government truly be popular.[1]

In the 1760s and 1770s, the British king and Parliament had provoked the colonies by limiting their ability to govern themselves. The revolution reestablished self-rule in the individual states. When the Federalists proposed a stronger national government in the Constitution, many Americans feared that this recentralization of power would threaten the popular governments established in the states, just as the British imperial government had threatened them in the previous decades. If Virginians and Rhode Islanders and Pennsylvanians would all be governed by the same set of laws, those laws would not reflect their individual state's culture. If the laws did not reflect the interests and values of a state, could it really be a government "of the people"? Tyranny could just as easily be imposed from an American capital as it had been from London. In objecting to the Constitution, the Anti-federalists hoped to preserve state autonomy against another external assault. They literally thought that they were conserving the result of the American Revolution.

In 1776, each individual state had declared independence; they did not declare independence as the collected "people of the United States."[2] In subsequent years, state autonomy had been preserved by the first American constitution, the Articles of Confederation. Under it, each state retained its own final decision-making power or sovereignty.[3] For example, the Congress authorized by the Articles could not tax the states; it could only request funds from them. Only the individual states possessed the power to tax. Each state also possessed a single vote in the Congress, emblematic of their equal status as independent political bodies. Thus, when it came to important decisions, a small state had as much say in the Confederation as a large one because they were both sovereign. As long as that was the case, no combination of states could coerce another one into taking a step so momentous as adopting a new constitution. But by writing "We the People of the United States," the Federalists implied that a majority of Americans could coerce the inhabitants of all the constituent states. The initial words of the Constitution signified that the nation and *its* people were sovereign, rather than the individual states and their people. Throughout the document, Antifederalists found a good deal more evidence that Federalists hoped to consolidate the thirteen states into a single political entity, thus threatening popular government.

The Constitution was ratified despite Antifederalist objections. Nevertheless, the Antifederalists are not merely of interest as historical figures; they helped shape the American regime along with the Federalists. Attention to this group gives us greater insight into the Constitution and a richer perspective on why the American government developed as it did. Further, the ratification fight is a particularly instructive episode in learning how politics works. Both Federalists and Antifederalists came to their respective positions because of a complex mix of personal interests, values, and the more systematic, abstract thinking about politics that academics label "political theory." Forging a collective outcome from a vast array of individual positions required painstaking effort. Each side needed to compromise internally as well as with the other camp to be successful. Both groups attempted to simultaneously outflank and discredit their opponents. All practiced politics—the art or skill of producing a defined, preferred outcome when faced with countless options.

The interaction between political theory and political practice that took place during this era is particularly interesting. Evolving political contexts altered responses even from those who consistently held to a single set of political ideals. While many possessed coherent ideals, the compromises that are inherently a part of practical politics induced them to order and prioritize among their ideals. For the Antifederalists, ratification ultimately confirmed how important it was to preserve the Union, to respect the rule of law, to act as "good citizens," and to avoid civil war. These core values led the Antifederalists to abide by the Constitution once ratified, despite its flaws. They vowed to work for change from within the system, and it is that pledge that earns them the title of "men of great faith and forbearance."[4] They toiled to create a workable government from a plan they thought very inadequate. They did so by trying to obtain amendments, but they also did so more subtly, by defining the meaning of the document.

The contest over the Constitution's meaning continued long after the Antifederalists passed from the political stage. Redefining the Constitution continues to this day; it is a distinctive aspect of American politics that the Antifederalists were the first to pursue. Thus, the final lesson to be learned from ratification is that events we consider great landmarks of political life are not fully determinative. We might think of the Constitution's ratification as an event with a very well-defined meaning, but ratification was in many ways nebulous. In writing the Constitution, the Federalists avoided many issues that threatened to split their coalition apart. Antifederalists exploited this vagueness. They also adopted Federalist reassurances about the document to construct a vision of American politics in which the states and the nation shared sovereignty and in which national powers were strictly limited. The Jeffersonian Republican party, with many former Antifederalists among them, gained majority status after the watershed election of 1800. In subsequent decades, the Constitution would be used in a way that satisfied Antifederalists more than Federalists.

This book elaborates on these themes. Particular attention will be paid to different forms of Antifederalism and to the chronological development of the ratification fight. By doing so, I hope to develop a more well-rounded picture of Antifederalist political thinking than has previously been presented in a work like this and a better feel for the politics of the era. To develop a sense of the figures we are dealing with, the first chapter of the book consists of my commentary on the Antifederalists. Its opening section defines who the Antifederalists were. I then stake out their basic position, focusing on what united all—or nearly all—of the Constitution's critics. After that, I'll complicate things a bit by discussing matters about which they did not agree. These disagreements point to three distinct strands of Antifederalism.[5] Subsequently, I'll describe the evolving political context faced by the Antifederalists. This section will show how the critics of the Constitution adjusted their arguments to fit with the changing situations they faced and at the same time remained true to their core political principles. Finally, I will comment on the strengths and weaknesses of the Antifederalist argument and its importance to American politics today.

The remaining six chapters consist of excerpts from Antifederalist writings and speeches with brief introductions about them. In chapter 2, I present excerpts from speeches presented at the Philadelphia convention. Those who would become its critics could not have known they would spearhead a movement against the Constitution, but their arguments in Philadelphia are consistent with the lines of commentary they would develop in the succeeding months. Chapter 3 collects the most widely known and reprinted Antifederalist commentaries as a "contemporaneous canon." As today, many citizens paid only slight attention to politics. If such citizens were to read just a few Antifederalist arguments, these were likely the ones they read. Chapters 4, 5, and 6 are devoted to the three major strands of Antifederalist commentary. Chapter 4 offers a middle-class, populist version of Antifederalism. The next chapter presents a much more virulent strain of commentary, which treated the Constitution as a conspiracy of the "well-born" to subvert democracy. These writers doubted that even an amended Constitution could usher in a national regime that was "democratical" in nature. A different view is offered in chapter 6, in which elite politicians critique the Constitution. This last group also faulted the Constitution for being aristocratically oriented, but they would have been content with a single democratic branch in the national government. These men hoped the House of Representatives would be that democratic branch and that it would be balanced by the more aristocratic Senate and an independent Executive. The main thrust of this last group's commentary was that the Constitution could be salvaged as long as representation in the House was increased to better reflect popular desires. A final chapter explores the post-ratification reactions of the Antifederalists as indicative of their moderate, forbearing nature.

This book also has three appendixes. The first appendix presents two "spurious" letters, representing two kinds of documents: those written by Federalists posing as Antifederalists and those that Antifederalists penned while pretending to be Federalists. These letters indicate that the ratification era was not always high-toned but that it also contained its share of political trickery and even mudslinging. The second appendix is a ratification chronology, which lists important milestones and the dates of publication for the items included in this volume. Referencing this chronology will help to keep straight the different contexts faced by the Antifederalists. Finally, a copy of the Constitution is included. When a writer references a specific clause of the Constitution, I will provide a citation so that you can find the precise words being discussed.

"We the People" should be familiar with the Antifederalists' arguments. They presented visions of how to preserve government "of the people." In our cynical age, their faith in and concern for popular government is worth reconsidering.

NOTES

1. Notice that I have used the qualifiers "many" and "most" when dealing with the Antifederalists. Though it is fair to say that all Antifederalists wanted to preserve some form of state autonomy, going beyond that statement is tricky. As will be noted in this preface, theirs was a diverse group, as were the Federalists. Some Antifederalists were mildly opposed to the Constitution; others were much more vehement. A big reason for this variance was the degree to which they wished to preserve state sovereignty. Some argued that the states should be sovereign, independent unto themselves; most were willing to cede some defined sovereign powers to the national government, as long as the states retained the bulk of their independent abilities to legislate; a few were comfortable with a relatively powerful national government as long as it was properly constituted.

2. In the first week of July, 1776, twelve states declared independence simultaneously, but separately. New York abstained because the state's delegation to the Second Continental Congress had not received authorization from the state government to declare independence. Almost immediately upon hearing of the issuance of the Declaration of Independence, New York declared independence as well.

3. Many disputed whether the Articles of Confederation in fact preserved the sovereign independence of the individual states entirely. The nation arguably had sovereign powers too, particularly in the ability to prosecute the Revolutionary War. Nevertheless, the states did retain the majority of key powers. Though it was not clearly settled by the Articles or by common agreement, the Articles did allow Antifederalists to believe and make a plausible claim that each state was a separate, fully sovereign entity.

4. My title is intended to be a counterpoint to Cecelia Kenyon's oft-repeated view that the Antifederalists were "Men of Little Faith," to quote from the title of her influential *William & Mary Quarterly* article.

5. These three strands of Antifederalism correspond to those identified by Saul Cornell in his book *The Other Founders*.

Acknowledgments

Time is our most precious commodity and I would like to thank those who gave of this valuable resource to help me write this book. Sid Milkis first suggested that I compile a volume of Antifederalist writings. To Sid it probably seemed an obvious suggestion because of the research I did for an earlier book, *Ratifying the Republic* (Stanford University Press, 2002), but it had not crossed my mind. This book would not exist without his encouragement.

My knowledge of the Antifederalists was honed at the Center for the Study of the Constitution in Madison, Wisconsin. While I have aimed to present a well-rounded picture of Antifederalist thought in this short volume, their series, *The Documentary History of the Ratification*, is the definitive comprehensive source for ratification debate documents. John Kaminski, the director of the Center, knows more about the ratification process than anyone ever has—or likely ever will again. He is a great resource. I thank him for encouraging my interest in the Antifederalists, for suggesting I publish with Rowman & Littlefield, and for his substantive comments on chapter and document introductions.

Curtis Cook, Laura Olson, and Adam Fink each read the first chapter and provided suggestions that clarified my prose and strengthened my argument. Curtis led me to take more care in using terminology describing the exercise of power. Laura recognized where my argument lacked punch and made valuable remedial suggestions. Adam helped me understand and alter what might not have made sense to an undergraduate audience. Each of them helped me improve the introductory chapter, for which I am grateful, as I am for their friendship. Booth Fowler also read the original introductory chapter and gave it the good wringing out it deserved. My expression is much clearer as a result of his suggestions.

My father, Roger Siemers, proofread the document with a keen eye and helped me compile the index. I am now indebted to him professionally, as I am in every other way.

Several scholars spurred my interest in the Antifederalists and I would be remiss to not mention Gordon Wood and Lance Banning as foremost among them. I also relied heavily on Saul Cornell's argument about the Antifederalists from his book *The Other Founders* (University of North Carolina Press, 1999) and I appreciate our continuing dialogue on the early republic. The staff at Rowman & Littlefield, particularly my editor Mary Carpenter, have been both helpful and easy to work with. Above all, I thank them for recognizing that a new collection of Antifederalist documents was needed.

Three institutions deserve thanks. I have spent countless hours in the Wisconsin State Historical Society. Their resources and staff have been a great help to me for years. I received a faculty research grant from The Colorado College enabling me to travel to Madison to finalize the documents I have included here. I can't think of a better place to have worked. A faculty development grant from the University of Wisconsin–Oshkosh enabled me to concentrate on writing the volume's introduction. I am proud that my home institution recognizes the value of scholarship and the value of this project in particular.

Needless to say, this book would not exist without the Antifederalists. I admire and respect their patriotism, even as I simultaneously judge them as a scholar. Finally, I dedicate this book to my students. Alexis de Tocqueville once wrote that "without politics the Americans would lose half of their existence." Absent my students, present and past, I would surely lose as much.

Editing Note

The ratification debate occurred at a time before spelling had been systematized. Thus, when reading the original documents contained here, you will often find spellings different from those accepted today. Except where there were obvious typographical errors, I have retained the original spellings used by those who first wrote or printed these documents. Additionally, some of the wording might strike students as arcane, but I have retained original language, believing this practice necessary to preserving the ideas of the ratification era. Occasionally, abbreviations are used, and where the full word is not obvious, I have supplicd the missing letters in brackets. I have added ellipses to denote where I have edited the text.

The Antifederalists:
Men of Great Faith and Forbearance

Who were the Antifederalists? The Antifederalists were simply those who opposed the unamended Constitution as a proposal. Notice the two qualifiers in that last sentence. First, note that the Constitution was opposed as a *proposal*. The Constitution was formulated in Philadelphia during the spring and summer of 1787, and it was made public in mid-September. Nine states had to ratify the document for it to go into effect among the ratifying states, and the ninth state to do so was New Hampshire in June 1788. New Hampshire's ratification meant that in the nine ratifying states, the Constitution was no longer a proposal but a legal document, even though it was not yet implemented. This change in status altered how Antifederalists treated the Constitution. They noted that the document had been sanctioned by a popular political process, and they reasoned that citizens in popular governments could not oppose laws created by proper means simply because they disagreed with them.[1] To continue to dispute the Constitution, even though it was severely flawed, would set an anarchical precedent and probably lead to civil war.[2] Responsible citizens, like they were, would not risk provoking civil war. For all but a very few, the legal status of the Constitution meant that the document would have to be accepted. Changes would have to be fought for from within its bounds.

This change in approach is so significant, that to continue to label these individuals Antifederalists would be misleading. After New Hampshire's ratification, it is proper to call them "former Antifederalists."[3] This label has the advantage of recognizing that the group remained true to its principles while responding to a changed context by accepting the Constitution's requirements. The nation and its leaders had moved forward from the particular context where Antifederalists opposed Federalists on whether to ratify.[4] Thus, in most states, the period in which one could be an Antifederalist was relatively short, about nine months—but there were exceptions. Virginia and New York ratified the Constitution rather quickly after the ninth state did so. North Carolina and Rhode Island took much longer, only entering the Union in late 1789 and mid-1790, respectively, after the new government was already underway. While the Antifederalist movement lasted a short time, the political careers of most of its leaders included the years before and after ratification.

Antifederalists also opposed the *unamended* Constitution. They did not like the document as it was written. Federalists initially offered ratification as an either/or proposition: either states could accept the Constitution, or they could reject it. Because the Articles of Confederation were considered fundamentally flawed by almost everyone, this tactic proved to be shrewd. Rejecting the Constitution meant continuing to operate under the flawed Articles of Confederation, thus making it appear as if critics were defending the indefensible. When presented with such a choice, Antifederalists chose to reject the Constitution anyway. However, many hoped for a third alternative: improve the Constitution by amending it. While some thought the document was flawed beyond redemption, milder Antifederalists were satisfied simply by the promise of a few key amendments. Starting with Massachusetts' ratification in February 1788, ratifying states recommended amendments along with ratification. These amendments were not legally binding; they were simply suggestions the new Congress was expected to consider. The so-called recommendatory amendments allowed ratification to occur in several states—where the Antifederalists were probably a majority, albeit a slim one—including the critical, populous states of Virginia and Massachusetts, as well as New Hampshire and New York. In these and the late-ratifying states (where political pressure was mounting), the mildest of the Antifederalists actually voted to ratify.

The label "Antifederalist" can be applied to both political leaders and average citizens, but it is usually easier to identify whether a political elite opposed the Constitution. First, evidence of a leader's position was more likely to have been recorded and preserved. Second, on such a visible issue, it was necessary for public figures to take a stand, whereas average citizens might pay little attention or simply equivocate. Although the positions of some public figures are obscure, some of America's best-known political figures were among those who opposed the unamended Constitution. The great organizer of the Revolution, Samuel Adams of Massachusetts, was an Antifederalist.[5] So too was Virginia's renowned orator Patrick Henry. George Clinton, New York's longtime governor, led the Antiferalists there. A key voice in the convention that declared independence in 1776, Richard Henry Lee, was also an Antifederalist. These individuals were just one level below the stature of the nation's two best-known and most respected figures, George Washington and Benjamin Franklin, both of whom favored the Constitution. Leaders who would later occupy the topmost offices in the land were among the Antifederalists as well. James Monroe, later president, opposed the Constitution as a young Virginia legislator, as did John Quincy Adams, who was studying to be a lawyer during the ratification debate. Hundreds of other active politicians opposed the Constitution. Although most are now obscure, they were nonetheless important political figures in their time.

Though it is harder to discern whether common citizens were Antifederalists, there were many of them, perhaps even a majority nationwide. Some wrote newspaper pieces. In a few towns, popular protests were staged against the Constitution. Rhode Island held a referendum in which citizens themselves voted directly on whether the document should be ratified (it lost overwhelmingly). The most important sign of public opinion, however, was who they elected to ratification conventions. Citizens who objected to the Constitution elected delegates who promised to oppose ratification. A pattern emerges from this kind of analysis, with a few exceptions: Federalists were concentrated on the Atlantic coast while the Antifederalist strongholds were inland.[6]

This "coastal versus inland" pattern is not a fluke. The Constitution promised to solidify the nation's economic health. Such an upturn would spur commerce. The nation's major commercial centers were its coastal cities and the areas immediately around them. People in these areas recognized that the Constitution would likely benefit their local economy. Away from the coast, the economy tended to be dominated by small farms, which would not immediately benefit from more commercial activity. In these areas, fears over losing local political control trumped any hope of economic benefit. Though the Antifederalists tended to win where small farms were predominant, it would be a mistake to conclude that they were simply a group of small farmers or that personal economics inevitably dictated individual positions. Artisans and craftsmen were included among the Antifederalists, as well as prominent lawyers and plantation owners. Elbridge Gerry was among the nation's wealthiest men, and he was a merchant who lived in coastal Massachusetts. All personal considerations would seem to dictate that Gerry would favor the Constitution, but he in fact opposed it (see chapters 2, 3, and 6). The "coastal versus inland" pattern hindered the Antifederalists. Most state capitals were situated on or very near the Atlantic coast, and with them the political power in most states was disproportionately concentrated along the coast. So too was capital, thus allowing newspapers to flourish on the coast, while they were scarce inland. Most of the ninety-plus newspapers in print during the ratification debate clearly favored the Constitution. Only a half-dozen were clearly against the Constitution, and another half-dozen or so printed items from both the Federalists and the Antifederalists. The Federalists won the newspaper war even before the ratification debate had begun, a critical factor in their success.

In addition to considerations of household economy, the states themselves had interests. Citizens and the politicians who represented them inevitably weighed these interests in their calculus of whether or not to support the Constitution. Because New Jersey lacked a good harbor, almost all of its imports came through New York City or Philadelphia. These goods were taxed heavily, particularly by New York. In the mid-1780s, New Jersey was experiencing a depression, greatly exacerbated because New York was bleeding revenue out of the state. The Constitution promised to lift this burden from New Jersey, as states would not be allowed to tax imports. Thus, when its state convention met, delegates unanimously favored ratification. Although leaders had certain qualms with the document, New Jersey's particular political situation made only one stance viable, given a forced choice of whether or not to ratify. Those standing for election to ratification conventions were politicians. Like politicians of today, they did not wish to be caught on the "wrong side" of a key debate. Taking an unpopular stance on such a visible issue could threaten their reputation and destroy their political careers.

New York, meanwhile, was strongly Antifederalist, precisely because the status quo's taxation arrangement benefited it. Cantankerous Rhode Island jealously guarded its autonomy and was overwhelmingly Antifederalist. North Carolina was also dominated by opponents of the Constitution. Its Outer Banks formed a barrier that kept the state's coast from being highly integrated with other coastal areas. Its geography thus encouraged an agrarian political economy, and even those in its coastal regions tended to oppose the Constitution. Every state but Delaware, New Jersey, and Georgia contained a significant Antifederalist presence. The critics of the Constitution were clearly outnumbered in four other states as well: Pennsylvania, Connecticut, Maryland, and South Carolina. Among the seven states that were clearly Federalist-oriented, only Pennsylvania was a large state in terms of population. Massachusetts, New Hampshire, and Virginia were tightly contested, with probable Antifederalist majorities absent an agreement to suggest amendments. Virginia was by far the most populous state, containing about a fifth of the nation's population. Massachusetts had the second-largest number of inhabitants. There were clear Antifederalist majorities in the fourth-largest state, North Carolina, the fifth-largest state, New York, and in little Rhode Island.[7]

Each state's political and economic context was different, and each contributed to how the Constitution was received. At the same time, political principles were important, too. Antifederalist leaders frequently referenced Enlightenment philosophers, British legal experts, the Bible, and even ancient Romans. The Antifederalists' purpose in referencing such works was to bolster their persuasiveness, of course, but their treatment of outside sources was generally cursory. The Antifederalists rarely drew out implications or fine shades of meaning, preferring to stick to the main thrust of an argument. Use of outside sources did far more than shore up their argument, though; it actively shaped it. The Antifederalists' most reliable themes and assumptions were based on the works that very many had read and that they thought provided timeless insights about politics. Even those who had not read the aforementioned authors had been influenced by their ideas, which were frequently voiced in "layman's terms."[8]

The Antifederalists did not choose their name. Shrewdly, the Federalists saddled them with a name that sounds negative. The word "federal" had a very positive connotation for post-Revolution Americans, and the Federalists appropriated it for themselves. The word "federal" was originally used to describe a league of sovereign states united in a military or trade alliance. The politicians of the ratification era might describe today's European Union or the NATO alliance as a federation. The Revolution was thought to have established a *federal* republic, and politicians in the late 1770s and early 1780s emphasized how beneficial it was to have a federal government, in contrast to the centralized government the British attempted to impose. Labeling someone "Antifederal" indicated that the person was against something commonly accepted as a great strength of the American system.[9]

In reality, the Federalists were the ones with a questionable commitment to a "federal" government as it was generally understood at the time, for they worked to make the tie between the states more than just a league or agreement among sovereign states. In appropriating the term "federal" for themselves, they redefined the word.[10] Today, we use the word "confederation" to describe what "federation" originally meant. The term "federal" is presently used to describe an arrangement where a national government shares power with geographical subunits, like states. Antifederalists grumbled about this propagandizing but never succeeded in redefining themselves with a more positive label. Many current commentators include a hyphen in their name (i.e., "Anti-Federalist" or "anti-Federalist") to make sure that readers know that the group simply opposed the Federalists rather than opposed federalism as a concept.

Needless to say, there was much to divide a group that included ordinary citizens and political elites, backcountry farmers and plantation owners, and individuals of thirteen different political communities, each with its own traditions, interests, and pressing issues. The Antifederalists were divided among themselves in a variety of ways, and their opponents exploited these fissures. Yet *any* significant political group contains divisions. American political parties, for instance, have always needed to balance disparate regional interests, cultural emphases, and socioeconomic ranks within their coalitions. The fact of Antifederalist diversity is not a stunning revelation, though it should be kept in mind.[11] Of greater value is discerning exactly how the group was divided and how the specific divisions affected the outcome of the ratification process.

The Federalists, too, were severely divided. Just how different James Madison's thinking was from his *Federalist* coauthor Alexander Hamilton became clear in the years immediately following ratification, as they led the opposing Republican and Federalist parties, respectively.[12] While we must acknowledge the diversity within the Antifederalist camp, we must also not lose sight of the fact that there were core objections to the Constitution that nearly all of them agreed upon. The next section describes those core objections and the reasoning behind them.

CORE POSITIONS

According to its critics, the Constitution contained two kinds of errors: errors of commission and errors of omission. They judged parts of it dangerous and in need of modification or elimination, but they also felt important safeguards were left out. The most frequently cited error of commission was the "necessary and proper" clause at the end of Article I, section 8, which defined the legislative powers of Congress. After a fairly lengthy list of specified powers (e.g., "to provide and maintain a navy"), the Constitution gave Congress the authority "to make all Laws which shall be necessary and proper for carrying into Execution the foregoing Powers vested by this Constitution in the Government of the United States." Objections to this clause were bottomed on the then-common assumption that a government's most awesome power was to legislate. Antifederalists considered the legislature the "first branch" of government, the one that was predominant.[13] The executive and judicial branches could enforce and adjudicate the law, but they did not make the law they applied, a key check on them. The legislature, on the other hand, *did* make the law, and if it were allowed to make any law whatsoever, there was theoretically no end to its power. The Antifederalists pointed out that authorizing Congress to make any law it considered "necessary and proper" put no check at all on the most powerful part of government.

The Federalists countered by pointing to the middle part of the clause, the qualifier "for carrying into Execution the foregoing powers." This qualifier meant the clause did not grant power arbitrarily. Rather, it simply confirmed that Congress had the ability to pass laws needed to effectively carry out the various powers listed. Those powers were specific. Congress could not go beyond them. Federalists reassured Americans that the full clause indicated the Constitution contained only defined powers and no implied ones.[14] But Antifederalists protested that the clause would not be used in this way. Its opening words were so clear and emphatic compared with the tangle of language in its middle, that the clause would simply be taken to sanction "all laws" that Congress would want to pass. Antifederalists observed that by design, constitutions were supposed to put limits on government. The key written compacts in British history, like the Magna Charta and English Bill of Rights, did so. Charters had limited England's control over the colonies.[15] To the Antifederalists, the Constitution was a major departure from previous governing charters in that it seemed primarily concerned with granting powers to government rather than defining its limits. The necessary and proper clause was the most egregious example of this newfangled constitutionalism.

True, certain powers were forbidden. Article I, section 9, which was less than half the length of the section that granted powers, listed them. For example, Congress was prohibited from issuing titles of nobility or detaining prisoners without a hearing, except in wartime. Far from being satisfied by these prohibitions, Antifederalist suspicions were aroused by them. If the Constitution had to list the things that Congress could *not* do, then by implication Congress could do all else. If it took an explicit clause of the Constitution to prevent Congress from granting titles of nobility, then it would take an explicit clause to prevent the Congress from limiting freedom of the press. But no such prohibition was in the Constitution, nor were many of the other prohibitions on government that Americans expected as a matter of right. This error was the Philadelphia convention's worst error of omission—the lack of a list, or "bill," of rights, including freedom of the press, freedom of assembly, and freedom of religious practice.

These were rights *against* government. That is, no governing body would have the authority to impose itself upon citizens in certain ways. Such a stance revealed a certain level of suspicion. From the Antifederalist perspective, suspicion of government was both a necessity and a virtue. Almost by definition, governments possess awesome powers: the ability to command armies, to appropriate money in the form of taxes, and to dispense justice. With these powers, governments can determine whether citizens are richer or poorer, whether they are imprisoned or free, and even whether they live or die. With this array of powers, Antifederalists were convinced of the need for a variety of checks on those doing the governing. Several of these checks were mechanical—they could be written into a constitution. A bill of rights was one such check. The clean separation of powers into three branches (legislative, executive, and judicial) was another. But vigilance, a habit of the people rather than a mechanically produced characteristic of government, was vital as well.

The Antifederalists believed themselves to be performing the crucial service of vigilance during the ratification debate, following the advice of a long line of political theorists who warned that if citizens were not vigilant, government would quickly turn from serving the people to serving itself. In forming a constitution, then, a certain amount of rancor was to be expected and would prove to be beneficial. Writing in Boston's *Independent Chronicle*, an Antifederalist who called himself "Candidus" (most Antifederalist and Federalist writers used pseudonyms) noted that "it must be a melancholy crisis when the people are tired of guarding their liberties and are resigned to whatever government is dealt to them."[16] Patrick Henry expressed a similar sentiment at the Virginia convention: "Sir, suspicion is a virtue, as long as its object is the preservation of the public good and as long as it stays within proper bounds."[17] Antifederalists hoped to inspire popular vigilance toward the proposed Constitution. Through their vigilance, the Constitution might be improved, as they could build structural checks into the system of government.

The Antifederalist essayist "Federal Farmer" (see chapter 6) noted what was at stake if such checks were not forced by citizen vigilance:

> If the constitution or social compact be vague and unguarded, then we depend wholly upon the prudence, wisdom and moderation of those

who manage the affairs of government; or on what, probably, is equally uncertain and precarious, the success of the people oppressed by the abuse of government, in receiving it from the hands of those who abuse it, and placing it in the hands of those who use it well.

Without placing checks on leaders, one would have to rely on their native benevolence and selflessness. Certainly there were some leaders who could be trusted to pursue the common good. George Washington was thought to be one such leader, but Washingtons were recognized as rare. It is much more common, Antifederalists thought, for power to be addictive, like a drug. And more often than not, the more expansive the powers an individual or small group possessed, the more likely those powers would be used for self-service. A century before Lord Acton wrote it, the Antifederalists were devotees of the sentiment that "power tends to corrupt and absolute power corrupts absolutely." When the self-serving possess power, the Federal Farmer implies that revolution will be required to place it in better hands—and then the only guarantee is bloodshed, not a successful popular revolution. A proper constitution would make a public-regarding government much more probable, but that required altering the document formulated in Philadelphia, removing some clauses, and adding others not there. After the necessary and proper clause, the Antifederalists trained their suspicion on three general powers that were "vague and unguarded": military power, the ability to tax, and judicial authority.

The nation would have to defend itself at various times, to be sure, and thus would need the ability to raise an army. But the Constitution had granted Congress this power without qualification. Allowing a "standing army" in time of peace would be both expensive and dangerous. Soldiers trained to fight might get restless without an enemy and could be turned on American citizens. Many Antifederalists suggested that a limit be included on how large the armed forces could be in peacetime.

To add insult to possible injury, Antifederalists noted that the national government was not restricted in its ability to tax.[18] The government could oppress its own citizens with its army and also make them pay for that oppression. Most Antifederalists were comfortable with allowing the national government a secure source of revenue; however, the Constitution authorized the national government to levy "direct taxes" on individual citizens. Under this arrangement, Antifederalists feared that the national government's thirst for tax revenue would limit state revenues. To remain viable governments, states needed a secure source of revenue. Antifederalists suggested a logical division between state and national taxation powers: the national government should have exclusive power to tax imports and exports, while the states could tax their citizens directly.

The courts were another cause for concern. Article III, which dealt with the federal courts, was agonizingly vague and brief. It gave federal courts the power to determine both the law and facts of the cases it heard, and it allowed Congress to create such inferior federal courts as it thought necessary. The error of commission here was in giving federal courts jurisdiction over the law and facts of cases.[19] In other words, the federal courts could determine guilt or innocence not merely as an interpreter of the legal and constitutional issues involved, but also by reexamining the particulars of a case. If the federal government degenerated into tyranny, its courts could be used to pass whatever sentences were wished for. Antifederalists also feared that trials would take place outside the parties' local area. There was no guarantee that a federal court would exist even reasonably close to where citizens lived. Not having a case heard reasonably close to home was more than an inconvenience. Removed from one's locality, a person on trial had no guarantee of getting the "jury of one's peers" so indispensable for a fair trial. Jury trials themselves were guaranteed in criminal cases, but not in civil cases, and the Antifederalists objected vehemently to that omission.

The national government's trump card over the states was the "supremacy clause."[20] Its language, coupled with the previously mentioned "unguarded" powers, reinforced the Antifederalists' sense that there would be no limits on the national government and that it would eventually reduce the states to mere administrative units. The clause stated that "this Constitution, and the Laws of the United States which shall be made in Pursuance thereof . . . shall be the supreme Law of the Land; and the Judges in every State shall be bound thereby, any Thing in the Constitution or Laws of any State to the Contrary notwithstanding." The national government could not only raise an army of unlimited size (even in peacetime), tax citizens until they were penniless, and drag them before courts far from their home, but it could also make any law it deemed "necessary and proper" and have that law supersede any contradictory state laws. This writ was not a prescription for sharing powers between levels of government, as the Federalists had promised; it was a prescription for a single consolidated national government.

All this worrying revolved around a rather simple premise: representation would fail on the national level. Antifederalists had few illusions about the potential selfishness of human nature. Politicians in particular were viewed skeptically. Critics of the Constitution thought the states were better suited to checking the inherent ambition of politicians and the tendency of power to corrupt. State legislators returned to their home districts between legislative sessions, allowing them to get a sense of what their constituents were thinking on the issues of the day. Mingling with ordinary citizens exerted beneficial peer pressure on the representatives. State legislators would want their neighbors to continue to think highly of them and would thus favor laws that promoted the good of their constituents. For most national representatives, the national capital would take weeks to travel to, no matter where it was placed. This logistical difficulty would likely prevent them from frequently mingling with their constituents. Representatives would find it more difficult to discern what constituents were thinking, and they would feel less social pressure to pursue the people's interests.

Further, long terms would also serve to limit attention to the public's wishes. In many states, elections were held annually to allow or to force the populace to assess how their representatives were performing. Connecticut and Rhode Island had even shortened their legislative terms to six months. But the Constitution set Senate terms at six years and the president's at four. With such lengthy terms, a politician's prospects were not tied so securely to the pursuit of the common good. A senator might easily get away with many votes cast at the expense of his constituents, even on measures where he stood to gain personally from the legislation. Critics suggested shortening term lengths, particularly for senators. They also proposed "rotation" out of office, or what we call term limits. Rotation would ensure that today's representative would be tomorrow's private citizen. The prospect of an inevitable return to one's home district would exert more beneficial, community-regarding peer pressure on them. The Antifederalists also feared that a chief executive who was "perpetually reeligible" could use the advantages of incumbency to be reelected over and over. Rotation would also ensure that the presidency would not develop into a monarchy.

Even with these modifications, the Antifederalists doubted that national representation would work. They were pessimistic for two reasons: they believed that Congress would be populated almost exclusively by a wealthy "aristocracy," and they also believed that the states were so different that an effective national government could not be composed of them. The Constitution set the number of senators at two per state and initially allotted each state a set number of seats in the House of Representatives. If all the states ratified the Constitution, the first Senate would consist of twenty-six individuals, and the first House would have sixty-five occupants. These numbers were far too small, particularly the sixty-five in the House of Representatives. Tiny Rhode Island had an assembly of seventy; Virginia had a House of Delegates of 150; and Massachusetts had a House of Representatives of 400. As Virginia's Richard Henry Lee put it, the House provided "a mere shred or rag of representation" (see chapter 3).

The Federalists noted that each chamber would grow along with the country, with each new state adding two to the total number in the Senate and with reapportionment expanding the House based on total national population following each census. This format, however, did not satisfy the Antifederalists. The First Congress was crucial, as it would set the tone and establish precedents for the new government. The Antifederalists believed that afterward there would still be too many constituents per legislator for effective representation. In New York's ratifying convention, Melancton Smith noted that "a substantial yeoman, of sense and discernment will hardly ever be chosen" (see chapter 4). The Federal Farmer added that "it is deceiving a people to tell them they are electors, and can choose their legislators, if they cannot, in the nature of things choose men from among themselves and genuinely like themselves" (see chapter 6). How were these observers so sure that few "average" people would be chosen to serve in Congress? In the Senate, elections were indirect. The people did not vote for Senators; rather, the state legislatures selected them. Antifederalists suspected they would select two of the most eminent and wealthy men in each state, who would have different interests from most citizens.[21]

The House would consist of no more than one member for every thirty thousand citizens. Antifederalists reasoned that only prominent lawyers, or military heroes, or the most prosperous merchants in a state could possibly be known by enough people to get elected. The Congress would not be a representative cross-section of American society. The small size of the House dictated that it would also be aristocratically skewed. At the very least, Antifederalists agreed, the House needed to be significantly expanded to allow average citizens an opportunity to have a hand in government policy and to reflect the tremendous diversity among the states.

A larger House would prove beneficial, but it could not solve a more fundamental problem. As noted earlier, the Antifederalists were very aware of each state's distinctive nature. Although the states were relatively homogeneous internally, they were unlike one another. Thirteen distinctive states could only be brought together if the particular values and interests of each state were compromised. Only a broad coalition of states could pass any legislation on the national level. Forging these broad coalitions would require so much compromise from each state that the result could hardly be said to reflect their people's wishes. John Francis Mercer succinctly summarized this view (see chapter 3):

> We are persuaded that the People of so large a Continent, so different in Interests, so distinct in Habits, cannot in all cases legislate in one Body by themselves or their representatives—By themselves it is obviously impracticable—By their Representatives it will be found on Investigation equally so—for if these representatives are to pursue the general Interest . . . it must be done by a mutual sacrifice of the Interests, wishes, and prejudices of the parts they represented—and then they cannot be said to represent those Parts, but to misrepresent them.[22]

Such misrepresentation could be prevented by securing state power. Many Antifederalists suggested that an amendment be ratified explicitly acknowledging the Federalist pledges that the national government was one of specified powers and that all powers not mentioned in the Constitution were reserved to the states or the people. Such an amendment would keep the state governments viable, protecting their "interests, wishes, and prejudices."

With aristocratic national representatives, Antifederalists doubted that the American people would consider the new national government "theirs." Some wealthy individuals would champion popular causes, but they would likely be overwhelmed by those who would promote policies that benefited themselves. Some Antifederalists thought this was a Federalist conspiracy, but most believed it would naturally result from a legislature populated by the well-off. They matter-of-factly quoted Britain's Judge Blackstone who had written, "it is not to be expected in human nature, that the few should always be attentive to the good of the many" (see chapter 3).

Aristocratically tilted policies, whether a result of a self-serving conspiracy or not, would take a toll on the confidence Americans would have in their government. That word, *confidence,* was used over and over by Antifederalists to indict the Constitution. The Antifederalists reasoned that the people would consider the government and its laws "theirs," or they would not. Once they realized how skewed toward the rich the new government was, they would almost surely *not* consider it theirs. And when that happened, the laws would have to be forced on the people rather than be willingly obeyed. The great promise that there could be viable popular governments would give way to another type of state all too familiar in human history, the military regime.

A final objection to the Constitution was its unfortunate mixing of legislative and executive powers. The ideas of the British political philosopher John Locke played a key role in the shape of this complaint. Locke, like the Antifederalists, felt that the concentration of power was particularly dangerous. He reasoned that preventing tyranny required that governmental powers should be strictly separated into legislative and executive functions. If this separation were accomplished, no one person or group could both make the law and enforce it, thus lessening the possibility of tyranny. To Antifederalists, the problem with the Constitution was that it often combined legislative and executive functions in a single institution. The Senate was given the responsibility of giving "Advice and Consent" to the president on treaties and in filling national offices, both executive and judicial.[23] The president was dealt a legislative role: the Constitution explicitly asked him to "recommend to their [Congress'] consideration such Measures as he shall judge necessary and expedient" and granted him veto power over legislation.[24] The vice president, an executive officer, was the presiding officer of the Senate, a legislative body.[25] These combined powers frightened the Antifederalists. They frequently expressed fears that the president and Senate would combine to dominate the new government, or even that the Senate could dominate by itself.

Two other matters of agreement among Antifederalists are often overlooked because they are not criticisms of the Constitution. First, almost all agreed that the Articles of Confederation were in need of significant reforms. Two reforms in particular were thought necessary: granting the national government a secure source of revenue and allowing it to regulate interstate commerce. Through the 1780s, a near-national consensus favored granting the central government "impost" power, or the power to tax imports. The practice of asking (or "requisitioning") funds from states was not working particularly well. The delinquency of certain states kept the national government constantly starved for revenue and unable to pay its soldiers and creditors. In turn, this practice damaged the nation's credit, limiting its ability to establish a sound economy. The Articles' mechanism for amendment required the unanimous agreement of the state legislatures. Twice during the decade, twelve states had agreed to an impost amendment, only to have a thirteenth (once Rhode Island and once New York) object and scuttle the plan. Most Antifederalists favored the impost.

Even many from New York and Rhode Island admitted to its utility, even if they felt their state's interests dictated opposing it. Regulating interstate commerce was necessary to prevent predatory taxation and commercial schemes between the states. New York was clearly taking advantage of New Jersey and Connecticut, for instance, but absent national regulatory power, nothing could be done to stop that practice.

Antifederalists also agreed it was the duty of citizens to abide by the results of legitimate political processes. Popular government required submission to the law. Any other stance seemed to make popular government unworkable. If individuals were allowed to choose which laws to accept, anarchy would result.[26] If the Constitution were ratified, they believed it would have to be accepted. Several Antifederalists even included pledges to abide by the Constitution in their preratification writings. Others spelled out their reasoning after ratification, including Pennsylvania's James Hanna, who reasoned, "the worst that we can expect from a bad form of government is anarchy and confusion . . . and by an opposition in the present situation of affairs, we are sure of it" (see chapter 7). John Quincy Adams expressed a similar sentiment in his diary: "I find myself on the weaker side, [and therefore] I think it is my duty to submit without murmuring against what is not to be helped. In our Government, opposition to the acts of a majority of the people is rebellion to all intents and purposes" (see chapter 7).[27]

MIDDLING, VIRULENT PLEBEIAN, AND ELITE ANTIFEDERALISM

No two individuals who opposed the Constitution were precisely alike. Some Antifederalists were so different from each other that it was only natural to doubt whether a national government could satisfy them all. Take Patrick Henry and Consider Arms, for instance. Henry had built the most successful law practice in Virginia by 1770 and ultimately served as governor. From independence to ratification, Henry influenced Virginia politics more than anyone, including George Washington and Thomas Jefferson. Henry was well-off; his holdings included numerous tracts of land and over a hundred slaves. The Constitution was problematic in his eyes because it threatened the liberty of free men. But he also judged it to be particularly bad for Virginia. The state, like all others under a stronger national government, would lose considerable influence. In the Senate, the state would be coequal with tiny states like Rhode Island and Delaware. Small states could combine to prevent Virginia from influencing national policies in proportion to its population. Henry also feared that the more numerous Northern states would pass legislation harmful to the South. Animating these fears was the possibility that slavery would be abolished, thus crippling the Southern economy. Diminished state power also spelled a loss of influence for Henry personally, a prospect he did not relish.

Conversely, Consider Arms was virtually unknown outside of Conway, Massachusetts, which selected him to be one of nearly four hundred delegates to the state's ratifying convention. Arms had served as a captain during the Revolutionary War. He had also participated in Shays' Rebellion, a lawless uprising of debt-ridden Massachusetts farmers who shut down civil courts, temporarily ending foreclosing procedures in them. His participation in Shays' Rebellion was not an unusual occurrence for a small farmer from the Bay State's Connecticut River valley, but it surely lowered his stature among fellow delegates. His participation likely meant that he was a debtor and perhaps in danger of losing his small farm. There is no record of Arms ever holding other elective positions. In a postconvention letter to his fellow citizens, Arms, like Henry, cited the possibility that citizens might lose their liberty under the new Constitution, but he also indicted the Constitution for sanctioning and protecting slavery.[28] Voting to ratify would have made him complicit in a despicable practice diametrically opposed to the core American principle of liberty. Ironically, while Henry opposed the Constitution for not offering sufficient protection to slavery, Arms opposed it because it protected slavery.

However, there is nothing paradoxical about Henry and Arms rejecting the Constitution for opposite reasons. Either would have clearly been dissatisfied by a single comprehensive national policy on slavery. Both were satisfied with the way their states approached the issue (Massachusetts had outlawed slavery by judicial decree just a few years earlier, and Virginia's law sanctioned and protected it), but neither was confident that slavery policy would remain primarily a state power under the Constitution. If Congress could pass whatever laws it thought necessary and proper, as the Antifederalists believed it could, and if those laws automatically trumped state laws, then the gradual nationalization of slavery policy was likely and both feared the results of that nationalization.

In its diversity of views, Antifederalism resembled a political party. The modern Republican and Democratic parties are often referred to as "big tents," where many different identifiable groups are welcome and needed for success. Republicans simultaneously aim to appeal to social conservatives, the probusiness constituency, and to libertarians. Democrats, meanwhile, have often relied on the constituencies of the "New

Deal coalition," consisting of blue-collar workers, African Americans, immigrants, and liberal intellectuals.[29]

Historian Saul Cornell has identified and labeled three main Antifederalist groups: a middle class (or "middling" perspective), a more virulent group of commoners (or "plebeians"), and a smaller but more prominent set of political "elites."[30] According to Cornell, authors representing the elite perspective were most likely to reference works of political philosophy. They also generally accepted the idea of a "natural aristocracy," that the most successful and intelligent men in a polity should be involved in government by virtue of their acuity. They also did not champion democracy. On the contrary, some of these elite Antifederalists feared the nationalization of politics because it could be a step toward excessive democracy. Politics in their view was "a perennial struggle between the many and the few."[31] The natural aristocracy and the democratic element exerted mutual restraints on each other. A constitution should recognize and maintain this balance. The elite Antifederalists initially favored curtailing democracy, which they thought was an overbearing presence in the states. As the Constitution took shape, they speculated that it would be too aristocratic in nature (chapter 6).

The middling Antifederalists were not hostile to the idea of a "natural aristocracy," but they were, however, unwilling to grant it a privileged status in government. To the middling Antifederalists, it only made sense that government should be responsive to the majority. Middle-class influence was palpable to them in each state, but they felt it would be significantly reduced by the Constitution because average citizens would not be elected to Congress. Their writings were less likely than elite texts to include a broad array of references; instead, they quoted more familiar sources, like John Locke or the Bible. These authors asserted that the middle class possessed characteristics that would lead to good governance, like industry and frugality. New Yorker Melancton Smith, for instance, opined that "the circumstances in which men are placed in a great measure give cast to the human character. Those in middling circumstances have less temptation; they are inclined by habit, and the company with whom they associate, to set bounds to their passions and appetites" (chapter 4). To an extent that probably made elite Antifederalists cringe, their goal was popular government, the translation of popular wishes into public policy.

While the middling group's tone was fairly moderate, "plebeian" commentators were more adamant in their criticism of the Constitution. I call these individuals "virulent Antifederalists." Often calling the drive for ratification a "conspiracy," they feared and loathed aristocracy. According to this view, when the well-off achieved political power, there was reason for grave suspicion. For example, Centinel asserted that "the present conspiracy is a continental exertion of the well-born of America to obtain that darling domination, which they have not been able to accomplish in the states" (chapter 5). Virulent essays often struck this kind of accusatory tone. In these writings, few references were made to renowned political thinkers; their rhetoric fit their more common, folksy style. Because these essays tended to come from the "backcountry," away from the highly populated coast, they were also not as widely reprinted as those of the other types.

In short, according to Cornell, "Anti-Federalist support depended on three crucial groups in American society: backcountry farmers and artisans [the virulent Antifederalists], the middling sort who dominated politics in the Middle Atlantic, and a small but highly influential group of elite politicians."[32] Many writings clearly fall into these categories. Centinel's hard-edged essays featured in chapter 5 are of the virulent plebeian variety, while chapter 4's Brutus is an example of the middling perspective. Some of the future Antifederalists who participated in the Philadelphia convention express their fears about unfettered democracy in chapter 6 and are safely classified as proponents of the elite perspective. Other essays are less easy to categorize.

Adding to Cornell's observations about how to distinguish between these three forms of Antifederalist argument, the specific institutional arrangements favored by various authors provide a distinguishing clue. Elite Antifederalists favored a British-style "mixed republic," in which the interests of the aristocratic few and the democratic many would be balanced by constructing the government in a certain way. Balancing aristocratic and popular impulses in government institutions was an idea that went back more than two millennia, to the Greek philosopher Aristotle. This idea was particularly popular in England, where institutions seemed consciously constructed to achieve this balancing act. In fact, members of the House of Lords were aristocrats; the House of Commons, however, was elective and thus representative of the people. In the minds of the elite Antifederalists, the American legislature should have approximated this balancing act. The two-chambered Congress was a positive starting point. In their view, the upper chamber, the Senate, should be populated by a "natural aristocracy" of the nation's best and brightest. The House of Representatives should be far different—a popular, democratic institution to balance the elite Senate. But according to the elite Antifederalists, the framers of the Constitution had not struck that balance correctly.

Middling Antifederalists rejected the mixed regime. To them, it was contrary to the spirit of the Revolution to reserve an entire branch of the legislature for a small minority, even if some of them were the nation's best and brightest. At the same time, they were willing to give these individuals their due, admitting that many elective officials would be of the natural aristocracy and that their presence might prove beneficial as long as they did not dominate. These authors did not reject having a two-chambered legislature. Many of the plebeian populists did, however, preferring a single-chambered legislature. The virulent Antifederalists hypothesized that such a "unicameral" legislature would be more democratic and more responsive to the people than a bicameral one. Rejecting any sort of expertise provided by elites, they wished for unfettered popular rule.[33]

These factions were disagreeing on what governing arrangements were sanctioned by the American Revolution. The elites believed they rightly had a permanent, institutionalized place in American government, as elites did in Britain. The other groups did not aim to replicate British practices. Middling authors hoped for majority rule with the elites invited to join in governance but accorded no special privileges. Virulent Antifederalists hoped for populist governance untainted by any influence exerted by wealth. Each of these three visions were critically important to their proponents. Each group felt it was conserving the accomplishment of the Revolution, yet there was no consensus among them on what exactly that accomplishment was. They also achieved no consensus that democracy was a worthwhile goal, something that would no doubt surprise many contemporary Americans.

The peculiar composition of any large political movement challenges its members. Different factions vie for supremacy while often settling for compromises. Assorted versions of Antifederalism did jockey for position and compromise with each other. But to a surprising extent, the elite, middling, and virulent strands of these arguments could be presented without bothering to reconcile them. At the time, the critical matter was to oppose the Constitution: reconciling one's views with the other Antifederalists was important but secondary. Ratification was also a one-time occurrence, which meant that the Antifederalists did not have to keep rebalancing their coalition and redefining themselves to fit changing times in the way that a political party must, engaged as they are in a sequence of elections. Finally, theirs was an age without instantaneous remote communication or speedy cross-country travel. This relative isolation lessened the need to form a single coherent message. For instance, a Kentucky newspaper would print virulent pieces while an Albany paper published middling essays. Both appealed to those who populated the two areas served by their respective papers. These arguments would have been much more obviously at odds with each other if communication had been easier or if travel had been more efficient.

As you read the documents contained in this book, keep the three strands of Antifederalism in mind. Consider also formulating a series of questions through which you can judge these arguments. Are they coherent and plausible? What makes them so? Each vision implies something different about what American politics *should* be like. Ask yourself which best describes what American politics should strive for and why? The Antifederalists offered predictions about what American politics would be like under the Constitution. Which predictions were most accurate? Are their suggestions for making politics better valid?

THE PROGRESS OF CONSTITUTIONAL TIME: ANTIFEDERALISTS AND POLITICAL CONTEXT

The American founding did not happen all at once. The founding was a process, defined by a series of changing political contexts. Tensions between Britain and the colonies escalated in the period from 1765 to 1775. "Committees of Correspondence" were formed during this period in which leaders of the several colonies became acquainted with each other, shared their grievances, and discussed possible remedies. By 1774, the colonists were sufficiently agitated to discuss their grievances face-to-face, meeting in a "Continental Congress." Armed conflict began in Massachusetts in 1775, and the Second Continental Congress declared independence from Great Britain the next year. The colonies worked together as a de facto alliance until the Articles of Confederation were formally adopted in 1781. Though the progress of these events could not have been foreseen, they occurred in a logical order. Further, different behaviors were appropriate in the different contexts. For instance, no one advocated declaring independence in 1770—that suggestion would have been premature. Independence was precipitated only by the drastic event of British soldiers engaging in a sustained armed conflict with the colonists.

Similarly, an unforeseeable but logical progression of contexts occurred during the later portion of the founding, when the ratification of the Constitution took place. Each step forward in "constitutional time" produced its own understandable behaviors from those involved, but the behaviors appropriate in one context were not necessarily appropriate in another. By 1786, it was acknowledged that the first American constitution, the Articles of Confederation, needed revision. Representatives from several states met in Annapolis that year to discuss changes in commercial policy. Without any prospect of all states being involved, the Annapolis convention quickly disbanded, but not before suggesting that another convention be held in Philadelphia the next year. Later in 1786, Shays' Rebellion occurred in western Massachusetts. Its lawlessness caused great concern among the nation's political elite, ensuring that the Philadelphia convention would be well attended, particularly by those who favored wide-ranging changes. The convention suggested major, nationalizing changes, issuing an entirely new constitution. Five states approved the Constitution quickly, but then the march toward ratification slowed. The ratification of Massachusetts acted as something of a catalyst, though. Massachusetts recommended actual amendments along with its ratification. Subsequent states eventually did likewise. By the end of summer 1788, eleven states, all but North Carolina and Rhode Island, had ratified. Elections for the new federal offices were held late in 1788 and early in 1789. Congress convened in early April. George Washington was sworn in as the nation's first president on April 30. North Carolina joined the Union in November, and Rhode Island completed the Union by ratifying the Constitution in May 1790. Though Antifederalists behaved differently in these various contexts, these different behaviors logically sprang from the same coherent but multifaceted worldview they possessed all along.

Shays' Rebellion disturbed the future Federalists far more than those who would be Antifederalists. The latter group interpreted the disturbance in western Massachusetts as short-lived and, by and large, peaceful. They did not infer that state-based popular government in general was unstable. Unlike the Federalists, then, the future Antifederalists were not particularly motivated to populate the Philadelphia convention. Influential figures like Patrick Henry, Samuel Adams, and George Clinton, who would have restrained the convention's nationalizing inclinations, did not attend. Their nonappearance was a tremendous advantage for the Federalists, as they were able to design a government more far-reaching in its changes than almost any outsider imagined they would. Additionally, the future Antifederalists who were at the convention did not act in concert. For instance, Elbridge Gerry fought every contestable point to the end of the convention; Robert Yates and John Lansing left in disgust halfway through its proceedings, leaving arch-nationalist Alexander Hamilton as New York's sole representative; and Virginia's Governor Edmund Randolph displayed a kind of resigned acceptance. Afterward, Randolph equivocated so much that it is impossible to say if he even was an Antifederalist. In short the Antifederalists began the ratification fight a step behind the more aggressive Federalists.

When the Constitution was first made public, in September 1787, the immediate goals of those who opposed it were straightforward. First, they needed to ensure a healthy debate about the document would take place. Accordingly, they urged the public to carefully consider it for themselves and not accept the convention's work just because of the eminence of its delegates. They also bought time for consideration by reminding citizens that there was no crisis; despite the flaws of the Articles, the country need not act precipitously. Second, Antifederalists offered reasons for opposition. Pointing out the sparse limitations on federal power was critical. They insisted the Federalists would have to clarify their intent. If they failed to calm fears about a runaway central government, the groundwork would be laid for amendments. Third, Antifederalists proposed remedies to these flaws, including changes in the document's language. These suggestions provided a ready-made agenda for a second convention, which many Antifederalists suggested to perfect the work of the first one. Naturally, the Antifederalists would have made sure to turn out in full force at this second convention to counter the Federalists.

From the initial volley of accusations against the Constitution, a Federalist response emerged that played a crucial role in the course of American constitutionalism. On October 6, 1787, Federalist James Wilson responded to the Antifederalists' charge that the powers of the federal government were limitless. Wilson's speech, delivered in Philadelphia, received nationwide press coverage. It was, in fact, the most widely printed and best-known argument from the ratification debates. Wilson observed that the federal Constitution was different from state constitutions in that it was formulated with existing political compacts, the state constitutions, already in force. As original compacts, state constitutions allowed state governments to wield all powers except what they specifically prohibited, a very broad grant of power. The federal Constitution took from the states (or the people) only expressed powers, which were clearly spelled out in Article I, section 8. In contrast to the state constitutions, the national Constitution granted limited, defined powers. Most Antifederalist fears were unfounded, Wilson argued, because the central government was not authorized to do what the Antifederalists feared would be done. Could Congress abridge the freedom of speech? No, because there was no explicit grant of such a power in the Constitution.

In the weeks and months after the Constitution was made public, state legislatures authorized conventions as well as elections for delegates who would attend those conventions.[34] Within a month, starting on December 7, 1787, five states—Delaware, Pennsylvania, New Jersey, Georgia, and Connecticut—ratified the Constitution. Of these, only Pennsylvania's ratification was marked by controversy, but it was a significant one. Proponents of the Constitution in the state legislature were not sufficiently numerous to conduct business. With the legislative term in its final days, Antifederalists simply played hookey, absenting themselves from the assembly to prevent it from calling a convention. Knowing that they needed only two members of the opposition to form a quorum, Federalists encouraged a mob to forcibly bring two Antifederalists to the chamber. The Antifederalists were dragged to the Assembly and held there against their will, where a resolution for a state convention passed. During the convention, the Federalist majority reluctantly allowed opponents to speak, but then refused to allow their objections to become part of the official proceedings of the convention. These controversial actions led many Pennsylvania Antifederalists to argue that their state's ratification was illegitimate, thus justifying continued opposition. In western Pennsylvania, a petition demanding that the state's ratification be voided netted six thousand signatures. Ardent essayists from the state, like Centinel, continued to denounce the Constitution (chapter 5). This series of events was far different from what occurred in the other four states.

As the first five states ratified, others considered holding conventions. Of the remaining states, Massachusetts was the first to call for a convention. Delegates from Massachusetts gathered in Boston in early January. After three weeks of debate, Federalists knew they were short of a majority and thus courted a prominent fence-sitter, Governor John Hancock, to offer amendments. To Federalists, the form of these amendments was crucial. Massachusetts' ratification was not made contingent on the adoption of the amendments; rather, the amendments were offered as recommendations to the new Congress. This precedent was followed by all but one of the remaining seven states. It enabled ratification to occur in states where the Federalists were not necessarily a majority, which was the case in New Hampshire, the ninth state to ratify. Thus, the Constitution ultimately attained legal status in the states that had ratified with the help of the mildest Antifederalists. Most Antifederalists continued to be wary of the Constitution, however, warning that the mere promise of consideration by Congress was little guarantee that perfecting amendments would be passed.

Once momentum coalesced behind the referral of recommended amendments to Congress, the Antifederalist hope for a second convention became less realistic. Nevertheless, the Antifederalists did not leave the ratification fight empty-handed. The need for amendments was widely publicized, there was a ready-prepared agenda of amendments to be dealt with by Congress—including some which many states had recommended. Additionally, James Wilson's argument allowed the Antifederalists to hold Federalists to their reassurances that the central government wielded only specific, limited powers. As the Constitution neared ratification, the opposition in Pennsylvania moderated, and New Yorkers, sensing that the best chance to amend the Constitution would be in a Congress with New York represented in it, reluctantly considered ratification. A month after Virginia ratified, New York Antifederalists agreed to allow ratification with recommendatory amendments.

The Constitution itself stated that if nine states ratified, it would go into effect among the ratifying states. With this occurrence, the nation entered another political context. No longer was the Constitution a proposal; it was law, even if it was not yet implemented. This progression in constitutional time yielded a very different approach to the Constitution by the Antifederalists. They had been reluctant to scrap the Articles of Confederation because doing so required extralegal action; to them, the sanctity of the rule of law was just too important. This aspect of the Antifederalist mind-set now dictated acceptance of the Constitution. The critics' objections to the Constitution had not changed, but they recognized that it was now the law of the land. The fight for amendments would have to be joined from within the bounds set by the Constitution itself.

To many, it appeared as if the Antifederalists had turned 180 degrees. Naturally, the Federalists exploited their opponents' seeming about-face. But what casual observers failed to understand was that the new political context triggered a different part of the preexisting Antifederalist ideology. Elbridge Gerry tried to set the record straight in the First Congress by saying "those who, whilst [the Constitution] was depending, were for critically examining and correcting it, will now be among the last to give it up, because they well know we cannot always be new-modelling our system."[35]

Antifederalists worked very hard to publicize their acceptance of the ratified Constitution. Many feared that the adamant nature of their critique could inspire discord, even to the point of sparking a civil war. Reminding citizens that they were duty-bound to accept the Constitution would prevent such an occurrence. Additionally, in the wake of

Shays' Rebellion, they wanted to avoid the stigma of being portrayed like the Shaysites, who had been condemned for their willingness to pursue extralegal remedies to their plight. Electioneering also occurred in this interim period. Former Antifederalists argued that the "friends of amendments" should be elected to Congress to ensure that the Constitution would be altered. Their attempts at winning office failed miserably, however: the public found the Federalists' plea that proponents of the Constitution be elected to build the new government much more convincing.

Implementation of the Constitution brought yet another context. In the initial Congress, some Federalists aggressively brought the new government into existence, thus alienating their opponents, who asserted that they had forgotten James Wilson's pledge that the Constitution authorized only specific, enumerated powers. The former Antifederalists did their best to uphold a static, concrete vision of the Constitution.[36] They were joined in this effort by a breakaway group of Federalists, who were serious about following Wilson's pledge. As stated by one of them, Maryland's Michael Jenifer Stone (see chapter 7):

> Never did a country more completely unite in any sentiment than America in this—That Congress ought not to exercise, by implication, powers not granted by the Constitution. . . . The people said to the ministers of this country, "We have given you what we think [are] competent powers; but if experience proves them inadequate, we will enlarge them—but in the meantime dare not usurp those which we have reserved."

The First Congress had even formulated two amendments, shortly to become the ninth and tenth amendments, which seemed to confirm that this view was constitutional law. The remaining Federalists seemed increasingly prone to ignore these limits, cementing the alliance between the former Antifederalists and the breakaway Federalists, and thus inaugurating the first American party system. In this capacity, the Antifederalists played a critical role in defining the nature of the new government.

COMMENTARY

Interest in the Antifederalists has never been higher. After many years of neglect or simplified treatments, their critique of the American government and their contribution to it are now being appreciated, and there are several reasons for this resurgent interest. Primary among them is renewed attention to the federal relationship. The relationship between the national government and the states has always been a defining aspect of the American regime. Which government should possess which powers has always been contentious, but it has been particularly so in the past several decades. Ronald Reagan began his presidency in 1981 by stating that "government is not the solution to our problem. Government *is* the problem," thus sparking a heated debate on whether the national government had become too powerful. In the same year, Herbert Storing published *The Complete Antifederalist*, a seven-volume compilation of Antifederalist writings. This reference, along with *The Documentary History of the Ratification of the Constitution* (which is now at nineteen volumes), made the Antifederalists' work much easier to access.

But why did the Antifederalists need to be rediscovered in the first place? In the early years of the new republic, Federalists downplayed their opponents' significance and caricatured them for their own political advantage. The Constitution's early success allowed them to claim that the Antifederalists had been on the "wrong side" of ratification, and some even equated them with the disgraced Shaysites. For their part, the former Antifederalists did not try to rehabilitate themselves *as* Antifederalists. Given the high esteem the American public quickly developed for the Constitution, it would have been counterproductive for Antifederalists to point out that they had opposed the document. As they related it to the American public, the fight to ratify was over; there were no more Antifederalists. There was, however, a contest to define the meaning of the Constitution, though, and they were doing so as Jeffersonian Republicans.

Nineteenth-century commentators tended to view the Antifederalists through the lens of contemporary politics. During the first six decades of the century, the possibility of disunion grew and ultimately culminated in the Civil War. During this era, most historians were pro-Union and took it upon themselves to emphasize the heroism of the Federalists and the benefits of their paramount goal, a strengthened union. By contrast, they displayed either antipathy or open hostility to the Antifederalists.[37] For more than a century after ratification, then, an accurate picture of the Antifederalists was obscured.

Historians of the twentieth century often treated the Antifederalists more kindly, but not always more accurately. Charles Beard rehabilitated the Antifederalists by implication. In *An Economic Interpretation of the Constitution*, Beard famously argued that the Federalists were motivated by self-interest. Wealthy individuals were owed money by the central government, which was not paying it back to them. To remedy that situation, they constructed a stronger national government that could raise revenue. Without saying so directly, Beard implied that the Antifederalists were more representative of the people and more honest than the Federalists. Progressive-era historians later dealt more directly with the Constitution's critics than had Beard, stressing their agrarian roots and democratic leanings. Not coincidentally, these virtues were precisely the ones the Progressives often championed.

Several decades later, Cecelia Kenyon critiqued the Progressive interpretation by noting that these historians were more influenced by intellectual trends than "by a study of the political beliefs current in 1787."[38] Kenyon countered by writing that the Antifederalist commitment to democracy was dubious. It was for this reason that she labeled them "men of little faith." Despite their differing assessments, the Progressive thinkers and Kenyon suffered from the same tendency, treating the Antifederalists monolithically. In truth, some Antifederalists were committed democrats while others were not; many were farmers, many were not. Because of Antifederalist diversity, both the Progressive-era historians and Kenyon were able to point to certain authors who bolstered their claims, yet their reading of Antifederalism was selective. Both presented a vital part, but only a part, of the Antifederalists' thinking. The Progressives, in the main, presented a view of the Antifederalists that was more generally true; Kenyon's portrayal added the caveat that certain of their number—that is, the elite Antifederalists—did not consider themselves democrats at all.

A testament to the Antifederalists' diversity is their ability to appeal to those who criticize the American national government from both conservative and liberal perspectives. Many conservatives argue that the national government has accrued too much power. Antifederalists lend weight to these complaints by showing that their intellectual lineage goes back more than two hundred years. But Antifederalist ideas also help conservatives to imagine solutions to this problem. After ratification, they argued for a version of constitutionalism that limited national power. Many modern conservatives have also adopted this way of viewing the Constitution. "Strict construction," limiting the national government to the powers expressly written into the Constitution, allows them to argue that many actions of the national government are not authorized and should either be done by the states or not done by government at all.

Liberal thinkers also turn to the Antifederalists for intellectual support. Many of them argue that in the United States, power is retrenched and the government is unresponsive. They point out that Antifederalists warned of this very occurrence: citizens would lose the ability to influence government under the Constitution. Who would influence the government? The wealthy would, precisely those whom many on the left argue control government policy. Though their focus is generally on corporate wealth rather than individual wealth, the Antifederalists' views still resonate with them and lend credence to the idea that the structure of government is to blame. Vigilant grass-roots participation, something the Antifederalits engaged in and advocated, is presented as a possible remedy.

Thus, many Americans feel an intellectual kinship with the Antifederalists. In part, this connection is due to the prescience of the group's arguments, but it is also because American wariness of government is traditionally strong. This ideological predisposition has its roots in immigration. Settlers who came to the New World were often fleeing repressive regimes. Antifederalists reflected and reinforced what was already a very strong public sentiment. That their arguments resonate with us today is an indication that wariness of government penetrated deep into the American psyche.

The identification of conservative and liberal critics with the critics of the Constitution is rooted in what the United States is *not*, their view is that the Antifederalists point to a path not taken. Another perspective, however, deserves mention, and it is one that stresses Antifederalist influence on American politics. Gordon Wood, for example, notes that the Federalists feared institutions dominated by and reflective of popular interests, and he suggests that this is the very kind of politics that prevails in the United States. The real prophets of the founding age, in Wood's view, were the men who came to grips with popular politics on a national scale, like many of the former Antifederalists. Wood therefore doubts the oft-asserted claim that we live under a Federalist regime because the Federalist preference for policy created by a natural aristocracy did not last.

The American regime is a hybrid. Neither the Federalists nor the Antifederalists controlled the outcome of the ratification process, but both groups affected it mightily. Their legacy can still be felt, even after more than two hundred years. With a hybrid regime, it is no wonder that critics can point out practices that the Antifederalists would not—and that they do not—like. But in part, the existence of these various practices is some evidence that we do have a government that encompasses a wide variety of views; compromises must be made for any such government to succeed. And pointing out the necessity of coming to grips with other political actors—accepting political outcomes that favor others while exploring new ways to achieve one's own favored outcomes—is one of the enduring legacies of the Antifederalists.

Most Antifederalists had faith in a more popular brand of government than the Federalists did. For all its flaws in coordinating between the states, the Articles of Confederation allowed for much popular input in the individual states. Most Antifederalists thought that popular government could not exist without such direct participation. Washington and his Federalist colleagues feared that the Articles allowed government to be too reflective of human nature's troubling impulses.[39] Particularly in the wake of Shays' Rebellion, they believed that if popular wishes were not corralled, representative government would self-destruct. The Constitution was consciously designed to keep government from being too responsive to the general public. Certain key powers were taken from the states. The national government was given the power to restrain states with force when necessary. Federalists also intended that a natural aristocracy would provide expert representation in Congress, thus countering popular impulses as needed. The Federalists thought introducing these impediments to democracy was the only way to preserve popular government. Most Antifederalists believed that such restraints were unnecessary and that in the long run they would only produce discontent and cynicism. In short, Antifederalists had more faith than Federalists did that popular government could work.

Many believe this vision naive, citing low voter turnout rates to argue that people don't care to participate in politics. A dim view of the political competence of average citizens is also frequently expressed. The Antifederalists would not be surprised that many Americans hold such a view, but they would point out that this perspective is colored by the present political context, a context in which it makes little sense for average citizens to educate themselves about politics because they have so little say in national policies. "A Farmer" put it this way: "Men no longer cultivate, what is no longer useful—should every opportunity be taken away, of exercising their reason, you will reduce them to that state of mindlessness in which they appear in nine-tenths of this globe . . . give them power and they will find the understanding to use it."[40] This is hardly the sentiment of a man "of little faith." Rather, the Farmer's attitude expresses much more faith in people than the average American possesses today.

Most who participated in the ratification debate had taken part in the American Revolution. To put it bluntly, the Antifederalists had been revolutionaries and had risked their lives to combat tyranny during the war. As mentioned, many thought the Constitution threatened what they had risked their lives for. It is striking that with the stakes so high and with a successful example of combating tyranny through armed resistance fresh in their memory, that this group so assiduously avoided extralegal resistance. The Constitution's errors were egregious. Further, the flaws in the ratification process were many: the Philadelphia convention was only authorized to propose modifications to the Articles of Confederation, not scrap it entirely; the Articles' requirement of unanimous approval of major political changes was ignored; the use of specially convened ratification conventions was unprecedented and probably formulated to avoid state legislatures; there were signs of mail tampering in certain states; Antifederalist newspapers did not circulate freely in many areas; there was significant malapportionment in several ratification conventions that systematically disadvantaged Antifederalists; in Pennsylvania, the minority was rudely treated, prevented from having any say over the proceedings of the state convention, and left out of its official record. Surely, cases for not abiding by a new constitution have been built on less. The Antifederalists displayed restraint and forbearance in the wake of ratification.

Coming to grips with the ratified Constitution was tricky for them politically. It threatened to make the Antifederalists look weak-kneed or as if they had not taken their original position seriously. Certainly, it was difficult to explain to constituents why they should abide by a document that might lead to tyranny. In many ways, they would have saved face by not accepting ratification. Antifederalist office seekers were disadvantaged at the polls for almost ten years after the ratification debates. Certain promising Antifederalist politicians like Melancton Smith and Jonathan J. Hazard had their careers cut short because of their agreement to abide by the Constitution.[41] At a political cost to themselves, the Antifederalists avoided plunging the nation into civil war. Pennsylvanian James Hanna summed up the Antifederalist view at ratification as follows: "the worst that we can expect from a bad form of government is anarchy and confusion . . . and by an opposition in the present situation of affairs we are sure of it" (see chapter 7). By historical standards, this forbearance was extraordinary for a group of revolutionaries.

For better or for worse, the Antifederalists possessed greater faith in the accepted political thinking of their day than did the Federalists, who were undergoing a transformation during the 1780s. Many had originally believed that popular republics needed to be small in size, but Shays' Rebellion and other civic disturbances caused them to doubt the wisdom of this position. The Federalists were struggling to reconstruct popular government when, in their minds, the ideas of certain respected political theorists had been tested and had failed. Federalists often described their efforts as an experiment, which was indicative of their feeling that no precedent or readily applicable political theory was available to guide them. The Federalists had to formulate their own political theory on the fly, and they were frequently brilliant in doing so. Less brilliance was displayed by the Antifederalists, but less brilliance was required of them.

A decided strength of the Antifederalists was their sensitivity to an issue subsequent generations have largely ignored. They were keenly aware that population size can affect the public's relationship with government. The Antifederalists argued that transferring government from entities that presided over tens or hundreds of thousands to an entity that ruled more than three million people would reduce how much citizens would identify with the state. The population of the United States has increased nearly a hundredfold since. At the least, political observers should be discussing whether that immense growth has led to a corresponding psychological distance between Americans and their government.[42] More generally, as countries grow in size, might their citizens lose confidence in them? This issue is one of great importance in a world where population growth seems to be an inexorable trend. If the Antifederalists are correct, in the long term we might see populations become increasingly restive—particularly in the largest and the most rapidly growing nations. Perhaps modern communication and travel can offset this perceived distance; perhaps universal suffrage is a mitigating factor; perhaps feelings of regime legitimacy are produced by factors that are unrelated to polity size. But it could also be that the Antifederalists were right. We might exist at the beginning of a very curious era in human history that they foresaw, where the trappings of popular government (like elected representatives) exist while its benefits are not readily perceived.

Although the political theory accepted by the Antifederalists had its strengths, it also contained some identifiable weaknesses. Critics of the Constitution were particularly prone to repeating certain commonly accepted either–or fallacies. Recall what many hypothesized: that either the people would consider the laws "theirs" and voluntarily abide by them; or they would not identify with the law, and obedience would thus have to be enforced. Reality in the American regime seems much more muddled. Do Americans obey laws cheerfully, believing the law to be of a piece with themselves? Not exactly. Do they have laws forced on them at the point of a bayonet? Rarely. Reality lies somewhere in between, with citizens who frequently grumble about certain laws and regulations but choose in the main to put up with them. Perhaps a certain resigned apathy represents a third possibility that is more indicative of public attitudes in modern regimes.

Some Antifederalists repeated the well-known maxim that there could not be an "imperium in imperio," or a sovereign power within a sovereign power. They believed that either the states were sovereign or the federal government was sovereign and that there was no possibility of permanently sharing powers between them. Others argued with great foresight that sovereignty *could* be split between the state and the nation, as long as the Constitution was explicit about what powers resided where. While the national government has surely accrued power in the last two hundred years, states have too. States are still very meaningful political organizations, with primary responsibility for administering justice, educating citizens, and looking after their inhabitants' welfare. The presumption that the balance of power would tip wholly to the national government because only one entity could possess sovereignty was faulty. The Federalists did indeed introduce a new kind of government, with powers divided between constituent states and the nation. After ratification, the Antifederalists readily embraced this new vision because they recognized it was the only way to preserve state power.[43]

A third fallacy that the Antifederalists stuck to was that powers were inherently either executive or legislative in nature and should be strictly possessed only by their respective institutions of government. In other words, executive powers would remain the exclusive province of the president, and legislative powers would be exclusively housed in Congress. Federalists ignored this maxim of John Locke's, which had been accepted for a century. Veto power allowed the executive a major hand in legislation. The vice president, an executive officer, was also made the leader of the Senate. The Senate was allowed to approve or reject presidential appointments within the executive and judicial branches. Antifederalist objections to this unorthodox practice of "separated institutions sharing powers" were nearly endless. But the Federalists divided powers for a reason the Antifederalists should have been very comfortable with—so no one entity of government could have exclusive power that could be abused. However, the opposition was convinced that the president and representatives would share an upper-class mentality. Thus, the sharing of powers was not viewed as an innovative way of checking government. Rather, it was viewed as allowing the upper class to possess and coordinate both executive and legislative power. Given their sensitivity to the differences between the cultures of the different states, they might have realized that there could be no single nationwide upper-class mentality. For the new government to work, the president and Congress would inevitably have to compromise, a vital check on the power of each.

The Antifederalists believed that for government to succeed, citizens needed to possess confidence in it. But combining confidence toward government with skepticism is a tricky business, and in the heat of battle, the Antifederalists never fully explained how to reconcile these two potentially contradictory impulses. Ideally, they would have taken more care in working out when and how suspicion toward government should manifest itself. Perhaps certain criteria could have been developed by which to judge whether the government was indeed popular; if those criteria were met, then citizens could go about their business confident that the government was still "theirs."[44] But formulating such criteria is an exceedingly challenging enterprise, difficult to do in a lifetime of theorizing about politics, let alone in a nine-month dispute over a constitution.

While the Antifederalists reinforced a healthy skepticism about government, one may wonder whether this skepticism has gone too far. Fears of government have been reinforced in recent decades by the living memories of the Vietnam War, Watergate, and the highly partisan, accusatory nature of politics left in their wake. No doubt the negative preconceptions of government harbored by many citizens are reinforced by Antifederalist influences. Americans are more reluctant to grant their central government power than the people of any other advanced industrialized nation. To many in those other nations, it seems as if the United States exists in a time warp, with an obsolete eighteenth-century mentality guiding the politics of the twenty-first century. In some cases, the national government fails precisely because it is not trusted to solve certain societal ills. Adhering strictly to the Antifederalist vision of government would have prevented some of the greatest accomplishments of the past century, including the broader application of civil rights, the introduction of pure food and pure drug legislation, and the protection of the environment to name a few. Local legislators often find it difficult to resist local prejudices. As a body, the national government can sometimes resist those parochial impulses and produce legislation directed at a more general good than the states can.

Even so, we still divide power between the national government and the states, and we still should divide power between them. New York differs from Utah; Massachusetts differs from Nebraska. Each should have its own laws reflecting its own circumstances and culture. Debate will always exist over where to draw boundaries between state and national authority and why. That argument will never be settled with finality. The Antifederalists had their views, as did the Federalists, as do many today. As much as anything, the debate over federalism defines America. It is America's challenge; it is America's genius. And it is a debate that the Antifederalists began.

NOTES

1. Reasons were available to dispute the legitimacy of the ratification process, and many Antifederalists pointed them out while the Constitution was being debated. Nevertheless, almost all Antifederalists accepted and worked within the process. Once the document was ratified, they accepted the process as legitimate and therefore the result as binding. This conclusion, however, was not an inevitability. The Antifederalists could have continued their opposition. They could have cited many flaws in the ratification process, and I mention several of them in the Commentary section of this chapter.

2. Had the Antifederalists chosen to reject the ratified Constitution and thus precipitate civil war, they may well have been successful. Antifederalists were sufficiently numerous and geographically concentrated that at the very least, they could have successfully resisted incorporation into the Union for many years. Ultimately, they may have been able to split the union and establish their own republics in areas like upstate New York and western Pennsylvania.

3. Many of those involved in the ratification debate were later involved in the early republic's party politics. While many of the figures I write about here are reliably identified with the "Republican" or "Federalist" parties, it is also misleading to apply these labels until political parties appear on the scene. The great majority of former Antifederalists became Republicans (also called Democratic-Republicans or Jeffersonian Republicans) once that party formed. To put it another way, most Antifederalists were future Republicans; however, to be precise, one cannot be both a Republican and an Antifederalist simultaneously. Both labels apply only to specific political contexts that are closely associated both in terms of ideas and time, but still distinct.

4. Until they accepted the Constitution as legitimate, the few critics who refused to acquiesce upon ratification might continue to be called Antifederalists.

5. Adams eventually did vote in favor of the Constitution at the Massachusetts' ratification convention, but he had clearly opposed the document as it was formulated. At least two factors induced Adams to vote to ratify: the recommendatory amendments formulated and passed by the convention and his Boston constituents, who almost universally favored the document and gathered informally at the Green Dragon Tavern to "instruct" Adams to vote in favor of it.

6. The tendency of Federalists to be coastal and Antifederalists to be from the backcountry was well known to participants in the ratification debate. These tendencies were, however, largely forgotten and had to be rediscovered. Orrin G. Libby was the first to compile systematic evidence on the *Geographical Distribution of the Vote of the Thirteen States on the Federal Constitution*. Jackson Turner Main's *The Antifederalists* popularized Libby's findings and added that river basins provided inland tongues of Federalism because of the ease with which goods could find their way to market in these areas.

7. For a more comprehensive treatment of how the politics of each individual state affected their approach to the Constitution, see Patrick T. Conley and John P. Kaminski, eds., *The Constitution and the States*, which includes a separate chapter on each state's ratification process.

8. It deserves mention that the ratification debate was a conversation among white males. Discrimination (including the practice of slavery) kept African Americans and others from participating in the debate. Though there were occasional letters and essays written by women that touched on politics, such writings were relatively rare. Formal political participation by women was taboo. The best-known political essay written by a woman during the ratification period is Mercy Otis Warren's "Columbian Patriot." Warren also later wrote a multivolume *History of the Rise, Progress and Termination of the American Revolution* (1805) under her own name, which was quite favorably received.

9. In labeling themselves "Federalist," the Federalists may have taken a cue from publisher and lexicographer Noah Webster, who used the term "federal men" in 1786 to indicate those who were continentally minded.

10. See James Farr's contribution to Richard Beeman, Stephen Botein, and Edward C. Carter II, eds., *Beyond Confederation*.

11. In the last two decades, commentators have stressed heavily Antifederalist diversity. Doing so corrected the monolithic views presented by Progressive scholars like Vernon Louis Parrington and some who disputed their vision such as Cecelia Kenyon. The Progressives portrayed the critics of the Constitution as long-suffering yeoman farmers who favored democracy but were taken advantage of by selfishly motivated Federalists. To counter this Progressive view, Kenyon labeled the Antifederalists "Men of Little Faith." She stressed the Antifederalists' discomfort with popular government. As this chapter progresses, these views should appear oversimplified at the least and perhaps even severely misleading at the most. Though I stress Antifederalist diversity as a counterpoint, I also aim to not overstress it. Antifederalists did agree on certain substantive matters, and despite their diversity, they did work together to win some key concessions during the ratification process.

12. See James H. Read, *Power versus Liberty*, particularly chapters 2 and 3, and David J. Siemers, *Ratifying the Republic*, chapters 4 and 5.

13. Many casually assert that the American founders created three coequal branches of government. To my knowledge, no political figure of the time believed they were doing so, or even could do so.

14. In fact, the Federalists' most widely known and most frequently reprinted argument made this point. The argument was presented by Philadelphian James Wilson in an October 6, 1787, speech. In the speech, Wilson made a distinction between state constitutions and the federal Constitution: in state constitutions, all powers not expressly reserved to the people were retained by the state. The proposed Constitution, coming after these already exisiting compacts, reserved to the states and people all powers not explicitly delegated to the national government. Thus, Congress had no ability to restrict freedom of the press, for instance, because that power was not explicitly given to the national government.

15. This sentiment was widely accepted in the colonies but was not the British understanding of charters. The British felt they had granted the colonies

autonomy for practical considerations and at the pleasure of the crown. The British assumed that they could revoke colonial autonomy, but the Americans viewed colonial self-government as a right. This misunderstanding was the basis of the rift that led to independence.

16. Herbert Storing, ed., *The Complete Antifederalist*, vol. 4, p. 126.

17. Herbert Storing, ed., *The Complete Antifederalist*, vol. 5, p. 213.

18. Article I, section 8 begins with the statement "The Congress shall have the Power To lay and collect Taxes, Duties, Imposts and Excises." Not directly stated, but implicit in this clause, is the ability of the central government to directly tax individuals. The Constitution did contain an important prohibition on the central government's taxation power: items exported from any state (Article I, section 9, clause 5) ensuring open interstate commerce; but crucially for the Antifederalists, there was no prohibition on direct taxation.

19. Article III, section 2, clause 1.

20. Article VI, section 1, clause 2.

21. For reasons I will explain in the next section, a few Antifederalists were comfortable with an aristocratically oriented Senate. None, however, were comfortable with an aristocratically oriented House.

22. This argument might sound vaguely familiar to students of the ratification debate. James Madison's well-known "Federalist #10" essay works from a similar observation about diversity in the states to a very different conclusion. One of Madison's hopes for the Constitution was that it would restrain "majority factions" that could form in the states because of their relative homogeneity, but would likely not form in the nation as a whole because of its relative diversity. Groups that had been able to zealously pursue their values or interests in the states—trampling the rights of others in the process—would not be able to do so on a national scale.

23. Article II, section 2, clause 2.

24. Article II, section 3.

25. Article I, section 3, clause 4.

26. The ratification debate occurred before the formulation of the theories of civil disobedience offered by Henry David Thoreau, Mohandas K. Gandhi, and Dr. Martin Luther King Jr. Civil disobedience is a way of doing what the founding generation thought impossible: selectively flaunting the law to improve the regime. In "Civil Disobedience," Thoreau makes a point of telling readers that though he refused to pay a poll tax, he did pay his highway tax because he agreed that roads needed to be built. Gandhi selectively disobeyed only the British laws he felt were unjust. King's "Letter from a Birmingham Jail" describes criteria that must be satisfied for a law to be disobeyed. He also writes that laws should be broken "lovingly," in a way that does not call into question the need for laws or government itself. These ideas represent ways of dealing with the dilemma that Antifederalists concluded to have no available solution.

27. For a fuller treatment of Antifederalist actions after ratification, see Lance Banning, "Republican Ideology and the Triumph of the Constitution, 1789–1793"; and David J. Siemers, "'It Is Natural to Care for the Crazy Machine': The Antifederalists' Post-Ratification Acquiescence."

28. Arms wrote two letters along with Malachi Maynard and Samuel Field that appeared in the Northampton *Hampshire Gazette* of April 9 and 16, 1788 (*The Complete Antifederalist*, vol. 4, pp. 255–66).

29. Since white males dominated politics (free blacks could vote in some states, but they did not have the numbers to grant them any clout), the divisions within Antifederalism were socioeconomic and ideological rather than ethnic and racist, but they were no less clear than the divisions in modern American political parties.

30. Saul Cornell, *The Other Founders*, chapters 2 and 3.

31. Saul Cornell, *The Other Founders*, p. 68.

32. Saul Cornell, *The Other Founders*, p. 48.

33. Focusing on these preferred institutional arrangements is of particular relevance for this work in that it puts the Federal Farmer into the elite category rather than among the middling group where Cornell places him. The Federal Farmer preferred a mixed regime, as indicated by the excerpts of his writings featured in chapter 6. In one of his letters he writes, "I am not among those men who think a democratic branch a nuisance." Unlike the middling Antifederalists, the Federal Farmer did not want a democratic government, but a democratic *branch* of government as a counterweight to the aristocratic branch housed in the Senate. Even with these various cues, it is not entirely clear where each particular Antifederalist fits in this typology. In certain cases, it may be helpful to think of these types as points on a continuum, with some perspectives mixing elite and middling views and others combining middling views with plebeian views.

34. The only state where a call to hold a convention was defeated was Rhode Island. Every other state authorized a convention in its initial session after the Constitution was transmitted to the states.

35. Charlene Bangs Bickford et al., eds., *Documentary History of the First Federal Congress*, House Debates, 2nd session, p. 952.

36. See Banning's "Republican Ideology and the Triumph of the Constitution."

37. Saul Cornell, "The Changing Fortunes of the Anti-Federalists," *Northwestern University Law Review* (1989): 45.

38. Cecelia A. Kenyon, "The Antifederalists: Men of Little Faith," p. 5.

39. Shortly before the Philadelphia convention met, George Washington wrote in a letter, "we have probably had too good a conception of human nature in forming our confederation." John C. Fitzpatrick, ed., *The Writings of George Washington*, vol. 28, p. 502.

40. Herbert Storing, ed., *The Complete Antifederalist*, vol. 5, p. 39.

41. See Robin Brooks, "Alexander Hamilton, Melancton Smith, and the Ratification of the Constitution in New York," and John P. Kaminski's "Political Sacrifice and Demise: John Collins and Jonathan J. Hazard, 1786–1790."

42. While the relationship between the size of a polity and governance has received little attention lately, many classical political theorists dealt extensively with the issue. Like the Antifederalists, Plato and Aristotle both thought that states with larger populations were more difficult to govern. Their ideal was the Greek city-state, a much smaller entity than the American states. In

The Laws, Plato even suggests an ideal size for a city: 5,040 "hearths" (or households). During the Enlightenment, Montesquieu gained renown for his argument that the size of a nation dictated the way it would be governed, with popular rule possible only in smaller nations. Jean-Jacques Rousseau took Montesquieu's idea a step further, reviving the city-state as an ideal. On the other hand, James Madison, following the lead of David Hume, argued the opposite, that only large polities could withstand the kind of factionalism that debilitated smaller regimes. Though these thinkers differ widely in their views, they all find that population size is a critical factor in governance.

43. The Antifederalists' quick reversal on whether a federal republic was viable raises the possibility that they had exaggerated their original claims.

44. Political theorists have developed such lists of criteria. Robert Dahl, in particular, specified criteria by which a government can be judged to be popular or not in *Democracy and Its Critics* (see, in particular, chapter 15).

2

The First Antifederalists: Objectors at the Philadelphia Convention

The Constitution was, famously, the result of compromises. The most important of these was an accommodation on representation. The small states pushed for the equal representation of each state, and the large states argued for representation proportionate to population. The "Great Compromise" (or "Connecticut Compromise") used the small state's plan in the Senate and the large state's plan in the House of Representatives. Northerners compromised with Southerners on slavery, which produced the three-fifths clause and a stipulation that the slave trade could not be outlawed before 1808, but it could be taxed. Those who wanted a strong executive compromised with those who were wary of executive power: they constructed an independently elected executive office, where the occupant would have to work in tandem with Congress.

With all these compromises, no delegate was perfectly pleased with the convention's work, but for most, successfully framing a more powerful national government was of overriding importance. Since the convention produced a document that clearly enhanced national power, most delegates were willing to put up with the parts of the Constitution they considered objectionable. Others, however, were not so satisfied. These delegates had particular objections, too, but what distinguishes these first Antifederalists from their colleagues was an assessment that the Constitution as a whole was too flawed to give it their assent.

Six Philadelphia convention delegates opposed the Constitution: Elbridge Gerry of Massachusetts; Robert Yates and John Lansing of New York; Luther Martin and John Francis Mercer of Maryland; and George Mason of Virginia. A seventh, Edmund Randolph, then governor of Virginia, openly voiced reservations but equivocated so much that to call him an Antifederalist would be misleading.[1] These individuals felt that the national government would be too strong under the Constitution. Despite this common thread, they differed on many particulars. In his "Genuine Information" letters, Luther Martin stressed that the large states ganged up on the smaller ones during the convention and would in the future dominate the new regime. This line of argument was completely foreign to Mason and Gerry, both residents of populous states. Mason, Gerry, and Randolph were wealthy and shared an elitist view of politics. They idealized the British system, which combined democratic and aristocratic elements in equal proportions. Yates and Lansing were middle-class politicians. They were disgusted by the idea that supposed aristocrats should be able to restrain democracy. Even before the Constitution was formulated, those who would oppose it were fractured.

Temperamental and stylistic differences also existed among the Antifederalists. Deeply disappointed by the direction the convention was headed, Yates and Lansing left it for good in early July. Meanwhile, the cantankerous Elbridge Gerry fought tooth and nail on almost every point to the end of the convention. He and George Mason were among the most active delegates, each speaking before the convention more than one hundred times. The other budding "Antis" were more reticent, particularly Yates, who apparently delivered just one speech before the convention. Mercer was not yet thirty years of age. His youthfulness presented a striking contrast to Gerry and Randolph, who had played key roles in the Revolution and who were among the nation's most eminent men. The Antifederalists never quite overcame these differences of substance and style.

Despite their fragmentation, these few Antifederalists greatly influenced the convention's work. Elbridge Gerry himself shaped many of the Constitution's provisions. Gerry recognized the absolute importance of formulating a new constitution. By mid-June, he feared that the convention was at an impasse over representation and was near disbanding. To break the impasse, Gerry was appointed chair of the committee which eventually suggested the Great Compromise. Yates, Martin, and Mason were also members of this critical committee. Gerry's proposal of how the presidential veto should operate was adopted and is still used to this day. He advocated an enumeration of Congress's powers, which was done in Article I, section 8, and he was also a key supporter of the Electoral College. Though he came to have objections to the constitutional system, Edmund Randolph introduced the Virginia Plan, which formed the template for debate and a blueprint (albeit significantly modified) for the Constitution. The convention's early endorsement of Randolph's suggestions indicated that it would make a decisive break from a strict confederation. Randolph and Mason helped determine that Representatives would serve two-year terms. Strangely, Luther Martin, a champion of state sovereignty, introduced language very similar to the supremacy clause. The language of his suggested clause was used, but it was modified to ensure national dominance over the states when a dispute arose.[2]

These Antifederalists also greatly influenced the ratification debate. Through their objections, they ensured that the Constitution would not simply be adopted by acclaim but would undergo serious examination. Citizens observing the process recognized the convention as an assemblage of well-respected politicians. When some of these well-respected men objected to the new Constitution, their dissents begged for explanation. Each of these seven dissenters explained why they opposed the Constitution in public letters. Most of those who commented on the Constitution employed pseudonyms. Issuing signed public letters sharply contrasted with that practice. Those who objected to the Constitution had to explain their position, and they did so. Because of their high profile, these letters were among the most widely reprinted Antifederalist writings. Gerry's letter was reprinted in nearly fifty newspapers, as frequently as any Antifederalist writing. Yates and Lansing (who wrote a joint letter), George Mason, and Edmund Randolph each had their objections printed in more than twenty newspapers. Several of these letters are included in chapter 3, where the most well-known and influentiual Antifederalist documents are printed. Such widespread arguments had to be countered, of course. A large proportion of the Federalists' commentary focused on refuting the convention's Antifederalists. The proceedings of the Philadelphia convention were secret; all members save one remained tight-lipped about its proceedings. Maryland's Luther Martin provided the only firsthand account of the convention made public during the ratification debate. In fact, Martin's "Genuine Information" was the only account written by a member to appear before 1808.

The Philadelphia convention marks the birth of the Federalist movement. It just as surely gave birth to the Antifederalists. The remarks of the seven dissenters contained here anticipate the major contours of the opposition's argument. Luther Martin's account of the convention is excerpted here, as are speeches and diary entries from the Philadelphia convention. Together they portray a wary minority, united in opposition, but far from united in their reasoning.

SPEECHES AND NOTES FROM
THE PHILADELPHIA CONVENTION

Delegates from twelve states, all but Rhode Island, met in Philadelphia from May to September 1787. The inadequacies of the Confederation were well known to the fifty-five men who met in the same room where the Second Continental Congress declared independence. Two events from 1786 gave impetus to the proceedings: the Annapolis convention and Shays' Rebellion. The Annapolis convention gathered to add to the Confederation's nearly nonexistent powers over commerce. It failed to do so because too few states attended. Nevertheless, it signaled to all the states that a convention might be a viable means of revising the confederation. Delegates at Annapolis suggested that a convention be held in Philadelphia the next year. Shays' Rebellion, the uprising of agrarian debtors in western Massachusetts, induced many political elites to support a strong national government that would bring order to the potentially lawless states.

The target date for meeting in Philadelphia was May 14. Many delegates were late in arriving, however, and a quorum of states was reached on May 25. The trajectory of the convention was set by the Virginia Plan, which was introduced by that state's governor, Edmund Randolph, on May 29. The Virginia Plan, written mainly by James Madison, proposed a bicameral legislature with representation proportionate to population or taxes paid, and an independent executive. Randolph's stated intent was to go beyond a mere confederation to form a national government. The convention spent the next two weeks debating the Virginia Plan point by point, tentatively adopting many of its suggestions. The New Jersey Plan, an alternative supported by delegates from several small states, was offered on June 15. This plan added powers to the confederation but retained its essential form: each state would have equal power. For the next several days, the New Jersey Plan was compared and contrasted with the Virginia Plan, but a majority of the convention clearly favored a radical departure from the Confederation and thus rejected the New Jersey Plan on June 19. This rejection led to an impasse, with representatives from the small states fearing that a new national government would be dominated by the populous states.

To bridge this impasse, a "grand committee" of one delegate from each state was formed. On July 5, the committee suggested that representation be by population in one part of a two-

chambered legislature and that states would be equally repre-
sented in the other chamber. This was the Great Compromise,
which was adopted by the convention on July 16 and still en-
dures as part of the American system of government. By the end
of July, the convention had come to a tentative agreement on a
system of representation for a national regime, and members
appointed a committee to draw up an early draft of a constitu-
tion. A lull in the proceedings occurred from July 26 to August
6 while this Committee of Detail did its work. Their specific
recommendations were debated in the next month, including
the tricky issue of slavery. The last major difficulty to be
worked out was the method of selection and the length of
tenure for the executive, which was determined with finality on
September 5. A Committee of Style wrote the specific wording
of the Constitution, which was eventually adopted on Septem-
ber 17, after which the convention disbanded.

Several members of the convention took notes on its pro-
ceedings. James Madison's were the most complete and accu-
rate. The summaries of Antifederalist speeches reproduced in
the following section are his unless indicated otherwise by a
name in parentheses at the end of the excerpt. Robert Yates took
notes as well, helping us to discern how this budding Antifederal-
ist viewed the proceedings. But Yates left the convention in early
July, along with John Lansing, his colleague from New York, so
his commentary ends then. Further, portions of Yates's notes
were doctored later for partisan effect by Edmond Genet, a one-
time French emissary to the United States and later the son-in-
law of New York's Governor George Clinton. Among the seven
who came to oppose the Constitution, only Mason, Randolph,
and Gerry were in attendance through the end of the convention.
As noted, Luther Martin's attendance was spotty, and John Fran-
cis Mercer appeared at the convention for less than two weeks.
Since Mason, Randolph, and Gerry were also the most outspo-
ken of these men, there is far more documentary material on
their ideas and opinions than the other four. Madison took notes
on 136 separate speeches by Mason and 119 by Gerry. Randolph
apparently spoke about half as many times as Mason. Martin
and Mercer each spoke approximately twenty-five times, with
Martin tending to speak at great length. Lansing and Yates
hardly gave any speeches.

Reconstructing exactly what these delegates thought on all
the issues discussed is impossible. General positions do emerge,

however. Most of these dissenters offered overarching views of the convention's work as it proceeded. The result is fascinating. A clear division among those who would become Antifederalists emerges. Martin, Lansing, and Yates are adamant in their unwillingness to part with state sovereignty and a strict federation. They insist that each state remain equal in a unicameral national legislature. The convention's majority dismissed this option. Mason, Randolph, and Gerry did, too. They were willing to vest some sovereign authority in a national government. These three envisioned the division of power between the states and the national government, an extraordinary development in the history of politics, something most of their generation—including Martin, Lansing, and Yates—thought impossible. None of these latter three felt a necessity to remain at a convention committed to such an unpalatable result, one they were not commissioned to produce. Mason, Randolph, and Gerry, meanwhile, did their utmost to put limits on the national government. They ultimately decided the national government was too strong and too aristocratic in nature, and thus they refused to sign the document.[3]

Tuesday, May 29, 1787

His excellency Governor Randolph, a member from Virginia, got up, and in a long and elaborate speech, shewed the defects in the system of the present federal government as totally inadequate to the peace, safety and security of the confederation, and the absolute necessity of a more energetic government. He closed these remarks with a set of resolutions, fifteen in number, which he proposed to the convention for their adoption, and as leading principles whereon to form a new government—He candidly confessed that they were not intended for a federal government—he meant [to propose] a strong *consolidated* union, in which the idea of states should be nearly annihilated (Yates).[4]

Thursday, May 31, 1787

Mr. Mason argued strongly for an election of the larger branch by the people. It was to be the grand depository of the democratic principle of the Govt. It was, so to speak, to be our House of Commons—It ought to know & sympathise with every part of the community; and ought therefore to be taken not only from different parts of the whole republic, but also taken from different districts of the larger members of it, which had in several instances particularly in Virga., different interests and views arising from difference of produce, of habits &c &. He admitted that we had been too democratic but was afraid we s[houl]d. incautiously run into the opposite extreme. We ought to attend to the rights of every class of people.[5]

Mr. Randolph disclaimed any intention to give indefinite powers to the national Legislature, declaring that he was entirely opposed to such an inroad on the State jurisdictions, and that he did not think any considerations whatever could ever change his determination. His opinion was fixed on this point.

Tuesday, June 5, 1787

Mr. Gerry. Observed that in the Eastern States the Confedn. had been sanctioned by the people themselves. He seemed afraid of referring the new system to them. The people in that quarter have (at this time) the wildest ideas of Government in the world. They were for abolishing the Senate in Massts. And giving all the other powers of Govt. to the other branch of the Legislature.[6]

Wednesday, June 6, 1787

Col. Mason.[7] Under the existing Confederacy, Congs. represents the *States* not the *people* of the *States*: their acts operate on the States not on the individuals. The case will be changed in the new plan of Govt. The people will be represented; they ought therefore to choose the Representatives. The requisites in actual representation are that the Reps. should sympathize with their constituents; shd. think as they think, & feel as they feel; and that for these purposes shd. even be residents among them. Much he sd. had been alledged agst. democratic elections. He admitted that much might be said; but it was to be considered that no Govt. was free from imperfections & evils; and that improper elections in many instances, were inseperable from Republican Govts. But compare these with the advantage of this Form in favor of the rights of the people, in favor of human nature. He was persuaded there was a better chance for proper elections by the people, if divided into large districts, than by the State Legislatures. Paper money had been issued by the latter when the former were against it. Was it supposed to be that the State Legislatures then wd. not send to the Natl. legislature patrons of such projects. If the choice depended on them.

Thursday, June 7, 1787

Mr. Gerry insisted that the commercial & monied interest wd. be more secure in the hands of the State Legislatures, than of the people at large.[8] The former have more sense of character, and will be restrained by that from injustice. The people are for paper money when the Legislatures are agst. it. In Massts. the County Conventions had declared a wish for a *depreciating* paper that wd. sink itself. Besides, in some States there are two Branches in the Legisature, one of which is somewhat aristocratic.

Col. Mason. whatever power may be necessary for the Natl. Govt. a certain portion must necessarily be left to the States. It is impossible for one power to pervade the extreme parts of the U.S. so as to carry equal justice to them. The State Legislatures also ought to have some means of defending themselves agst. encroachments of the Natl. Govt. In every other department we have studiously endeavored to provide for its self-defense. Shall we leave the States alone unprovided with the means for this purpose? And what better means can we provide than the giving them some share in, or rather to make them a constituent part of, the Natl. Establishment. There is danger on both sides no doubt; but we have only seen the evils arising on the side of the State Govts. Those on the other side remain to be displayed. The example of Cong: does not apply. Congs. had no power to carry their acts into execution as the Natl. Govt. will have.

Friday, June 8, 1787

Mr. Gerry c[oul]d. not see the extent of such a power [the Virginia Plan's proposal to allow the national legislature to veto state legislation], and was agst. every power that was not necessary. He thought a remonstrance agst. unreasonable acts of the States wd. reclaim them. If it shd. not, force might be resorted to. He had no objection to authorize a negative to paper money and similar measures. When the confederation was depending before Congress, Massachusetts was then for inserting the power of emitting paper money am[on]g. the exclusive powers of Congress. He observed that the proposed negative wd. extend to the regulations of the militia, a matter on which the existence of a State might depend. The Natl. Legislature with such a power may enslave the States. Such an idea as this will never be acceded to.

Saturday, June 16, 1787

Mr. Lansing moved to have the first article of the last plan of government [the New Jersey Plan] read; which being done, he observed, that this system is fairly contrasted with the one ready to be reported [the Virginia Plan]—the one federal, and the other national. In the first, the powers are exercised as flowing from the respective state governments—The second, deriving its authority from the people of the respective states—which latter must ultimately destroy or annihilate the state governments. To determine the powers on these grand objects with which we are invested, let us recur to the credentials of the respective states, and see what the views were of those who sent us. The language is there expressive—it is, upon the revision of the present confederation, to alter and amend such parts as may appear defective, so as to give additional strength to the union. And he would venture to assert, that had the legislature of the state of New-York, apprehended that their powers would have been construed to extend to the formation of a national government, to the extinguishment of their independency, no delegates would have here appeared on the part of that state. This sentiment must have had its weight on a former occasion, even in this house; for when the second resolution of Virginia, which declared, in substance, that a federal government could not be amended for the good of the whole, the remark of an honorable member of South-Carolina, that by determining the question in the affirmative their deliberative powers were at an end, induced this house to wave the resolution.[9] It is in vain to adopt a mode of government, which we have reason to believe the people gave us no power to recommend—as they will consider themselves on this ground to be authorized to reject it. . . . If we form a government, let us do it on principles which are likely to meet the approbation of the states. Great changes can only be gradually introduced. The states will never sacrifice their essential rights to a national government. New plans, annihilating the rights of the states (unless upon evident necessity) can never be approved. I may venture to assert, that granting additional powers to congress would answer their views; and every power recommended for their approbation exceeding this idea, will be fruitless (Yates).

Tuesday, June 19, 1787

Mr. Martin. When the states threw off their allegiance on Great Britain, they became independent of her and each other. They united and confederated for mutual defense, and this was done on principles of perfect reciprocity—They will now again meet on the same ground. But when a dissolution takes place, our original rights and sovereignties are resumed.—Our accession to the union has been by states. If any other principle is adopted by this convention, he will give it every opposition (Yates).

Wednesday, June 20, 1787

Mr. Lansing. . . . if we devise a system of government which will not meet with the approbation of our constituents, we are dissolving the union—but if we act within the limits of our power, it will be approved of; and should it upon experiment prove defective, the people will entrust a future convention again to amend it. Fond as many are of a general government, do any of you believe it can pervade the whole continent so effectually as to secure the peace and harmony and happiness of the whole? The excellence of the British model of government has been much insisted on; but we are endeavoring to complicate it with state governments, on principles which will gradually destroy the one or the other. You are sowing the seeds of rivalship, which must at last end in ruin (Yates).

Mr. Mason. The material difference between the two plans has already been clearly pointed out. The objection to that of Virginia arises from the want of power to carry it into effect. Will the first objection apply to a power merely recommendatory? In certain seasons of public danger it is commendable to exceed power.[10] The treaty of peace, under which we now enjoy the blessings of freedom, was made by persons who exceeded their powers. It met the approbation of the public, and thus deserved the praises of those who sent them. The impracticability of the plan is still groundless. These measures are supported by one who, at his time of life, has little to hope or expect from any government.[11] Let me ask, will the people entrust their dearest rights and liberties to the determination of one body of men, and those not chosen by them, and who are invested both with the sword and purse?[12] They never will—they never can—to a conclave, transacting their business secret from they eye of the public. Do we not discover by their public journals of the years 1778-9, and 1780, that factions and party spirit had guided many of their acts? The people of America, like all other people are unsettled in their minds, and their principle fixed to no object, except that a republican government is the best, and that the legislature ought to consist of two branches. The constitutions of the respective states, made and approved of by them, evince this principle. Congress, however, from other causes received a different organization. What, would you use military force to compel the observance of a social compact? It is destructive to the rights of the people. Do you expect the militia will do it, or do you mean a standing army? The first will never, on such occasion, exert any power; and the latter may turn its arms against the government which employs them. I never will consent to destroy the state governments, and will ever be as careful to preserve the one as the other. If we should, in the formation of the latter, have omitted some necessary regulation, I will trust my posterity to amend it. That the one government will be productive of disputes and jealousies against the other, I believe; but it will produce mutual safety. I shall close with observing that though some gentlemen have expressed much warmth on this and former occasions, I can excuse it, as the result of sudden passion; and hope that although we may differ in some particular points, if we mean the good of the whole, that our good sense upon reflection, will prevent us from spreading our discontent further (Yates).[13]

Mr. Martin. I know that the government must be supported; and if the one was incompatible with the other, I would support the state government at the expense of the union—for I consider the present system as a system of slavery. Impressed with this idea, I made use, on a former occasion, of expressions rather harsh. If gentlemen conceive that the legislative branch is dangerous, divide them into two. They are as much the representatives of the states, as the state assemblies are the representatives of the people. Are not the powers which we here exercise given by the legislatures? . . . I confess when the confederation was made, congress ought to have been invested with more extensive powers; but when the states saw that congress indirectly aimed at sovereignty, they were jealous, and therefore refused any farther concessions. The time is now come that we can constitutionally grant them not only new powers, but to modify their government, so that the state governments are not endangered. But whatever we have now in our power to grant, the grant is a state grant, and therefore it must be so organized that the state governments are interested in supporting the union. Thus systematized, there can be no danger if a small force is maintained (Yates).

Tuesday, July 3, 1787

Many of the members, impressed with the utility of a general government, connected with it the indispensible necessity of a representation from the states according to their numbers and wealth; while others, equally tenacious of the rights of the states, would admit of no other representation but such as was strictly federal, or in other words, equality of suffrage. This brought on a discussion of the principles on which the house had divided, and a lengthy recapitulation of the arguments advanced in the house in support of these opposite propositions. As I had not openly explained my sentiments on any former occasion on this question, but constantly in giving my vote, showed my attachment to the national government on federal principles, I took this occasion to explain my motives . . . (Yates).[14]

Saturday, July 7, 1787

Mr Gerry thought it would be proper to proceed to enumerate & define the powers to be vested in the Genl. Govt. before a question on the report should be taken as to the rule of representation in the 2d. branch.

Tuesday, July 10, 1787

Mr. Gerry was for increasing the number [of members in the initial House of Representatives] beyond 65. The larger the number the less danger of their being corrupted. The people are accustomed to & fond of a numerous representation, and will consider their rights as better secured by it. The danger of excess in the number may be guarded agst. by fixing a point within which the number shall always be kept.

Col. Mason admitted that the objection drawn from the consideration of expence, had weight both in itself, and as the people might be affected by it. But he thought it outweighed by the objections agst. the smallness of the number. 38, will he supposes, as being a majority of 65, form a quorum.[15] 20 will be a majority of 38. This was certainly too small a number to make laws for America. They would neither bring with them all the necessary information relative to the various local interests nor possess the necessary confidence of the people. After doubling the number, the laws might still be made by so few as almost to be objectionable on that account.

Saturday, July 14, 1787

Mr. L. Martin denies that there were ever [two-thirds] agst. the equality of votes [i.e., two-thirds of the convention favoring a departure from maintaining the equality of states]. The States that please to call themselves large, are the weekest in the Union. Look at Masts. Look at Virga. Are they efficient States? He was for letting a separation take place if they desired it. He had rather there should be two Confederacies, than one founded on any other principle than an equality of votes in the 2d branch at least.[16]

Tuesday, July 17, 1787

Mr. Luther Martin moved the following resolution "that the Legislative acts of the U.S. made by virtue & in pursuance of the articles of Union, and all treaties made & ratified under the authority of the U.S. shall be the supreme law of the respective States, as far as those acts or treaties shall relate to the said States, or their Citizens and inhabitants—& that the Judiciaries of the several States shall be bound thereby in their decisions, any thing in the respective laws of the individual States to the contrary notwithstanding" which was agreed to nem: con:[17]

Monday, August 6, 1787

Saw Mr. Mercer make out a list of the members names who had attended or were attending the convention with for and against marked opposite most of them—asked carelessly what question occasioned his being so particular upon which he told me laughing that it was no question but that those marked with a "for" were for a king. I then asked him how he knew that—to which he said no matter, the thing is so. I took a copy with his permission, and Mr. Martin seeing me about it asked what it was. I told him, in the words Mr. Mercer had told me, when he begged me to let him copy the list . . . I did (McHenry).

Tuesday, August 7, 1787

Mr. Mercer. The Constitution is objectionable in many points, but in none more than the present [requiring a property qualification to vote]. He objected to the footing on which the qualification was put, but particularly to the *mode of election* by the people. The people can not know & judge of the characters of the Candidates. The worst possible choice will be made. He quoted the case of the Senate in Virga. as an example in point—The people in Towns can unite their votes in favor of one favorite; & by that means always prevail over the people of the Country, who being dispersed will scatter their votes among a variety of candidates.

Wednesday, August 8, 1787

Mr. Mason thought 7 years [residency before a candidate is eligible for federal office] too long, but would never agree to part with the principle.[18]

It is a valuable principle. He thought it a defect in the plan that the Representatives would be too few to bring with them all the local knowledge necessary. If residence be not required, Rich men of neighbouring States, may employ with success the means of corruption in some particular district and thereby get into the public Councils after having failed in their own State. This is the practice in the boroughs of England.

Monday, August 13, 1787

Col. Mason. . . . the Senate did not represent the *people*, but the *States* in their political character. It was improper therefore that it should tax the people. The reason was the same agst. their doing it; as it had been agst. Congs. doing it. Nor was it in any respect necessary in order to cure the evils of our Republican system. He admitted that notwithstanding the superiority of the Republican form over every other, it had its evils. The chief ones, were the danger of the majority oppressing the minority, and the mischievous influence of demagogues. The Genl. Government of itself will cure these. As the States will not concur at the same time in their unjust & oppressive plans, the general Govt. will be able to check & defeat them, whether they result from the wickedness of the majority or from the misguidance of demagogues. Again, the Senate is not like the H. of Reps. chosen frequently and obliged to return frequently among the people. They are to be chosen by the St[ate]s for 6 years, will probably settle themselves at the seat of Govt. will pursue schemes for their own aggrandizement—will be able by weary[in]g out the H. of Reps and taking advantage of their impatience at the close of a long Session, to extort measures for that purpose. If they should be paid as he expected they would be yet determined & wished to be so, out of the Natl. Treasury, they will particularly extort an increase of their wages. A bare negative was a very different thing from that of originating bills. The practice in Engld was [a case] in point. The House of Lords does not represent nor tax the people, because not elected by the people. If the Senate can originate, they will in the recess of the Legislative Sessions, hatch their mischievous projects, for their own purposes, and have their money bills ready cut & dried, (to use a common phrase) for the meeting of the H. of Reps. . . . He did not mean by what he had said to oppose the permanency of the Senate. On the contrary he had no repugnance to an increase of it—nor allowing it a negative, though the Senate was not by its present constitution entitled to it. But in all events he would contend that the pursestrings should be in the hands of the Representatives of the people.[19]

Tuesday, August 14, 1787

Mr Mercer. It is a first principle in political science, that whenever the rights of property are secured, an aristocracy will grow out of it. Elective Governments also necessarily become aristocratic, because the rulers being few can & will draw emoluments for themselves from the many. The Governments of America will become aristocracies. They are so already. The public measures are calculated for the benefit of the Governors, not of the people. The people are dissatisfied & complain. They change their rulers, and the public measures are changed, but it is only a change of one scheme of emolument to the rulers, for another. The people gain nothing by it, but an addition of instability & uncertainty to their other evils.—Governmts. can only be maintained by force or influence. The Executive has not force; deprive him of influence by rendering the members of the (Legislature) ineligible to Executive offices, and he becomes a mere phantom of authority. The Aristocratic part will not even let him in for a share of the plunder. The Legislature must & will be composed of wealth & abilities, and the people will be governed by a Junto. The Executive ought to have a Council, being members of both Houses. Without such an influence, the war will be between the Aristocracy & the Executive. Nothing else can protect the people agst. those speculating Legislatures which are now plundering them throughout the U. States.

Saturday, August 18, 1787

Mr Gerry took notice that there was (no) check here agst. standing armies in time of peace. The existing Congs. is so constructed that it cannot of itself maintain an army. This wd. not be the case under the new system. The people were jealous on this head, and great opposition to the plan would spring from such an omission. He suspected that preparations of force were now making agst. it. (he seemed to allude to the activity of the Govr. of N. York at this crisis in disciplining the militia of that State.) He thought an army dangerous in time of peace & could never consent to a power to keep up an indefinite number. He proposed that there shall not be kept up in time of peace more than _____ thousand troops. His idea was that the blank should be filled with two or three thousand.[20]

Mr. Gerry thought this [allowing the national government to regulate the state militias] the last point remaining to be surrendered. If it be agreed to by the Convention, the plan will have as black a mark as was set on Cain. He had no such confidence in the Genl. Govt. as some Gentlemen possessed, and believed it would be found that the States have not.

Wednesday, August 22, 1787

Mr. Gerry & Mr. McHenry moved to insert after the 2d. sect. art: 7. the clause following, to wit, "The Legislature shall pass no bill of attainder nor (any) ex post facto law."[21]

Thurday, August 23, 1787

Mr. Gerry thought [allowing the national government control over state militias] was rather taking out of the right hand & putting into the left.[22] Will any man say that liberty will be as safe in the hands of eighty or a hundred men taken from the whole continent, as in the hands of two or three hundred taken from a single State?

Mr. Gerry. Let us at once destroy the State Govts have an Executive for life or hereditary, and a proper Senate, and then there would be some consistency in giving full powers to the Genl. Govt. but as the States are not to be abolished, he wondered at the attempts that were made to give powers inconsistent with their existence. He warned the Convention agst pushing the experiment too far. Some people will support a plan of vigorous Government at every risk. Others of a more democratic cast will oppose it with equal determination. And a Civil war may be produced by the conflict.[23]

Friday, August 31, 1787

Col. Mason 2ded. the motion [to postpone transmitting the Constitution to the states offered by Gerry], declaring that he would sooner chop off his right hand than put it to the Constitution as it now stands. He wished to see some points not yet decided brought to a decision, before being compelled to give a final opinion on this article. Should these points be improperly settled, his wish would then be to bring the whole subject before another general Convention.[24]

Monday, September 3, 1787

Mr. Randolph considered it as strengthening the general objection agst. the plan, that its definition of the powers of the Government was so loose as to give opportunities of usurping all the State powers. . . .

Monday, September 10, 1787

Mr. Gerry urged the indecency and pernicious tendency of dissolving in so light a manner, the solemn obligations of the articles of confederation. If nine out of thirteen can dissolve the compact, Six out of nine will be just as able to dissolve the new one hereafter.

Mr. Randolph took this opportunity to state his objections to the System. They turned on the Senate's being made the Court of Impeachment for trying the Executive—on the necessity of [three-fourths] instead of [two-thirds] of each house to overrule the negative of the President—on the smallness of the number of the Representative branch,—on the want of limitation to a standing army—on the general clause concerning necessary and proper laws—on the want of some particular restraint on Navigation acts—on the power to lay duties on exports—on the Authority of the general Legislature to interpose on the application of the Executives of the States—on the want of a more definite boundary between the General & State Legislatures—and between the General and State Judiciaries—on the unqualified power of the President to pardon treasons—on the want of some limit to the power of the Legislature in regulating their own compensations. With these difficulties in his mind, what course he asked was he to pursue? Was he to promote the establishment of a plan which he verily believed would end in Tyranny? He was unwilling he said to impede the wishes and Judgment of the Convention—but he must keep himself free, in case he should be honored with a Seat in the Convention of his State, to act according to the dictates of his judgment. The only mode in which his embarrassments could be removed, was that of submitting the plan to Congs. to go from them to the State Legislatures, and from these to State Conventions having power to adopt, reject or amend; the process to close with another general Convention with full power to adopt or reject the alterations proposed by the State Conventions, and to establish finally the Government—He accordingly proposed a Resolution to this effect.[25]

Wednesday, September 12, 1787

Mr. Gerry urged the necessity of Juries to guard agst. corrupt Judges. He proposed that the Committee last appointed should be directed to provide a clause for securing the trial by Juries.

Saturday, September 15, 1787

Col: Mason thought the plan of amendments exceptionable & dangerous. As the proposing of amendments is in both the modes to depend,
in the first immediately, and in the second, ultimately, on Congress,
no amendments of the proper kind would ever be obtained by the people, if the Government should become oppressive, as he verily believed would be the case.

Mr. Randolph . . . made a motion importing "that amendments to the
plan might be offered by the State Conventions, which should be submitted to and finally decided on by another general Convention"
Should this proposition be disregarded, it would he said be impossible
for him to put his name to the instrument. Whether he should oppose
it afterwards he would not then decide but he would not deprive himself of the freedom to do so in his own State, if that course should be
prescribed by his final judgment—[26]

Col: Mason 2ded. & followed Mr. Randolph in animadversions on the
dangerous power and structure of the Government, concluding that it
would end either in monarchy, or a tyrannical aristocracy; which, he
was in doubt. But one or other, he was sure. This Constitution had
been formed without the knowledge or idea of the people. A second
Convention will know more of the sense of the people, and be able to
provide a system more consonant to it. It was improper to say to the
people, take this or nothing. As the Constitution now stands, he could
neither give it his support or vote in Virginia; and he could not sign
here what he could not support there. With the expedient of another
Convention as proposed, he could sign.

Mr. Gerry, stated the objections which determined him to withhold
his name from the Constitution. 1. the duration and re-eligibility of
the Senate. 2. the power of the House of Representatives to conceal
their journals. 3—the power of Congress over the places of election.
4. the unlimited power of Congress over their own compensations.
5. Massachusetts has not a due share of Representatives allotted to
her. 6. [Three-fifths] of the Blacks are to be represented as if they were
freemen 7. *Under* the power over commerce, monopolies may be established. 8. The vice president being made head of the Senate. He
could however he said get over all these, if the rights of the Citizens
were not rendered insecure 1. by the general power of the Legislature
to make what laws they may please to call necessary and proper.
2. raise armies and money without limit. 3. to establish a tribunal with-

out juries, which will be a Star-chamber as to Civil cases. Under such a view of the Constitution, the best that could be done he conceived was to provide for a second general Convention.[27]

Monday, September 17, 1787

Mr Gerry described the painful feelings of his situation, and the embarrassment under which he rose to offer any further observations on the subject wch. had been finally decided. Whilst the plan was depending, he had treated it with all the freedom he thought it deserved—He now felt himself bound as he was disposed to treat it with the respect due to the Act of the Convention— He hoped he should not violate that respect in declaring on this occasion his fears that a Civil war may result from the present crisis of the U.S.— In Massachusetts, particularly he saw the danger of this calamitous event— In that State there are two parties, one devoted to Democracy, the worst he thought of all political evils, the other as violent in the opposite extreme. From the collision of these in opposing and resisting the Constituition, confusion was greatly to be feared. He had thought it necessary for this & other reasons that the plan should have been proposed in a more mediating shape, in order to abate the heat and opposition of parties— As it had been passed by the Convention, he was persuaded it would have a contrary effect— He could not therefore by signing the Constitution pledge himself to abide by it at all events. The proposed form made no difference with him. But if it were not otherwise apparent, the refusals to sign should never be known from him.[28] Alluding to the remarks of Docr. Franklin, he could not he said but view them as levelled against himself and the other gentlemen who meant not to sign.

LUTHER MARTIN'S "GENUINE INFORMATION"

"Genuine Information" was written as a series of letters to the Speaker of Maryland's House of Delegates. In all, twelve letters were produced serially in the Maryland Gazette *from December 28, 1787, to February 8, 1788. This unique firsthand account of the late convention attracted a great deal of notice, and each letter was reprinted in several other newspapers, some as many as eight or ten times.[29] Martin's writing was also collected into a pamphlet that had widespread readership. The work consists of two major parts: a relation of events from the convention and a systematic digest of Martin's objections to the Constitution. The latter portion is nearly*

twice the length of the former, but it is of less interest because his objections are not generally out of the ordinary. It is his willingness to discuss the convention's proceedings that is extraordinary, and it is what I have focused on here.

The tone of the letters is combative. Martin readily portrays his adversaries as holding one of two positions destructive of a federal republic: some were monarchists; others relentlessly pursued the interests of their own prominent states. The former group's intent was so obviously at odds with popular government—where legislatures, not executives should predominate—that they had to conceal their design. Martin does not explain in detail how monarchical preferences were concealed or how he saw through their misdirection. Such commentary would have provided an important link in the argument and thus made it significantly more persuasive. The latter group advocated proportional representation. This idea struck at the heart of Martin's conception of a federal order. His view was that the states were equal contracting partners, dictating that each should have the same power over collective decisions. Many Antifederalists made this argument, but it was a problematic one. It meant that Maryland would have as much power in the federation as Virginia, which struck even the Virginians who were against the Constitution as absurd. Clinging to the position that each was equal meant a continuation of the most obvious defect of the Confederation. If states fully retained sovereignty, then any one of them could prevent changes to the confederation. Rhode Island, with one-eightieth of the population of Virginia, could prevent changes considered necessary by all the other states to the obvious detriment of the national regime.

Despite the logic of Martin's position and its potential appeal to Marylanders, it did not square with the times. When it became clear that the national government would have legislative powers of its own rather than simply act as an agent of sovereign states, those in the large states naturally advocated proportional representation. Any hope that "Genuine Information" would serve to rally all Antifederalists foundered on this point. Virginians, Pennsylvanians, and Massachusetts residents—even those opposed to the Constitution—could hardly endorse Martin's position because it risked too great a loss of power for their own state. If the national regime's powers were to remain strictly limited, they could then side with Martin. According to Martin's own assessment, however, the Constitution had already gone well beyond improving the confederation. Indeed, it had set up a government that would annihilate the states. A further difficulty is Martin's spotty attendance. He missed the first three weeks of the convention, absented himself for two weeks in late July and and early August, and left two weeks before its conclusion.[30] Thus, the account he gives is far from systematic.

Nevertheless, Martin's views are still remarkable. "Genuine Information" expresses the legitimate frustrations of one who went to the convention to do what he was commissioned to do—amend the Articles of Confederation—and found the convention exceeding that charge. It also presents a cogent picture of Federalism as most Antifederalists understood it theoretically. His argument is not a dispassionate analysis of what transpired in Philadelphia. On the contrary, a good deal of the value of this work rests in its passion. "Genuine Information" is an important vocalization of the fears of a small-state politician with a unique insight into the convention. Martin believed that the political world he knew and cherished would be fundamentally altered by the new government. He wrote to alert his fellow citizens to this possibility. He also pointed out that this fundamental change in the character of the confederation was the design of the convention from the start. In that, he largely succeeds.[31]

. . . on our meeting in Convention, it was soon found there were among us three parties of very different sentiments and views:—

One party, whose object and wish it was to abolish and annihilate all state governments, and to bring forward one general government over this extensive continent, of a monarchical nature, under certain restrictions and limitations. Those who openly avowed this sentiment were, it is true, but few; yet it is equally true, sir, that there was a considerable number who did not openly avow it, who were, by myself and many others of the Convention, considered as being in reality favorers of that sentiment, and, acting upon those principles, covertly endeavoring to carry into effect what they well knew openly and avowedly could not be accomplished. The second party was not for the abolition of the state governments, nor for the introduction of a monarchical government under any form; but they wished to establish such a system as could give their own states undue power and influence, in the government, over the states.

A third party was what I considered truly federal and republican. This party was nearly equal in number with the other two, and was composed of the delegations from Connecticut, New York, New Jersey, Delaware, and in part from Maryland; also of some individuals from other representations. This party, sir, were for proceeding upon terms of federal equality; they were for taking our present federal system as the basis of their proceedings, and, as far as experience had shown that other powers were necessary to the federal government, to give those powers. They considered this the object for which they were sent by their states and what their states expected from them. They urged that if, after doing this, experience should show that there still were defects in the system, (as no doubt there would be,) the same good sense that induced this Convention to be called, would cause the states, when they found it necessary, to call another; and if that convention should act with the same moderation, the members of it would proceed to correct such errors and defects as experience should have brought to light—that, by proceeding in this train, we should have a prospect at length of obtaining as perfect a system of federal government as the nature of things would admit.

On the other hand, if we, contrary to the purpose for which we were intrusted, considering ourselves as master-builders, too proud to amend our original government, should demolish it entirely, and erect a new system of our own, a short time might show the new system as defective as the old, perhaps more so. Should a convention be found necessary again, if the members thereof, acting upon the same principles, instead of amending and correcting its defects, should demolish that entirely, and bring forward a third system, that also might soon be found no better than either of the former; and thus we might always remain young in government, and always suffering the inconveniences of an incorrect, imperfect system.[32]

But, sir, the favorers of monarchy, and those who wished the total abolition of state governments,—well knowing that a government founded on truly federal principles, the bases of which were the thirteen state governments preserved in full force and energy, would be destructive of their views; and knowing they were too weak in numbers openly to bring forward their system; conscious, also that the people of America would reject it if proposed to them, —joined their interest with that party who wished a system giving particular states the power and influence over the others, procuring, in return, mutual sacrifices from them, in giving the government great and undefined powers as to its legislative and executive; well knowing that, by departing from a federal system, they paved the way for their favorite object—the destruction of the state governments, and the introduction of monarchy.

. . . states, when once formed, are considered, with respect to each other, as individuals in a state of nature; that, like individuals, each state is considered equally free and equally independent, the one having no right to exercise authority over the other, though more strong, more wealthy, or abounding with more inhabitants—that, when a number of states unite themselves under a federal government, the same principles apply to them as when a number of individual men unite themselves under a state government—that every argument which shows one man ought not to have more votes than another, because he is wiser stronger, or wealthier, proves that one state ought not to have more votes than another, because it is stronger, richer, or more populous; and that, by giving one state, or one or two states, more votes than the others, the others thereby are enslaved to such state or states, having the greater number of votes, in the same manner as in the case before put of individuals, when one has more votes than the others—that the reason why each individual man, in forming a state government, should have an equal vote is, because each individual, before he enters into a federal government, are entitled to an equal vote, because, before they entered into such a federal government, each state was equally free and equally independent—that adequate representation of men, formed into a state government, consists in each man having an equal voice; either personally, or if by representatives, that he should have an equal voice in choosing the representatives—so adequate representation of states in a federal government consists in each state having an equal voice, either in person or by its representative, in every thing which relates to the federal government. . . .[33]

. . . Upon this compromise [the Great Compromise], a great number of the members so far engaged themselves, that, if the system was progressed upon agreeably to the terms of compromise, they would lend their names, by signing it, and would not actively oppose it, if their states should appear inclined to adopt it. Some however,—in which number was myself,—who joined in that report and agreed to proceed upon those principles, and see what kind of a system would ultimately be formed upon it, yet reserved to themselves, in the most explicit manner, the right of finally giving a solemn dissent to the system, if it was thought by them inconsistent with the freedom and happiness of their country. This, sir, will account for why the gentlemen of the Convention so generally signed their names to the system;—not because they thought it a proper one; not because they thoroughly approved, or were unanimous for it; but because they thought it better than the system attempted to be forced upon them.[34] This report of the select committee was, after long dissension, adopted by a majority of the Convention, and the system was proceeded in accordingly. I believe near a fortnight—perhaps more—was spent in the discussion of this business, during which we were on the verge of dissolution, scarce held together by the strength of a hair, though the public papers were announcing our extreme unity. . . . Soon after this period, the Hon. Mr. Yates and Mr. Lansing, of New York, left us. They had uniformly opposed the system; and, I believe, despairing of getting a proper one brought forward, or of rendering any real service, they returned no more. The propositions reported by the committee of the whole house having been fully discussed by the Convention, and, with many alterations, having been agreed to by the majority, a committee of five was appointed to detail the system according to the principles contained in what had been agreed to by that majority. This was likely to require some time, and the Convention adjourned for eight or ten days. Before the adjournment, I moved for liberty to be given to the different members to take correct copies of the propositions to which the Convention had then agreed, in order that, during the recess of the Convention, we might be prepared, again the Convention met, to bring them forward for discussion. But, sir, the same spirit which caused our doors to be shut, our proceedings to be kept secret, our Journals to be locked up, and every avenue, as far as possible, to be shut to public information, prevailed also in this case, and the poposal, so reasonable and necessary, was rejected by a majority of the Convention; thereby precluding even the members themselves from the necessary means of information and deliberation on the important business in which they were engaged.[35]

It has been observed, Mr. Speaker, by my honorable colleagues, that the debate respecting the mode of representation was productive of considerable warmth. This observation is true. But, sir, it is equally true, that, if we could have tamely and servilely consented to be bound in chains, and meanly condescended to assist in riveting them fast, we might have avoided all that warmth, and have proceeded with as much calmness and coolness as any Stoic could have wished. . . . it is the state governments which are to watch over and protect the rights of the individual, whether rich or poor, or of moderate circumstances, and in which the democratic and aristocratic influence or principles are to be so blended, modified, and checked, as to prevent oppression and injury—that the federal government is to guard and to protect the states and their rights, and to regulate their common concerns—that a federal government is formed by the states, as states, (that is, in their sovereign capacities,) in the same manner as treaties and alliances are formed—that a sovereignty, considered as a sovereignty, are the same, whether that sovereignty is monarchical, aristocratical, democratical, or mixed—that the history of mankind doth not furnish an instance, from its earliest history to the present time, of a federal government constituted of two distinct branches. . . .[36]

. . . [The Constitution] is in its very introduction, declared to be a compact between the people of the United States as individuals; and it is to be ratified by the people at large, in their capacity as individuals; all which, it is said, would be quite right and proper, if there were no state governments, if all the people of this continent were in a state of nature, and we were forming one national government for them as individuals; and is nearly the same as was done in most of the states, when they formed their governments over the people who composed them.

. . . they who advocate the system pretend to call themselves federalists, in Convention the distinction was quite the reverse; those who opposed the system were there considered and styled the federal party, those who advocated it the anti-federal.

Viewing it as a national, not a federal government,—as calculated and designed, not to protect and preserve, but to abolish and annihilate, the state governments,—it was opposed for the following reasons: It was said that this continent was much too extensive for one national government, which should have sufficient power and energy to pervade, and hold in obedience and subjection, all its parts, consistently with the enjoyment and preservation of liberty—that the genius and habits of the people of America were opposed to such a government—that, during their connection with Great Britain, they had been accustomed to have all their concerns transacted within a narrow circle, their colonial district; they had been accustomed to have their seats of government near them, to which they might have access, without much inconvenience, when their business should require it. . . . governments of a republican nature are those best calculated to preserve the freedom and happiness of the citizen . . . governments of this kind are only calculated for a territory but small in its extent—that the only method by which an extensive continent, like America, could be connected and united together, consistently with the principles of freedom, must be by having a number of strong and energetic state governments, for securing and protecting the rights of individuals forming those governments, and for regulating all their concerns; and a strong, energetic federal government over those states, for the protection and preservation, and for regulating the common concerns of the states.

Even if it was possible to effect a total abolition of the state governments at this time, and to establish one general government over the people of America, it could not long subsist, but in a little time would again be broken into a variety of governments of a smaller extent, similar, in some manner, to the present situation of this continent. The principal difference, in all probability, would be, that the governments so established, being effected by some violent convulsion, might not be formed on principles so favorable to liberty as those of our present state governments—that this ought to be an important consideration to such of the states who had excellent governments, which was the case with Maryland, and most others, whatever it might be to persons who, disapproving of their particular state government, would be willing to hazard every thing to overturn and destroy it. These reasons, sir, influenced me to vote against two branches in the legislature and against every part of the system which was repugnant to the principles of a federal government. Nor was there a single argument urged, or reason assigned, which, to my mind, was satisfactory to prove that a good government, on federal principles was unattainable; the whole of their arguments only proving, what none of us controverted—that our federal government, as originally formed, was defective, and wanted amendment. However, a majority of the Convention, hastily and inconsiderately, without condescending to make a fair trial, in their great wisdom decided that a kind of government which a Montesquieu and a Price have declared the best calculated of any to preserve internal liberty, and to enjoy external strength and security, and the only one by which a large continent can be connected and united, consistently with the principles of liberty, was totally impracticable; and they acted accordingly.[37] It was attempted to obtain a resolve that, if seven states, whose votes in the first branch, concurred in the adoption of the system, it should be sufficient, and this attempt was supported on the principle, that a majority ought to govern the minority; but to this it was objected that, although it was true, after a constitution and form of government is agreed on, in every act done under and consistent with that constitution and form of government, the act of the majority, unless otherwise agreed in the constitution, should bind the minority, yet it was directly the reverse in originally forming a constitution, or dissolving it—that, in originally forming a constitution, it was necessary that every individual should agree to it, to become bound thereby, and that, when once adopted, it could not be dissolved by consent, unless with the consent of every individual who was party to the original agreement—that, in forming our original federal government, every member of that government (that is, each state) expressly consented to it—that is part of the compact, made and entered into in the most solemn manner, that there should be no dissolution or alteration of that federal government without the consent of every state, the members of, and parties to, the original compact—that, therefore, no alteration could be made by the consent of a part of these states, or by the consent of the inhabitants of a part of the states, which could either release the states so consenting from the obligation they are under to the other states, or which could in any manner become obligatory upon those states that should not ratify such alterations. Satisfied of the truth of these positions, and not holding ourselves at liberty to violate the compact, which this state had solemnly entered into with the others, by altering it in a different manner from that which, by the compact, is provided and stipulated, a number of members, and among those the delegation of this state, opposed the ratification of this system in any other manner than by the unanimous consent and agreement of all states.[38]

By our original Articles of Confederation, any alterations proposed are, in the first place, to be approved by Congress. Accordingly, as the resolutions were originally adopted by the Convention, and as they were reported by the committee of detail, it was proposed that this system should be laid before Congress, for their approbation. But, sir, the warm advocates of this system, fearing it would not meet with the approbation of Congress and determined, even though Congress and the respective state legislatures should disapprove the same, to force it upon them, if possible, through the intervention of the people at large, moved to strike out the words "for their approbation," and succeeded in their motion; to which, it being directly a violation of the mode prescribed by the Articles of Confederation for the alteration of our federal government, a part of the Convention, and myself in the number, thought it a duty to give a decided negative.

Agreeably to the Articles of Confederation, entered into in the most solemn manner, and for the observance of which the states pledged themselves to each other, and called upon the Supreme Being as a witness and avenger between them, no alterations are to be made in those articles, unless, after they are approved by Congress, they are agreed to, and ratified, by the legislature of every state; but by the resolve of the Convention, this Constitution is not to be ratified by the legislatures of the respective states, but is to be submitted to conventions chosen by the people, and, if ratified by them, is to be binding.

This resolve was opposed, among others, by the delegation of Maryland. Your delegates were of opinion that, as the form of government proposed was, if adopted, most essentially to alter the Constitution of this state, and as our Constitution had pointed out a mode by which, and by which only, alterations were to be made therein, a convention of the people could not be called to agree to and ratify the said form of government without a direct violation of our Constitution, which it is the duty of every individual in this state to protect and support. In this opinion all your delegates who were attending were unanimous. I, sir, opposed it also upon a more extensive ground, as being directly contrary to the mode of altering our federal government, established in our original compact: and as such being a direct violation of the mutual faith plighted by the states to each other, I gave it my negative.

I was of opinion that the states, considered as states, in their political capacity, are the members of a federal government—that the states in their political capacity, or as sovereignties, are entitled, and only entitled, originally to agree upon the form of, and submit themselves to, a federal government, and afterwards, by mutual consent, to dissolve or alter it—that every thing which relates to the formation, the dissolution, or the alteration, of a federal government over states equally free, sovereign, and independent, is the peculiar province of the states in their sovereign or political capacity, in the same manner as what relates to forming alliances or treaties of peace, amity, or commerce; and that the people at large, in their individual capacity, in the same manner as what relates to forming alliances or treaties of peace, amity, or commerce; and that the people at large, in their individual capacity, have no more right to interfere in the one case than in the other—that according to these principles we originally acted [on] in forming our Confederation. It was the states as states, by their representatives in Congress, that formed the Articles of Confederation; it was the states as states, by their legislatures, who ratified those Articles; and it was there established and provided that the states as states (that is, by their legislatures) should agree to any alterations that should hereafter be proposed in the federal government, before they should be binding; and any alterations agreed to in any other manner cannot release the states from the obligation they are under to each other by virtue of the original Articles of Confederation. The people of the different states never made any objection to the manner in which the Articles of Confederation were formed or ratified, or to the mode by which alterations were to be made in that government: with the rights of their respective states they wished not to interfere. Nor do I believe the people, in their individual capacity, would ever have expected or desired to have been appealed to on the present occasion, in violation of the rights of their respective states, if the favorers of the proposed Constitution, imagining they had a better chance of forcing it to be adopted by a hasty appeal to the people at large, (who could not be so good judges of the dangerous consequence,) had not insisted upon this mode. Nor do these positions in the least interfere with the principle that all power originates from the people; because, when once the people have exercised their power in establishing and forming themselves into a state government, it never devolves back to them; nor have they a right to resume or again to exercise that power, until such events take place as will amount to a dissolution of their state government. And it is an established principle, that a dissolution or alteration of a federal government doth not dissolve the state governments which compose it.

. . . When I took my seat in the Convention, I found them attempting to bring forward a system which, I was sure, never had entered into the contemplation of those I had the honor to represent, and which, upon the fullest consideration, I considered not only injurious to the interest and rights of this state, but also incompatible with the political happiness and freedom of the states in general. From that time until my business compelled me to leave the Convention, I gave it every possible opposition, in every stage of its progression. I opposed the system there with the same explicit frankness with which I have here given you a history of our proceedings, an account of my own conduct, which in a particular manner I consider you as having a right to know. While there, I endeavored to act as a freeman, and the delegate of a free state. Should my conduct obtain the approbation of those who appointed me, I will not deny it would afford me satisfaction; but to me that approbation was at most no more than a secondary consideration: my first was, to deserve it . . .

NOTES

1. One commentator writes: "Between the Antifederalists and Federalists, Governor Edmund Randolph occupied the middle ground. He insisted that he was a friend to the Constitution (which he also refused to sign), but he argued that the way to prevent the document's outright rejection was to advocate prior amendments, particularly a bill of rights" (Alan Briceland in *The Constitution and the States*, ed. Conley and Kaminski, p. 209).

2. The first version of a supremacy clause was part of the New Jersey Plan introduced on June 15; because of the similarity in wording with his own proposal of July 17, it is believed Martin had probably written the language into the New Jersey Plan (Anderson, p. 81). He probably did so in part to make the alternative to the Virginia Plan sound more palatable to a convention ready to forge a powerful national government. But a careful review of his suggested

language reveals another purpose, in line with his state-centric outlook. Martin's concept of supremacy was much more circumscribed than that eventually adopted. His proposal read, "the Legislative acts of the U.S. made by virtue & in pursuance of the articles of Union, and all treaties made & ratified under the authority of the U.S. shall be the supreme law of the respective states. . . ." In this formulation, the states would be bound only to the laws and treaties of the national government authorized by the national Constitution. Presumably, the states would retain the ability to review the constitutionality of national laws and be able to declare them unconstitutional in their jurisdiction without being overridden by the national government. Article VI, section 2 explicitly states that the national Constitution trumps the state constitutions. Despite the best efforts of nullifiers like John C. Calhoun and interpositionists like Jefferson, most have agreed that the supremacy clause allows the national government to determine with finality what is constitutional and thus impose its will on states when the need arises.

3. These accounts were written as individuals were speaking, thus there are abbreviations in the text, most of which are easy to decipher. For those that are not, I have supplied brackets. A fuller picture of the contexts in which these speeches were delivered is provided by Max Farrand's *Records of the Federal Convention*, still an indispensible source more than ninety years after its initial publication.

4. Given Randolph's qualms about signing a Constitution that gave the national government indefinite powers (see his comments from September 10), this account either misunderstands Randolph's position or exaggerates the extent to which he was committed to the nationalization of power. From the text of the Virginia Plan, the notes of others, and Randolph's later speeches, it is clear that he hoped that the national government would be recognized as the superior of the state governments but that it would have only circumscribed powers (Farrand, vol. 1, 18–28, 53; vol. 2, 631, 644–46). Yates' notes indicate that he, like Luther Martin, considered any change in the power of states from strict equality to be a clear departure from a federation.

5. Note that this speech reflects Mason's preference for a British-style mixed regime. Mason is committed to democracy in one institution only, the House of Representatives. He believed that the Senate should approximate the House of Lords. If the House were democratic and the Senate aristocratic, he believed that the "rights of every class of people" could be safeguarded. The problem he saw with the convention was that it was too aristocratic in its leanings and thus constructed a government where all the institutions would be primarily influenced by the aristocracy.

6. Here Gerry, like Mason on May 31, displays his preference for a British-style mixed regime, with one branch of the federal legislature representative of the aristocratical element of society.

7. Mason had participated in the Revolutionary War as a colonel in the Virginia militia; thus, Madison refers to him by his military ranking.

8. This fear, a common one for both elite Antifederalists and Federalists, was solved by requiring Senators to be elected by state legislatives.

9. Here, Lansing refers to the discussion of May 30. In introducing the Virginia Plan the day before, Randolph mentioned that alterations to the confederation could not solve the problems they faced. South Carolina's Charles Cotesworth Pinckney wondered whether they could even discuss such a new system because their commission asked them only to propose alterations to the Articles of Confederation (Farrand, volume 1, 34). The convention apparently toyed with taking a definitive vote on whether they could proceed as Randolph suggested, but they ultimately decided not to. Lansing interprets that decision as a reluctance on the part of the convention to exceed their commissions, a reluctance that he thinks should still govern them.

10. This speech of Mason's is a direct response to Lansing's above it. It shows how different the thinking of these two budding Antifederalists were. Unlike Lansing, Mason clearly thinks that the convention is authorized to construct a national government and that the people will follow.

11. Mason is referring to himself. Since he is too old to personally benefit from the government and supports it anyway, it must be a good thing. Mason was born in 1725; this "old" man was sixty-two years of age.

12. Though it is unclear from accounts of his speeches, Lansing was, like Luther Martin, apparently still advocating a unicameral legislature at this point, which Mason thinks would be unable to check legislators' selfishness.

13. This plea for harmony seems curious from one who ultimately refused to sign the document. Mason's testy response to Lansing gives some indication of why he refused to go along in the end. Surely his expressed reasoning, the lack of a bill of rights, was a key factor in Mason's opposition. But it has also been noted by Stanley Elkins and Eric McKitrick that Mason himself proposed the inclusion of a bill of rights; thus, he was probably personally offended by the convention's refusal to consider one Elkins and McKitrick, *The Age of Federalism*, 59).

14. Unfortunately, there is no text of this speech, though Yates apparently wrote it out. Nor did Madison or any other convention scribe note what Yates said. It is likely that his sentiments were so different from what the convention was working with that his ideas were merely disregarded. Yates' last journal entry came on July 5, and he and Lansing left the convention shortly thereafter.

15. Mason was apparently poor at math, as a majority of sixty-five is thirty-three, not thirty-eight.

16. This kind of comment, intimating that Martin would accept a breakup of the Union, is a very rare argument for anyone to make around the time of ratification. The few such comments Antifederalists made were exploited by Federalists for their advantage. Alexander Hamilton, for instance, did so in "Federalist #1." As "Publius," Hamilton wrote that if the Constitution were not adopted, the union would likely split up into several rival republics.

17. *Nem. con.* is an abbreviation in Madison's notes for the Latin "nemine contradicente," literally meaning "no contrary votes." Thus, Martin's suggestion was unanimously agreed to.

18. In other words, Mason is arguing in favor of there being some residence requirement for national representatives, but he thinks seven years is too long.

19. Mason here supports Randolph's suggestion that the House be given exclusive power to originate bills that raise revenue. Like the Virginia governor, Mason believes the Senate should be able to modify such bills but not introduce them. Note again the importance of the British mixed system and its precedents to Mason.

20. A resolution to this effect was offered by Luther Martin and seconded by Gerry, but was opposed by each of the state delegations.

21. The prohibition on bills of attainder passed without dissent from any state delegation; the prohibition on ex post facto laws passed seven states to three. Both prohibitions are contained in Article I, section 9, of the Constitution.

22. Gerry here responds to New Hampshire's John Langdon, who said (in transferring powers from the state governments to the national government), "I only take out of my left hand what it cannot so well use, and put it into my right hand where it can be better used" (Farrand, volume 2, 386).

23. The first phrases are meant facetiously. This quote nicely captures Gerry's genuine fear that the proposed Constitution itself might prompt civil war.

24. See Mason's objections reprinted in chapter 3.

25. This passage is a fair summary of the objections Randolph raised in his public letter. Since the actual letter is lengthy and since Randolph's credentials as an Antifederalist are dubious, it is not reprinted in this volume.

26. Two days later, the convention's elder statesman, Benjamin Franklin, made a plea that all delegates sign the Constitution. Franklin related that as he gained experience, he found himself increasingly fallible. While he did object to some parts of the Constitution, his sense of fallibility kept him from thinking he was necessarily right. The nation clearly needed a "general government," and he would not stand in the way simply because he thought a few things were amiss. Franklin invited those threatening not to sign to "doubt a little of [their] own fallibility," too. He also allowed these objectors to maintain their opposition while signing, by moving that signing merely signified that all were witness to the fact that the convened states unanimously approved transmitting the document to the Confederation Congress (Farrand, volume 2, 641–43). Randolph, however, refused to be moved.

27. Compare this letter with Gerry's objections printed in chapter 3.

28. Gerry here rejects the form of signing Franklin proposed (as outlined in note 26) that would have allowed even those who objected to the Constitution to sign it. But he also pledges not to openly oppose the Constitution if names are not affixed to the document, implying that if delegates did sign the Constitution, he would have to make his objections public.

29. Cornell, *The Other Founders*, pp. 310–12.

30. Anderson, *Creating the Constitution*, xi.

31. The text of Martin's "Genuine Information" is reproduced from Jonathan Elliot's *Debates on the Adoption of the Federal Constitution*, first published 1827–1830. Reprinted in 1901, excerpts from volume 1, pp. 349–51; 352–53; 357–59; 360, 362–63; 386–88. Italics are used so frequently in the text as to be cumbersome and rather meaningless. They are not included, but original spelling and punctuation are retained.

32. In this paragraph, Martin displays an interesting take on government that is similar to Edmund Burke's. In *Reflections on the Revolution in France* (published two years after Martin's letters), Burke chides the French revolutionaries for their hubris. Thinking that they could build a successful political order from scratch, after having eliminated France's old institutions, was folly. To Burke, successful political orders were organic entities, with a logic of their own that did not easily correspond to rationalist attempts at refashioning them.

33. Making the analogy that the relations of states are like that of individuals in the state of nature is theoretically sound, but what is striking is how easily this argument can be turned against Martin. If people are considered "equal," a Federalist could respond that each individual Virginian should have as much say in the national government as each individual Rhode Islander, thus dictating that Virginia as a whole should have much more clout than tiny Rhode Island. In a popular appeal, Martin's abstract theoretical argument was probably less effective than if he would have straightforwardly asserted that the national government would swallow up the states.

34. If true, Martin's assertion would greatly change our view of the Philadelphia convention. Most believe the convention ultimately settled on a proposal that the vast majority of delegates thought to be very beneficial. Martin's belief is that many delegates went along despite deep reservations about the system in order to avoid a greater evil. He is probably thinking of the delegates, now mainly obscure, who pinned their hopes on the New Jersey Plan. If Martin is correct that they did not *really* support the Constitution, it means that relatively few vocal delegates dominated the convention in a way that is underappreciated and others became Federalists almost by default.

35. Martin proposed that delegates take the tentative conclusions of the convention to constituents on July 25. His suggestion narrowly lost: five state delegations voted in favor; six opposed. Had one opposing state favored the proposal, the ratification debate would have begun eight weeks earlier. Because of the radical departures made by the convention, a public debate about its proposals would likely have aided the Antifederalist cause. In the face of public pressure, the convention may have foundered.

36. Martin understands that a bicameral legislature is an indication that the new regime will be a government in itself rather than a mere confederation. In a true confederation, there would be no need for a bicameral legislature. Its powers would be greatly circumscribed, and it would be understood that each of the states confederating were, as sovereign entities, equal. Thus, a confederation would require no need for an elaborate system of checks and balances or a compromise scheme of representation, both of which were written into the Constitution. Bicameralism itself was an indication to Martin that the national regime was no longer a federation (as he understood that term).

37. Baron de Montesquieu was a famed political philosopher of the mid-eighteenth century whose most famous work was *The Spirit of the Laws*. Richard Price was an English pamphleteer who had achieved fame for his work titled "Observations on the Nature of Civil Liberty," which was published almost coincident with the American Revolution. In "Observations,"

Price argued that the Americans were justified in petitioning for their rights. He and Montesquieu both believed that a federation of republics was the best possible governing arrangement because it combined the possibility of popular government (of necessity available only in small republics) and the strength to repel external enemies. Martin thinks this form of government is precisely the kind the United States has and that it is one that it will not have if the Constitution is ratified.

38. Article VII of the Constitution required that nine states, not a bare majority or all of them, approve of the document before it could be put into effect in the ratifying states.

3

The Contemporaneous Canon

Thousands contributed to the ratification debate. *The Documentary History of the Ratification of the Constitution*, which provides a comprehensive digest of ratification debate documents, has already stretched to nineteen volumes and more than fifteen thousand pages. More than sixteen hundred individuals voted in the state ratification conventions, and hundreds of figures spoke or wrote against the proposed Constitution. The reason for this breadth of participation is readily apparent. The ratification question was recognized as the most momentous political decision that participants would make in their lifetime. It may have been the most important decision ever submitted to a popular vote in human history. It may still be. With so many voices involved, the debate might easily seem cacophonous, but for the fact that a relatively small number of writings were widely reprinted. Because of their wide distribution, the works in this chapter form a kind of "contemporaneous canon." The writings contained in this chapter arguably defined Antifederalism for most contemporary observers.

During the late 1700s, newspaper editors borrowed freely from each other. As a result, many essays, both Federalist and Antifederalist, were reprinted after their initial publication. Additionally, a large number of works were compiled and published as pamphlets, broadsides, or even books after their initial publication. In an appendix of *The Other Founders*, Saul Cornell lists 132 such Antifederalist tracts. This number is impressive, but it may even understate the amount of reprinting done, as this count relies on our imperfect knowledge of what was reprinted where. Nevertheless, Cornell's data on reprint frequency is a convenient way to assess how widespread various Antifederalist writings were distributed. He identifies seventeen works that were printed ten times or more after their initial appearance. Only nine of those were reprinted twenty times or more. Of these nine, six are included here.[1]

But why these works? Why were these Antifederalist writings more widely reprinted than the others? For at least four of the writings in this chapter, the answer is simple: these were letters authored by the members of the Philadelphia convention who decided to oppose the Constitution. Elbridge Gerry, Richard Henry Lee, and George Mason were men of national reputation even before the convention met. Their high-profile dissents begged for explanation. While Robert Yates and John Lansing were not national figures, their departure from the convention had been notable, as it left New York without an official vote for the remainder of the proceedings. They too needed to provide an explanation for their actions. The brevity of these letters also allowed them to be repinted quickly and cheaply, on a single page of newsprint.

The other two writings reproduced were both penned in Philadelphia, which was the largest city in the nation and a hub of printing activity. Its central location allowed printed material to be distributed quickly to the rest of the country. The first letter of "Centinel" appeared early in the ratification process, allowing it to become an exemplar for a virulent brand of Antifederalism. Centinel's accusatory tone at once encouraged reprintings in backcountry areas where the argument would be favorably received and in coastal areas where Federalist publishers could disapprove of its intemperate nature. As noted in the "Dissent of the Minority" of the Pennsylvania convention, the Quaker state's ratification was accompanied by significant irregularities, and Antifederalists wished to publicize these irregularities. Because the state had ratified so early in the process, there was ample time for this dissent to become widely distributed.

In this Antifederalist canon, the most frequent complaints about the Constitution are readily discerned: rights are not secured; legislative powers are vague and unlimited; powers are not separated among branches of government but mixed between them; the system is dangerously tilted toward aristocracy; and the national judiciary will pervert justice. Yet, careful readers of this "canon" will also discover tensions between the various writings. Centinel's virulence is readily apparent. He relates that "the wealthy and ambitious . . . think they have a right to lord it over their fellow creatures . . . and now triumphantly exult in the completion of their long meditated schemes of power and aggrandisement." These harsh words would have shocked the much more temperate Gerry, Mason, and Lee, themselves members of the nation's political and economic elite. Gerry hoped to defuse tensions, not arouse them, and he admonished people "not to be precipitate in their decisions." Lee thinks the Constitution can be perfected through amendments; Yates and Lansing believe it will destroy state sovereignty, implying that even an amended document would be unacceptable. Mason and Lee feel the South is made vulnerable by the Constitution, a concern the others look past. Gerry openly pledges to acquiesce to whatever is adopted; the Pennsylvania minority's qualms about the process's legitimacy are so deep that they don't think the ratification convention's actions are "binding on the people."[2]

The following essays are not the most detailed Antifederalist arguments, nor are they the most philosophical. They are, however, the criticisms of the Constitution that were most widely known in 1787–1788. These widespread ideas became part of the discourse of the time, and they were recognized even by many who did not read them. Their familiarity required Federalists to react to them in order to neutralize or deflect their criticisms. By this process, these writings shaped the course ratification took and even affected how the Constitution itself would be interpreted.

CENTINEL I

Philadelphia Independent Gazetteer, October 5, 1787

Centinel was written by Philadelphian Samuel Bryan. Years after the ratification debate, when Bryan applied for jobs in the Jefferson administration, he listed writing the letters of Centinel among his accomplishments. At the time of their appearance, Bryan was a young mathematics instructor at the University of Pennsylvania. His father, George Bryan, was a well-known politician who many erroneously suspected was Centinel. The elder Bryan had helped his son secure a position as clerk of the general assembly, a post Samuel Bryan held immediately prior to teaching math. Eighteen essays appeared in the series, and Bryan continued to write under the pseudonym even after ratification. This particular essay was reprinted at least twenty-seven times.

Centinel's first essay is one of his most careful. An argument is presented, rather than the polemic of many later essays. The political philosophy espoused by Centinel is a unique mix of classical republicanism, radical democratic views, and a Burkean sense of how politics works. "Time and habit," he writes, yield "stability and attachment" to governments. If a governing form is new or if the constitution of a state is unsettled, the "enlightened and aspiring few" have a greater chance to manipulate the government for their own benefit. After time, governments take on a definitive character.[3] Though John Adams' preference for a mixed regime might sound alluring, actual regimes either become aristocratic or democratic. Even Britain hasn't successfully combined aristocratic and democratic power. Furthermore, this kind of government is based on the participants' selfish motives: aristocrats seek aristocratic outcomes whereas the general public has its own set of "interests," requiring the two sets of interests to accommodate. By contrast, Centinel argues that there is a "common good." Every citizen, he hopes, will act for the good of the community regardless of his personal interest.

The aforementioned views are combined with a strong preference for a unicameral legislature. Pennsylvania had a single legislative body at the time, and it is Centinel's contention that such arrangements are much more democratic than two-chambered legislatures. After all, the will of the democratic majority cannot be stopped by an aristocratic upper chamber. In addition, the unicameral legislature is more "responsible"; that is, all citizens know who to praise or blame. Legislators cannot blame the other chamber for dragging their feet or being unreasonable. This argument is strikingly modern. It prefigures the views of many political scientists, from Woodrow Wilson to present-day scholars like Morris Fiorina. These observers all dislike the Constitution's inefficiency. They dispute the conventional wisdom that "checks and balances" are beneficial, saying that it leads to gridlock and a "blame game" among politicians.[4] Fitting these arguments together isn't always easy. Nevertheless, Centinel does so quite skillfully, and in so doing he prefigures the most persistent modern critique of the Constitution. Centinel was also one of the most provocative authors who wrote during the ratification debate. As such, many authors responded to his argument.

To the Freemen of Pennsylvania

Friends, Countrymen and *Fellow Citizens,* Permit one of yourselves to put you in mind of certain *liberties* and *privileges* secured to you by the constitution of this commonwealth, and to beg your serious attention to his uninterested opinion upon the plan of federal government submitted to your consideration, before you surrender these great and valuable privileges up forever. Your present frame of government, secures you to a right to hold yourselves, houses, papers, and possessions free from search and seizure, and therefore warrants granted without oaths or affirmations first made, affording sufficient foundation for them, whereby any officer or messenger may be commanded or required to search your house or seize your persons or property, not particularly described in such warrant, shall not be granted. Your constitution further provides "that in controversies respecting property, and in suits between man and man, the parties have a right *to trial by jury, which ought to be held sacred.*" It also provides and declares, "*that the people have a right of* FREEDOM OF SPEECH, *and of* WRITING *and* PUBLISHING *their sentiments, therefore* THE FREEDOM OF THE PRESS OUGHT NOT TO BE RESTRAINED." The constitution of Pennsylvania is yet in existence, as yet you have the right to *freedom of speech,* and of *publishing your sentiments.* How long those rights will appertain to you, you yourselves are called upon to say, whether your *houses* shall continue to be your castles; whether your *papers,* your *persons* and your *property,* are to be held sacred and free from *general warrants,* you are now to determine. Whether the *trial by jury* is to continue as your birthright, the freemen of Pennsylvania, nay, of all America, are now called upon to declare.

Without presuming upon my own judgment, I cannot think it an unwarrantable presumption to offer my private opinion, and call upon others for their's; and if I use my pen with the boldness of a freeman, it is because I know that *the liberty of the press yet remains unviolated,* and *juries yet are judges.*

The late Convention have submitted to your consideration a plan of a new federal government—The subject is highly interesting to your future welfare—Whether it be calculated to promote the great ends of civil society, viz. the happiness and prosperity of the community; it behoves you well to consider, uninfluenced by the authority of names. Instead of that frenzy of enthusiasm, that has actuated the citizens of Philadelphia, in their aprobation of the proposed plan, before it was possible that it could be the result of a rational investigation into its principles; it ought to be dispassionately and deliberately examined, and its own intrinsic merit the only criterion of your patronage. If ever free and unbiassed discussion was proper or necessary, it is on such an occasion. —All the blessings of liberty and the dearest privileges of freemen, are now at stake and dependent on your present conduct. Those who are competent to the task of developing the principles of government, ought to be encouraged to come forward, and thereby the better enable the people to make a proper judgment; for the science of government is

so abstruse, that few are able to judge for themselves; without such assistance the people are too apt to yield an implicit assent to the opinions of those characters, whose abilities are held in the highest esteem,
and to those in whose integrity and patriotism they can confide; not
considering that the love of domination is generally in proportion to
talents, abilities, and superior acquirements; and that the men of the
greatest purity of intention may be made instruments of despotism in
the hands of the *artful and designing.* If it were not for the stability and
attachment which time and habit gives to forms of government, it
would be in the power of the enlightened and aspiring few, if they
should combine, at any time to destroy the best establishments, and
even make the people the instruments of their own subjugation.

The late revolution having effaced in a great measure all former
habits, and the present institutions are so recent, that their exists not
that great reluctance to innovation, so remarkable in old communities, and which accords with reason, for the most comprehensive mind
cannot foresee the full operation of material changes on [a] civil polity;
it is the genius of the common law to resist innovation.

The wealthy and ambitious, who in every community think they
have a right to lord it over their fellow creatures, have availed themselves, very successfully, of this favorable disposition; for the people
thus unsettled in their sentiments, have been prepared to accede to any
extreme of government; all the distresses and difficulties they experience, proceeding from various causes, have been ascribed to the impo-
tency of the present confederation, and thence they have been led to expect full relief from the adoption of the proposed system of government;
and in the other event, immediate ruin and annihilation as a nation.
These characters flatter themselves that they have lulled all distrust and
jealousy of their new plan, by gaining the concurrence of the two men
in whom America has the highest confidence, and now triumphantly
exult in the completion of their long meditated schemes of power and
aggrandisement.[5] I would be very far from insinuating that the two illustrious personages alluded to, have not the welfare of their country at
heart; but that the unsuspecting goodness and zeal of the one, has been
imposed on, in a subject of which he must be necessarily inexperienced,
from his other arduous engagements; and that the weakness and indecision attendant on old age, has been practised on in the other.[6]

I am fearful that the principles of government inculcated in Mr.
Adams's treatise and enforced in the numerous essays and paragraphs in the news-papers, have misled some well designing members of the late Convention. —But it will appear in the sequel, that
the construction of the proposed plan of government is infinitely
more extravagant.[7]

I have been anxiously expecting that some enlightened patriot would, ere this, have taken up the pen to expose the futility, and counteract the baneful tendency of such principles. Mr. Adams's *sine qua non* of a good government is three balancing powers, whose repelling qualities are to produce an equilibrium of interests, and thereby promote the happiness of the whole community. He asserts that the administrators of every government, will ever be actuated by views of private interest and ambition, to the prejudice of the public good; that therefore the only effectual method to secure the rights of the people and promote their welfare, is to create an opposition of interests between the members of two distinct bodies, in the exercise of the powers of government, and balanced by those of a third. This hypothesis supposes human wisdom competent to the task of instituting three co-equal orders in government, and a corresponding weight in the community to enable them respectively to exercise their several parts, and whose views and interests should be so distinct as to prevent a coalition of any two of them for the destruction of the third. Mr. Adams, although he has traced the constitution of every form of government that ever existed, as far as history affords materials, has not been able to adduce a single instance of such a government; he indeed says that the British constitution is such in theory, but this is rather a confirmation that his principles are chimerical and not to be reduced to practice. If such an organization of power were practicable, how long would it continue? not a day—for there is so great a disparity in the talents, wisdom and industry of mankind, that the scale would presently preponderate to one or another body, and with every accession of power the means of further increase would be greatly extended. The state of society in England is much more favorable to such a scheme of government than that of America. There they have a powerful hereditary nobility, and real distinctions of rank and interests; but even there, for want of that perfect equallity of power and distinction of interests, in the three orders of government, they exist but in name; the only operative and efficient check, upon the conduct of administration, is the sense of the people at large.

Suppose a government could be formed and supported on such principles, would it answer the great purposes of civil society; If the administrators of every government are actuated by views of private interest and ambition, how is the welfare and happiness of the community to be the result of such jarring adverse interests?

Therefore, as different orders in government will not produce the good of the whole, we must recur to other principles. I believe it will be found that the form of government, which holds those entrusted with power, in the greatest responsibility to their constituents, the best calculated for freemen. A republican, or free government, can only exist where the body of the people are virtuous, and where property is pretty equally divided, in such a government the people are the sovereign and their sense or opinion is the criterion of every public measure; for when this ceases to be the case, the nature of the government is changed, and an aristocracy, monarchy or despotism will rise on its ruin. The highest responsibility is to be attained, in a simple struction of government, for the great body of the people never steadily attend to the operations of government, and for want of due information are liable to be imposed on.—If you complicate the plan by various orders, the people will be perplexed and divided in their sentiments about the source of abuses or misconduct, some will impute it to the senate, others to the house of representatives, and so on, that the interposition of the people may be rendered imperfect or perhaps wholly abortive. But if, imitating the constitution of Pennsylvania, you vest all the legislative power in one body of men (separating the executive and judicial) elected for a short period, and necessarily excluded by rotation from permanency, and guarded from precipitancy and surprise by delays imposed on its proceedings, you will create the most perfect responsibility, for then, whenever the people feel a grievance they cannot mistake the authors, and will apply the remedy with certain effect, discarding them at the next election. This tie of responsibility will obviate all the dangers apprehended from a single legislature, and will the best secure the rights of the people.

Having premised thus much, I shall now proceed to the examination of the proposed plan of government, and I trust, shall make it appear to the meanest capacity, that it has none of the essential requisites of a free government; that it is neither founded on those balancing restraining powers, recommended by Mr. Adams and attempted in the British constitution, or possessed of that responsibility to its constituents, which, in my opinion, is the only effectual security for the liberties and happiness of the people; but on the contrary, that it is a most daring attempt to establish a despotic aristocracy among freemen, that the world has ever witnessed.

I shall previously consider the extent of the powers intended to be vested in Congress, before I examine the construction of the general government.

It will not be controverted that the legislative is the highest delegated power in government, and that all others are subordinate to it. The celebrated *Montesquieu* establishes it as a maxim, that legislation necessarily follows the power of taxation. By sect. 8, of the first article of the proposed plan of government, "the Congress are to have power to lay and collect taxes, duties, imposts and excises, to pay the debts and provide for the common defence and *general welfare* of the United States; but all duties, imposts and excises, shall be uniform throughout the United States."[8] Now what can be more comprehensive than these words; not content by other sections of this plan, to grant all the great executive powers of a confederation, and a STANDING ARMY IN TIME OF PEACE, that grand engine of oppression, and moreover the absolute controul over the commerce of the United States and all external objects of revenue, such as unlimited imposts upon imports, &c. —they are to be vested with every species of *internal* taxation;—whatever taxes, duties and excises that they may deem requisite for the *general welfare*, may be imposed on the citizens of these states, levied by the officers of Congress, distributed through every district in America; and the collection would be enforced by the standing army, however grievous or improper they may be. The Congress may construe every purpose for which the state legislatures now lay taxes, to be for the *general welfare*, and thereby seize upon every object of revenue.

The judicial power by 1st sect. of article 3 "shall extend to all cases, in law and equity, arising under this constitution, the laws of the United States, and treaties made or which shall be made under their authority; to all cases affecting ambassadors, other public ministers and consuls; to all cases of admiralty and maritime jurisdiction, to controversies to which the United States shall be a party, to controversies between two or more states, between a state and citizens of another state, between citizens of different states, between citizens of the same state claiming lands under grants of different states, and between a state, or the citizens thereof, and foreign states, citizens or subjects."[9]

The judicial power to be vested in one Supreme Court, and in such Inferior Courts as the Congress may from time to time ordain and establish.[10]

The objects of jurisdiction recited above, are so numerous, and the shades of distinction between civil causes are oftentimes so slight, that it is more than probable that the state judicatories would be wholly superceded; for in contests about jurisdiction, the federal court, as the most powerful, would ever prevail. Every person acquainted with the history of the courts in England, knows by what ingenious sophisms they have, at different periods, extended the sphere of their jurisdiction over objects out of the line of their institution, and contrary to their very nature; courts of a criminal jurisdiction obtaining cognizance in civil causes.

To put the omnipotency of Congress over the state government and judicatories out of all doubt, the 6th article ordains that "this constitution and the laws of the United States which shall be made in pursuance thereof, and all treaties made, or which shall be made under the authority of the United States, shall be the *supreme law of the land*, and the judges in every state shall be bound thereby, any thing in the constitution or laws of any state to the contrary notwithstanding."[11]

By these sections the all-prevailing power of taxation, and such extensive legislative and judicial powers are vested in the general government, as must in their operation, necessarily absorb the state legislatures and judicatories; and that such was in the contemplation of the framers of it, will appear from the provision made for such event, in another part of it; (but that, fearful of alarming the people by so great an innovation, they have suffered the forms of the separate governments to remain, as a blind.) By sect. 4th of the 1st article, "the times, places and manner of holding elections for senators and representatives, shall be prescribed in each state by the legislature thereof; *but the Congress may at any time, by law, make or alter such regulations, except as to the place of chusing senators.*"[12] The plain construction of which is, that when the state legislatures drop out of sight, from the necessary operation of this government, then Congress are to provide for the election and appointment of representatives and senators.

If the foregoing be a just comment—if the United States are to be melted down into one empire, it becomes you to consider, whether such a government, however constructed, would be eligible in so extended a territory; and whether it would be practicable, consistent with freedom? It is the opinion of the greatest writers, that a very extensive country cannot be governed on democratical principles, on any other plan, than a confederation of a number of small republics, possessing all the powers of internal government, but united in the management of their foreign and general concerns.

It would not be difficult to prove, that anything short of despotism, could not bind so great a country under one government; and that whatever plan you might, at the first setting out, establish, it would issue in a despotism.

If one general government could be instituted and maintained on principles of freedom, it would not be so competent to attend to the various local concerns and wants, of every particular district; as well as the peculiar governments, who are nearer the scene, and possessed of superior means of information, besides, if the business of the *whole* union is to be managed by one government, there would not be time. Do we not already see, that the inhabitants in a number of larger states, who are remote from the seat of government, are loudly complaining of the inconveniences and disadvantages they are subjected to on this account, and that, to enjoy the comforts of local government, they are separating into smaller divisions.

Having taken a review of the powers, I shall now examine the construction of the proposed general government.

Art. I sect. I. "All legislative powers herein granted shall be vested in a Congress of the United States, which shall consist of a senate and a house of representatives." By another section, the president (the principle executive officer) has a conditional controul over their proceedings.

Sect. 2. "The house of representatives shall be composed of members chosen every second year, by the people of the several states. The number of representatives shall not exceed one for every 30,000 inhabitants."[13]

The senate, the other constituent branch of the legislature, is formed by the legislature of each state appointing two senators, for the term of six years.

The executive power by Art. 2, Sec. I. is to be vested in a president of the United States of America, elected for four years: Sec. 2. gives him "power, by and with the consent of the senate to make treaties, provided two thirds of the senators present concur; and he shall nominate, and by and with the advice and consent of the senate, shall appoint ambassadors, other public ministers and consuls, judges of the Supreme Court, and all other officers of the United States, whose appointments are not herein otherwise provided for, and which shall be established by law, &c."[14] And by another section he has the absolute power of granting reprievs and pardons for treason and all other high crimes and misdemeanors, except in case of impeachment.

The foregoing are the outlines of the plan.

Thus we see, the house of representatives, are on the part of the people to balance the senate, who I suppose will be composed of the *better sort*, the *well born*, &c. The number of the representatives (being only one for every 30,000 inhabitants) appears to be too few, either to communicate the requisite information, of the wants, local circumstances and sentiments of so extensive an empire, or to prevent corruption and undue influence, in the exercise of such great powers; the term for which they are to be chosen, too long to preserve a due dependence and accountability to their constituents; and the mode and places of their election not sufficiently ascertained, for as Congress have the controul over both, they may govern the choice, by ordering the *representatives* of a *whole* state, to be *elected* in *one* place, and that too may be the most *inconvenient*.

The senate, the great efficient body in this plan of government, is constituted on the most unequal principles. The smallest state in the union has equal weight with the great states of Virginia, Massachusetts, or Pennsylvania.—The Senate, besides its legislative functions, has a very considerable share in the Executive; none of the principal appointments to office can be made without its advice and consent. The term and mode of its appointment, will lead to permanency; the members are chosen for six years, the mode is under the controul of Congress, and as there is no exclusion by rotation, they may be continued for life, which, from their extensive means of influence, would follow of course. The President, who would be a mere pageant of state, unless he coincides with the views of the Senate, would either become the head of the aristocratic junto in that body, or its minion; besides, their influence being the most predominant, could the best secure his re-election to office. And from his power of granting pardons, he might skreen from punishment the most treasonable attempts on the liberties of the people, when investigated by the Senate.

From this investigation into the organization of this government, it appears that it is devoid of all responsibility or accountability to the great body of the people, and that so far from being a regular balanced government, it would be in practice a *permanent* ARISTOCRACY.

The framers of it; actuated by the true spirit of such a government, which ever abominates and suppresses all free enquiry and discussion, have made no provision for the *liberty of the press*, that grand *palladium of freedom*, and *scourge of tyrants*; but observed a total silence on that head. It is the opinion of some great writers, that if the liberty of the press, by an institution of religion, or otherwise, could be rendered *sacred*, even in *Turkey*, that despotism would fly before it. And it is worthy of remark, that there is no declaration of personal rights, premised in most free constitutions; and that trial by *jury* in *civil* cases is taken away; for what other construction can be put on the following, viz. Article III. Sect. 2d. "In all cases affecting ambassadors, other public ministers and consuls, and those in which a State shall be party, the Supreme Court shall have *original* jurisdiction. In all the other cases above mentioned, the Supreme Court shall have *appellate* jurisdiction, both as to *law and fact?*"[15] It would be a novelty in jurisprudence, as well as evidently improper to allow an appeal from the verdict of a jury, on the matter of fact; therefore, it implies and allows of a dismission of the jury in civil cases, and especially when it is considered, that jury trial in criminal cases is expressly stipulated for, but not in civil cases.

But our situation is represented to be so *critically* dreadful, that, however reprehensible and exceptionable the proposed plan of government may be, there is no alternative, between the adoption of it and absolute ruin.—My fellow citizens, things are not at that crisis, it is the argument of tyrants; the present distracted state of Europe secures us from injury on that quarter, and as to domestic dissentions, we have not so much to fear from them, as to precipitate us into this form of government, without it is a safe and a proper one. For remember, of all *possible* evils, that of *despotism* is the *worst* and the most to be *dreaded*.

Besides, it cannot be supposed, that the first essay on so difficult a subject, is so well digested, as it ought to be;—if the proposed plan, after a mature deliberation, should meet the approbation of the respective States, the matter will end; but if it should be found to be fraught with dangers and inconveniences, a future general Convention being in possession of the objections, will be the better enabled to plan a suitable government.

> "WHO'S HERE SO BASE, THAT WOULD A BONDMAN BE?
> "IF ANY, SPEAK; FOR HIM HAVE I OFFEN[D]ED.
> "WHO'S HERE SO VILE, THAT WILL NOT LOVE HIS COUNTRY?
> "IF ANY, SPEAK; FOR HIM HAVE I OFFENDED."[16]

LETTER CONTAINING THE REASONS OF ELBRIDGE GERRY FOR NOT SIGNING THE FEDERAL CONSTITUTION

Massachusetts Centinel, November 3, 1787

Elbridge Gerry was made profoundly uncomfortable by the ratification debate. He found the Constitution objectionable for the reasons outlined in this excerpt, but he also feared that the public would reject the Constitution and that that rejection might lead to anarchy.[17] What emerges from his writings, then, is a conservative opposition. He urged Americans not to act precipitously because he thought that the Constitution would be of benefit if properly amended. As outlined in the previous chapter, Gerry favored a mixed regime, and he felt that the Constitution departed from a mixed regime because its lower house was too aristocratic. Though that objection is offered here, it does not take center stage. Perhaps Gerry feared that drawing attention to this inadequacy would heighten tensions rather than reduce them. Instead, Gerry focuses on whether powers can be successfully divided between the national government and the states. He, like only a few others on each side, was an ardent proponent of dual sovereignty: most others believed that either the states or the nation would become dominant. Gerry himself was a wealthy merchant from Marblehead, Massachusetts. During the Revolutionary War, he had been a leading organizer of the Committees of Correspondence, which coordinated revolutionary activities. In addition to his service at the Philadelphia convention (see chapter 2), he would later be elected to Congress, become governor of Massachusetts, and eventually be vice president of the United States.[18] This letter was reprinted in nearly fifty newspapers nationwide.

Gentlemen: I have the honor to enclose, pursuant to my commission, the Constitution proposed by the federal Convention.

To this system I gave my dissent, and shall submit my objections to the honorable legislature.

It was painful for me, on a subject of such national importance, to differ from the respectable members who signed the Constitution; but conceiving, as I did, that the liberties of America were not secured by the system, it was my duty to oppose it.

My principal objections to the plan are, that there is no adequate provision for a representation of the people; that they have no security for the right of election; that some of the powers of the legislature are ambiguous, and others indefinite and dangerous; that the executive is blended with, and will have an undue influence over, the legislature; that the judicial department will be oppressive; that treaties of the highest importance may be formed by the President, with the advice of two thirds of a quorum of the Senate; and that the system is without the security of a bill of rights. These are objections which are not local, but apply equally to all the states.

As the Convention was called for "the sole and express purpose of revising the Articles of Confederation, and reporting to Congress, and the several legislatures, such alterations and provisions as shall render the Federal Constitution adequate to the exigencies of government, and the preservation of the Union," I did not conceive that these powers extend to the formation of the plan proposed; but the Convention being of a different opinion, I acquiesced in it, being fully convinced that, to preserve the Union, an efficient government was indispensibly necessary, and that it would be difficult to make proper amendments to the Articles of Confederation.

The Constitution proposed has few, if any, federal features, but is rather a system of national government. Nevertheless, in many respects, I think it has great merit, and, by proper amendments, may be adapted to the "exigencies of government, and preservation of liberty."

The question on this plan involves others of the highest importance: 1. Whether there shall be a dissolution of the federal government; 2. Whether the several state governments shall be so altered as in effect to be dissolved; 3. Whether, in lieu of the federal and state governments, the national Constitution now proposed shall be substituted without amendment. Never, perhaps, were a people called on to decide a question of greater magnitude. Should the citizens of America adopt the plan as it now stands, their liberties may be lost; or should they reject it altogether, anarchy may ensue.[19] It is evident, therefore, that they should not be precipitate in their decisions; that the subject should be well understood;—lest they should refuse to support the government after having hastily accepted it.

If those who are in favor of the Constitution, as well as those who are against it, should preserve moderation, their discussions may afford much information, and finally direct to a happy issue.

It may be urged by some, that an implicit confidence should be placed in the Convention; but, however respectable the members may be who signed the Constitution, it must be admitted that a free people are the proper guardians of their rights and liberties; that the greatest men may err, and that their errors are sometimes of the greatest magnitude.

Others may suppose that the Constitution may be safely adopted, because therein provision is made to amend it. But cannot this object be better attained before a ratification than after it? And should a free people adopt a form of government under conviction that it wants amendment?

And some may conceive that, if the plan is not accepted by the people, they will not unite in another. But surely, while they have the power to amend, they are not under the necessity of rejecting it.

I have been detained here longer than I expected, but shall leave this place in a day or two for Massachusetts, and on my arrival shall submit the reasons (if required by the legislature) on which my objections are grounded.[20]

I shall only add that, as the welfare of the Union requires a better Constitution than the Confederation, I shall think it my duty, as a citizen of Massachusetts, to support that which shall be finally adopted, sincerely hoping it will secure the liberty and happiness of America.

I have the honor to be, gentlemen, with the highest respect for the honorable legislature and yourselves, your most obedient and very humble servant,

E. GERRY

OBJECTIONS OF GEORGE MASON
TO THE PROPOSED CONSTITUTION

Massachusetts Centinel, November 21, 1787

Despite being a Virginian, Mason's objections were first printed in a Boston newspaper. His letter, however, had circulated throughout the colonies in manuscript form for two months before the Massachusetts Centinel *printed it. Other papers quickly followed suit. The essay was reprinted at least thirty times. The remarks here are an elaboration on the objections that Mason expressed at the close of the Philadelphia convention. Like Elbridge Gerry, Mason thinks the representation in the House of Representatives inadequate, but his objections seem to run deeper than Gerry's—or at least he is more willing to openly express his frustrations. George Washington was among those upset by Mason's frankness. After reading this letter, Washington commented that it seemed designed "to alarm the people."[21] Given how widely the letter was reprinted, Washington had reason for concern.*

Mason's own plantation was very close to Washington's Mount Vernon. Though a slaveholder and a key defender of slavery at the Virginia ratifying convention, Mason was a passionate advocate of individual rights.[22] He had written Virginia's "Declaration of Rights" in 1776, which became a model for other states and the Declaration of Independence. Mason did not wish to see his handiwork and his legacy threatened by a national government that did not respect or emulate those documents. Depite this unionwide concern, several of Mason's objections are regional or state-based. For instance, Mason objects to the Constitution treating "commercial and navigation laws" like any other legislation. The South, with its distinctive agriculture and slave-based economy, would be vulnerable to domination from the North because Northern states were a majority. Mason suggests that such laws should require approval of two-thirds of the states, which would give the South a veto power over laws that might harm their economy.[23] Mason died four years after ratification, living long enough to see the Bill of Rights ratified, another document modeled on his original Declaration of Rights.

There is no declaration of rights; and, the laws of the general government being paramount to the laws and constitutions of the several states, the declarations of rights in the separate states are no security.

Nor are the people secured even in the enjoyment of the benefit of the common law, which stands here upon no other foundation than its having been adopted by the respective acts forming the constitutions of the several states.

In the House of Representatives there is not the substance, but the shadow only, of representation, which can never produce proper information in the legislature, or inspire confidence in the people. The laws will, therefore, be generally made by men little concerned in, and unacquainted with, their effects and consequences.

The Senate have the power of altering all money bills, and of originating appropriations of money, and the salaries of the officers of their own appointment, in conjunction with the President of the United States, although they are not the representatives of the people, or amenable to them. These, with their other great powers, (viz., their powers in the appointment of ambassadors, and all public officers, in making treaties, and in trying all impeachments;) their influence upon, and connection with, the supreme executive from these causes; their duration of office; and their being a constant existing body, almost continually sitting, joined with their being one complete branch of the legislature,—will destroy any balance in the government, and enable them to accomplish what usurpations they please upon the rights and liberties of the people.

The judiciary of the United States is so constructed and extended as to absorb and destroy the judiciaries of the several states; thereby rendering laws as tedious, intricate, and expensive, and justice as unattainable, by a great part of the community, as in England; and enabling the rich to oppress and ruin the poor.

The President of the United States has no constitutional council, (a thing unknown in any safe and regular government.) He will therefore be unsupported by proper information and advice, and will generally be directed by minions and favorites; or he will become a tool of the Senate; or a council of state will grow out of the principal officers of the great departments—the worst and most dangerous of all ingredients for such a council, in a free country; for they may be induced to join in any dangerous or oppressive measures, to shelter themselves, and prevent an inquiry into their own misconduct in office. Whereas, had a constitutional council been formed (as was proposed) of six members, viz., two from the Eastern, two from the Middle, and two from the Southern States, to be appointed by vote of the states in the House of Representatives, with the same duration and rotation of office as the Senate, the executive would always have had safe and proper information and advice: the president of such a council might have acted as Vice-President of the United

States, *pro tempore*, upon any vacancy or disability of the chief magistrate; and long-continued sessions of the Senate would in a great measure have been prevented. From this fatal defect of a constitutional council has arisen the improper power of the Senate in the appointment of the public officers, and the alarming dependence and connection between that branch of the legislature and the supreme executive. Hence, also, sprang that unnecessary officer, the Vice-President, who, for want of other employment, is made president of the Senate; thereby dangerously blending the executive and legislative powers, besides always giving to some one of the states an unneccessary and unjust preeminence over the others.

The President of the United States has the unrestrained power of granting pardon for treason; which may be sometimes exercised to screen from punishment those whom he had secretly instigated to commit the crime, and thereby prevent a discovery of his own guilt. By declaring all treaties supreme laws of the land, the executive and the Senate have, in many cases, an exclusive power of legislation, which might have been avoided, by proper distinctions with respect to treaties, and requiring the assent of the House of Representatives, where it could be done with safety.

By requiring only a majority to make all commercial and navigation laws, the five Southern States (whose produce and circumstances are totally different from those of the eight Northern and Eastern States) will be ruined; for such rigid and premature regulations may be made, as will enable the merchants of the Northern and Eastern States not only to demand an exorbitant freight, but to monopolize the purchase of the commodities, at their own price, for many years, to the great injury of the landed interest, and the impoverishment of the people; and the danger is greater, as the gain on one side will be in proportion to the loss on the other. Whereas, requiring two thirds of the members present in both houses, would have produced mutual moderation, promoted the general interest, and removed an insuperable objection to the adoption of the government.

Under their own construction of the general clause at the end of the enumerated powers, the Congress may grant monopolies in trade and commerce, constitute new crimes, inflict unusual and severe punishments, and extend their power as far as they shall think proper; so that the state legislatures have no security for the powers now presumed to remain to them, or the people for their rights. There is no declaration of any kind for preserving the liberty of the press, the trial by jury in civil cases, nor against the danger of standing armies in time of peace.

The state legislatures are restrained from laying export duties on their own produce; the general legislature is restrained from prohibiting the further importation of slaves for twenty-odd years, though such importations render the United States weaker, more vulnerable, and less capable of defence. Both the general legislature and the state legislatures are expressly prohibited making ex post facto laws, though there never was, nor can be, a legislature but must and will make such laws, when necessity and the public safety require them, which will hereafter be a breach of all constitutions in the Union, and afford precedents for other innovations.

This government will commence in a moderate aristocracy: it is at present impossible to foresee whether it will, in its operation, produce a monarchy or a corrupt oppressive aristocracy; it will most probably vibrate some years between the two, and then terminate in the one or the other.

GEO. MASON

THE ADDRESS AND REASONS OF DISSENT
OF THE MINORITY OF THE CONVENTION OF THE
STATE OF PENNSYLVANIA TO THEIR CONSTITUENTS

Pennsylvania Packet, December 18, 1787

When he claimed authorship of the Centinel essays, Samuel Bryan also said he wrote the "Dissent of the Minority." This may well be the case, but the document was issued in the name of twenty-one dissenting members of the Pennsylvania ratification convention. Bryan was not among them because he was not a delegate to the convention. He was, however, well-connected to many of the delegates because of his service as clerk of Pennsylvania's general assembly. This essay does have a strident tone, similar to the Centinel essays. Among its unusual features is a statement that the minority does not consider the result of the ratification convention binding. The strange circumstances of the Pennsylvania assembly's call for a convention, explained in this piece, are responsible. At about this same time, Pennsylvania Antifederalists started circulating petitions asking the general assembly to nullify the convention's ratification. Months later, when it became clear that the Constitution would become the nation's supreme law, Pennsylvania's Antifederalists modified their view and acquiesced to the Constitution (see James Hanna's letter in chapter 7).

The dissent has three parts. First, the minority discusses the ratification process in Pennsylvania. Second, a list of amendments is offered. This list is one of the most detailed of its kind. If the Pennsylvania minority had its way, the Constitution would have even granted Americans a right to fish and hunt! This compilation is not just a list of rights, however. There are also suggestions for structural changes, including an executive council to aid the president and to remove some power from the Senate. Third, particular objections to the Constitution are discussed. Three major reasons for dissent are listed. They are not meticulously argued; rather, they are interspersed into a loosely organized narrative. These objectors to the Constitution ultimately feared that Pennsylvania would be swallowed up by a powerful national government of an aristocratic or despotic nature. This essay was reprinted in whole or in part at least twenty times.

The Continental convention met in the city of Philadelphia at the time appointed.[24] It was composed of some men of excellent characters; of others who were more remarkable for their ambition and cunning than their patriotism; and of some who had been opponents to the independence of the United States. The delegates from Pennsylvania were, six of them, uniform and decided opponents to the constitution of this commonwealth.[25] The convention sat upwards of four months. The doors were kept shut, and the members brought under the most solemn engagements of secrecy. Some of those who opposed their going so far beyond their powers retired, hopeless, from the convention, others had the firmness to refuse signing the plan altogether; and many who did sign it, did it not as a system they wholly approved, but as the best that could be then obtained, and notwithstanding the time spent on this subject, it is agreed on all hands to be a work of haste and accommodation.

Whilst the gilded chains were forging in the secret conclave, the meaner instruments of despotism without were busily employed in alarming the fears of the people with dangers which did not exist, and exciting their hopes of greater advantages from the expected plan than even the best government on earth could produce.

The proposed plan had not many hours issued forth from the womb of suspicious secrecy, until such as were prepared for the purpose were carrying about petitions for people to sign, signifying their approbation of the system, and requesting the legislature to call a convention. While every measure was taken to intimidate the people against opposing it, the public papers teemed with the most violent threats against those who should dare to think for themselves, and *tar and feathers* were liberally promised to all those who would not immediately join in supporting the proposed government be it what it would. Under such circumstances petitions in favor of calling a convention were signed by great numbers in and about the city, before they had leisure to read and examine the system, many of whom, now they are better acquainted with it, and have had time to investigate its principles, are heartily opposed to it. The petitions were speedily handed into the legislature.[26]

Affairs were in this situation when on the 28th of September last, a resolution was proposed to the assembly by a member of the house [George Clymer] who had been also a member of the federal convention, for calling a state election, to be elected within *ten* days for the purpose of examining and adopting the proposed constitution of the United States, though at this time the house had not received it from Congress. This attempt was opposed by a minority, who after offering every argument in their power to prevent the precipitate measure, without effect, absented themselves from the house as the only alternative left them, to prevent the measure taking place previous to their constituents being acquainted with the business. That violence and outrage which had been so often threatened was now practiced; some of the members were seized the next day by a mob collected for the purpose, and forcibly dragged to the house, and there detained by force whilst the quorum of the legislature, *so formed*, completed their resolution. We shall dwell no longer on this subject, the people of Pennsylvania have been already acquainted therewith. We would only further observe that every member of the legislature, previously to taking his seat, by solemn oath or affirmation, declares, "that he will not do or consent to any act or thing whatever that shall have a tendency to lessen or abridge their rights and privileges, as declared in the constitution of this state." And that constitution which they are so solemnly sworn to support cannot legally be altered but by a recommendation of the council of censors, who alone are authorized to propose alterations and amendments, and even those must be published at least *six months*, for the consideration of the people. The proposed system of government for the United States, if adopted, will alter and may annihilate the constitution of Pennsylvania; and therefore the legislature had no authority whatever to recommend the calling a convention for that purpose. This proceeding could not be considered as binding on the people of this commonwealth. The house was formed by violence, some of the members composing it were detained there by force, which alone would have vitiated any proceedings, to which they were otherwise competent; but had the legislature been legally formed, this business was absolutely without their power.

In this situation of affairs were the subscribers elected members of the convention in Pennsylvania. A convention called by a legislature in direct violation of their duty, and composed in part of members, who were compelled to attend for that purpose, to consider of a constitution proposed by a convention of the United States, who were not appointed for the purpose of framing a new form of government, but whose powers were expressly confined to altering and amending the present articles of confederation. Therefore the members of the continental convention in proposing the plan acted as individuals, and not as deputies from Pennsylvania. The assembly who called the state convention acted as individuals, and not as the legislature of Pennsylvania; nor could they or the convention chosen on their recommendation have authority to do any act or thing, that can alter or annihilate the constitution of Pennsylvania (both of which will be done by the new constitution) nor are their proceedings in our opinion at all binding on the people. . . .

The convention met, and the same disposition was soon manifested in considering the proposed constitution, that had been exhibited in every other stage of business. We were prohibited by an express vote of the convention, from taking any question on the separate articles of the plan, and reduced to the necessity of adopting or rejecting *in toto*. Tis true the majority permitted us to debate on each article, but restrained us from proposing amendments. They also determined not to permit us to enter on the minutes our reasons of dissent against any of the articles, nor even on the final question our reasons of dissent against the whole. Thus situated we entered on the examination of the proposed system of government, and found it to be such as we could not adopt, without, as we conceived surrendering up your dearest rights. We offered our objections to the convention, and opposed those parts of the plan, which, in our opinion, would be injurious to you, in the best manner we were able; and closed our arguments by offering the following propositions to the convention.

1. The right of conscience shall be held inviolable; and neither the legislative, executive, nor judicial powers of the United States shall have authority to alter, abrogate, or infringe any part of the constitution of the several states, which provide for the preservation of liberty in matters of religion.
2. That in controversies respecting property, and in suits between man and man, trial by jury shall remain as heretofore, as well in the federal courts, as in those of the several states.
3. That in all capital and criminal prosecutions, a man has a right to demand the cause and nature of his accusation, as well in the

federal courts, as in those of the several states; to be heard by himself and his counsel; to be confronted with the accusers and witnesses; to call for evidence in his favor, and a speedy trial by an impartial jury of his vicinage, without whose unanimous consent, he cannot be found guilty, nor can he be compelled to give evidence against himself; and that no man be deprived of his liberty, except by the law of the land or the judgment of his peers.

4. That excessive bail ought not to be required, nor excessive fines imposed, nor cruel nor unusual punishments inflicted.

5. That warrants unsupported by evidence, whereby any officer or messenger may be commanded or required to search suspected places, or to seize any person or persons, his or their property, not particularly described, are grievous and oppressive, and shall not be granted either by the magistrates of the federal government or others.

6. That the people have a right to the freedom of speech, of writing and publishing their sentiments, therefore, the freedom of the press shall not be restrained by any law of the United States.

7. That the people have a right to bear arms for the defense of themselves and their own state, or the United States, or for the purpose of killing game; and no law shall be passed for disarming the people or any of them, unless for crimes committed, or real danger of public injury from individuals' and as standing armies in the time of peace are dangerous to liberty, they ought not to be kept up; and that the military shall be kept under strict subordination to and be governed by the civil powers.

8. The inhabitants of the several states shall have liberty to fowl and hunt in seasonable times, on the lands they hold, and on all other lands in the United States not enclosed, and in like manner to fish in all navigable waters, and others not private property, without being restrained therein by any laws to be passed by the legislature of the United States.

9. That no law shall be passed to restrain the legislatures of the several states from enacting laws for imposing taxes, except imposts and duties on goods imported or exported, and that no taxes, except imposts and duties upon goods imported and exported, and postage on letters shall be levied by the authority of Congress.

10. That the house of representatives be properly increased in number; that elections shall remain free; that the several states shall have power to regulate the elections for senators and representatives, without being controlled either directly or indirectly by an interference on the part of Congress; and that elections of representatives be annual.

11. That the power of organizing, arming, and disciplining the militia (the manner of disciplining the militia to be prescribed by Congress) remain with the individual states, and that Congress shall not have authority to call or march any of the militia out of their own state, without the consent of such state, and for such length of time only as such state shall agree.

     That the sovereignty, freedom, and independency of the several states shall be retained, and every power, jurisdiction, and right which is not by this constitution expressly delegated to the United States in Congress assembled.

12. That the legislative, executive, and judicial powers be kept separate; and to this end that a constitutional council be appointed, to advise and assist the president, who shall be responsible for the advice they give, hereby the senators would be relieved from almost constant attendance; and also that the judges be made completely independent.

13. That no treaty which shall be directly opposed to the existing laws of the United States in Congress assembled shall be valid until such laws shall be repealed, or made conformable to such treaty; neither shall any treaties be valid which are in contradiction to the constitution of the United States, or the constitutions of the several states.

14. That the judiciary power of the United States shall be confined to cases affecting ambassadors, other public ministers and consuls; to cases of admiralty and maritime jurisdiction; to controversies to which the United States shall be a party; to controversies between two or more states—between a state and citizens of different states—between citizens claiming lands under grants of different states; and between a state or the citizens thereof and foreign states, and in criminal cases, to such only as are expressly enumerated in the constitution and that the United States in Congress assembled shall not have power to enact laws, which shall alter the laws of descents and distribution of the effects of deceased persons, the titles of lands or goods, or the regulation of contracts in the individual states.[27]

After reading these propositions we declared our willingness to agree to the plan, provided it was so amended as to meet those propositions, or something similar to them; and finally moved the convention to adjourn, to give the people of Pennsylvania time to consider the subject, and determine for themselves; but these were all rejected, and the final vote was taken, when our duty to you induced us to vote against the proposed plan, and to decline signing the ratification of the same. . . .

Our objections are comprised under three general heads of dissent, viz.:

We dissent, first, because it is the opinion of the most celebrated writers on government, and confirmed by uniform experience, that a very extensive territory cannot be governed on the principles of freedom, otherwise than by a confederation of republics, possessing all the power of internal government; but united in the management of their general, and foreign concerns. . . .

We dissent, secondly, because the powers vested in Congress by this constitution must necessarily annihilate and absorb the legislative, executive, and judicial powers of the several states, and produce from their ruins one consolidated government, which from the nature of things will be *an iron-handed despotism*, as nothing short of the supremacy of despotic sway could connect and govern these United States under one government.

As the truth of this position is of such decisive importance, it ought to be fully investigated. . . .

The powers of Congress under the new constitution are complete and unlimited over the *purse* and the *sword*, and are perfectly independent of, and supreme over, the state governments; whose intervention in these great points is entirely destroyed. By virtue of their power of taxation, Congress may command the whole, or any part of the property of the people. They may impose what imposts upon commerce; they may impose what land taxes, poll taxes, excises, duties on all written instruments, and duties on every other article that they may judge proper; in short, every species of taxation, whether of an external or internal nature is comprised in section the 8th, of Article the 1st, viz.: "The Congress shall have power to lay and collect taxes, duties, imposts, and excises, to pay the debts, and provide for the common defence and general welfare of the United States."

As there is no one article of taxation reserved to the state governments, the Congress may monopolize every source of revenue, and thus indirectly demolish the state governments, for without funds they could not exist. The taxes, duties, and excises imposed by Congress may be so high as to render it impracticable to levy further sums on the same articles; but whether this should be the case or not, if the state governments should presume to impose taxes, duties, or excises, on the same articles with Congress, the latter may abrogate and repeal the laws whereby they are imposed, upon the allegation that they interfere with the due collection of their taxes, duties, or excises, by virtue of the following clause, part of section 8th, Article 1st, viz.: "To make all laws which shall be necessary and proper for carrying into execution the foregoing powers, and all other powers vested by this constitution in the government of the United States, or in any department or officer thereof."[28]

The Congress might gloss over this conduct by construing every purpose for which the state legislatures now lay taxes, to be for the *"general welfare,"* and therefore as of their jurisdiction.[29]

And the supremacy of the laws of the United States is established by Article 6th, viz.: "That this constitution and the laws of the United States, which shall be made in pursuance thereof, and *all treaties* made, or which shall be made, under the authority of the United States, shall be the *supreme law* of the *land; and the judges in every state shall be bound thereby; any thing in the constitution or laws of any state to the contrary notwithstanding.*"[30] It has been alleged that the words "pursuant to the constitution" are a restriction on the authority of Congress; but when it is considered that by other sections they are invested with every efficient power of government, and which may be exercised to the absolute destruction of the state governments, without any violation of even the forms of the constitution, this seeming restriction, as well as every other restriction in it, appears to us to be nugatory and delusive; and only introduced as a blind upon the real nature of the government. In our opinion, "pursuant to the constitution" will be coextensive with the *will* and *pleasure* of Congress, which, indeed, will be the only limitation of their powers.

We apprehend that two coordinate sovereignties would be a solecism in politics. That therefore as there is no line of distinction drawn between the general and state governments; as the sphere of their jurisdiction is undefined, it would be contrary to the nature of things, that both should exist together, one or the other would necessarily triumph in the fullness of dominion. However the contest could not be of long continuance, as the state governments are divested of every means of defense, and will be obliged by "the supreme law of the land" *to yield at discretion. . . .*

The judicial powers vested in Congress are also so various and extensive, that by legal ingenuity they may be extended to every case, and thus absorb the state judiciaries, and when we consider the decisive influence that a general judiciary would have over the civil polity of the several states, we do not hesitate to pronounce that this power, unaided by the legislative, would effect a consolidation of the states under one government. . . .

In short, consolidation pervades the whole constitution. It begins with an annunciation that such was the intention. The main pillars of the fabric correspond with it, and the concluding paragraph is a confirmation of it. The preamble begins with the words, "We the people of the United States," which is the style of a compact between individuals entering into a state of society, and not that of a confederation of states. . . .

We dissent, thirdly, because if it were practicable to govern so extensive a territory as these United States includes, on the plan of a consolidated government, consistent with the principles of liberty and the happiness of the people, yet the construction of this constitution is not calculated to attain the object, for independent of the nature of the case, it would of itself, necessarily produce a despotism, and that not by the usual gradations, but with the celerity that has hitherto only attended to revolutions effected by the sword.

To establish the truth of this position, a cursory investigation of the principles and form of this constitution will suffice.

The first consideration that this review suggests is the emission of a BILL OF RIGHTS, ascertaining and fundamentally establishing those unalienable and personal rights of men, without the full, free, and secure enjoyment of which there can be no liberty, and over which it is not necessary for a good government to have the control. . . .

The legislature of a free country should be so formed as to have a competent knowledge of its constituests, and enjoy their confidence. To produce these essential requisites, the representation ought to be fair, equal, and sufficiently numerous, to possess the same interests, feelings, opinions, and views, which the people themselves would possess were they all assembled; and so numerous as to prevent bribery and undue influence, and so responsible to the people, by frequent and fair elections, as to prevent their neglecting or sacrificing the views and interests of their constituents, to their own pursuits. . . .

The house of representatives is to consist of 65 members; that is one for about every 50,000 inhabitants, to be chosen every two years. Thirty-three members will form a quorum for doing business, and 17 of these, being the majority, determine the sense of the house.

The senate, the other constituent branch of the legislature, consists of 26 members, being *two* from each state, appointed by their legislatures every six years—fourteen senators make a quorum; the majority of whom, eight, determines the sense of that body; except in judging impeachments, or in making treaties, or in expelling a member, when two-thirds of the senators present must concur.

The president is to have control over the enacting of laws, so far as to make the concurrence of *two*-thirds of the representatives and senators present necessary, if he should object to the laws.

Thus it appears that the liberties, happiness, interests, and great concerns of the whole United States may be dependent upon the integrity, virtue, wisdom, and knowledge of 25 or 26 men. How inadequate and un-safe a representation! Inadequate, because the sense and views of 3 or 4 millions of people over so extensive a territory comprising such various climates, products, habits, interests, and opinions cannot be collected in so small a body; and besides, it is not a fair and equal representation of the people even in proportion to its number, for the smallest state has as much weight in the senate as the largest, and from the smallness of the number to be chosen for both branches of the legislature; and from the mode of election and appointment, which is under the control of Con-gress; and from the nature of the thing, men of the most elevated rank in life will alone be chosen. The other orders in the society, such as farm-ers, traders, and mechanics, who all ought to have a competent number of their best-informed men in the legislature, will be totally unrepre-sented.

The representation is unsafe because in the exercise of such great powers and trusts, it is so exposed to corruption and undue influence, by the gift of the numerous places of honor and emolument, at the disposal of the executive; by the arts and address of the great and designing; and by direct bribery.

The representation is moreover inadequate and unsafe, because of the long terms for which it is appointed, and the mode of its appoint-ment, by which Congress may not only control the choice of the peo-ple, but may so manage as to divest the people of this fundamental right, and become self-elected. . . .

The next consideration that the constitution presents is the undue and dangerous mixture of the powers of government: the same body possessing legislative, executive, and judicial powers. The senate is a constituent branch of the legislature, it has judicial power in judging on impeachments, and in this case unites in some measure the char-acters of judge and party, as all of the principal officers are appointed by the president general, with the concurrence of the senate and there-fore they derive their offices in part from the senate. This may bias the judgments of the senators, and tend to screen great delinquents from punishment. And the senate has, moreover, various and great execu-tive powers, viz.: in concurrence with the president general, they form treaties with foreign nations, that may control and abrogate the con-stitutions and laws of the several states. . . .

Such various, extensive, and important powers combined in one body of men are inconsistent with all freedom. . . .

The president general is dangerously connected with the senate; his coincidence with the views of the ruling junto in that body is made essential to his weight and importance in the government, which will destroy all independency and purity in the executive department, and having the power of pardoning without the concurrence of a council, he may screen from punishment the most treasonable attempts that may be made on the liberties of the people, when instigated by his coadjutors in the senate. Instead of this dangerous and improper mixture of the executive with the legislative and judicial, the supreme executive powers ought to have been placed in the president, with a small independent council made personally responsible for every appointment to office or other act, by having their opinions recorded; and that without the concurrence of the majority of the quorum of this council, the president should not be capable of taking any step. . . .

From the foregoing investigation, it appears that the Congress under this constitution will not possess the confidence of the people, which is an essential requisite in a good government;[31] for unless the laws command the confidence and respect of the great body of the people, so as to induce them to support them, when called on by the civil magistrate, they must be executed by the aid of a numerous standing army, which would be inconsistent with every idea of liberty; for the same force that may be employed to compel obedience to good laws, might and probably would be used to wrest from the people their constitutional liberties. The framers of this constitution appear to have been aware of this great deficiency; to have been sensible that no dependence could be placed on the people for their support; but on the contrary, that the government must be executed by force. They have therefore made a provision for this purpose in a permanent STANDING ARMY, and a MILITIA that may be subjected to a strict discipline and government.

A standing army in the hands of a government placed so independent of the people may be made a fatal instrument to overturn the public liberties; it may be employed to enforce the collection of the most oppressive taxes, and to carry into execution the most arbitrary measures. An ambitious man who may have the army at his devotion may step into the throne, and seize upon absolute power.

The absolute unqualified command that Congress have over the militia may be made instrumental to the destruction of all liberty, both public and private; whether of a personal, civil, or religious nature. . . .

As this government will not enjoy the confidence of the people, but be executed by force, it will be a very expensive and burthensome government. The standing army must be numerous, and as a further support, it will be the policy of this government to multiply officers in every department: judges, collectors, tax gatherers, excisemen, and the whole host of revenue officers will swarm over the land, devouring the hard earnings of the industrious, like the locusts of old, impoverishing and desolating all before them.

We have not noticed the smaller, nor many of the considerable blemishes, but have confined our objections to the great and essential defects; the main pillars of the constitution, which we have shown to be inconsistent with the liberty and happiness of the people, as its establishment will annihilate the state governments, and produce one consolidated government, that will eventually and speedily issue in the supremacy of despotism.

In this investigation, we have not confined our views to the interests or welfare of this state, in preference to the others. We have overlooked all local circumstances; we have considered this subject on the broad scale of the general good; we have asserted the cause of the present and future ages, the cause of liberty and mankind.[32]

LETTER FROM RICHARD HENRY LEE TO HIS EXCELLENCY, EDMUND RANDOLPH, ESQ., GOVERNOR OF VIRGINIA

Petersburg Virginia Gazette, December 6, 1787

In June 1776, Richard Henry Lee introduced the motion for independence in the Second Continental Congress. "These united colonies are, and of right ought to be, free and independent states," he proclaimed. This action made Lee a national figure; he became the most renowned member of the most renowned family in the nation. Although elected to the Philadelphia convention, Lee turned down the appointment. He was, however, a member of the Confederation Congress in 1787 and a former president of that body as well. During the debate in Congress about sending the Constitution to the states, Lee wanted the Congress to amend the document. The great majority of Congressmen opposed that move and wished to recommend to the states that they ratify. Lee, with a few others, was able to prevent that recommendation, thus producing a compromise they could tolerate. The Constitution would be "neutrally transmitted" to the states; that is, the Congress would not recommend ratification but simply leave the decision up to the states. During the ratification debate, many speculated that key Antifederalist essays, most notably the essays of the "Federal Farmer," were actually being written by Lee, but these claims are dubious. Lee seems to have been content to write out his objections in this short private letter. Lee's letter is addressed to Virginia's governor, Edmund Randolph, and is dated October 16, 1787. In it, he tells Randolph to "make such use of this letter as you shall think to be for the public good." In other words, if Randolph thought it would do any good, he should make the letter available to the public. He did, and the result was that at least twenty papers printed it. Like George Mason, Lee's objections reflect his preference for a mixed regime that would protect Southern interests, with special emphasis accorded to the importance of guaranteeing trials by jury in federal courts.

It has hitherto been supposed a fundamental maxim, that, in governments rightly balanced, the different branches of the legislature should be unconnected, and that the legislative and executive powers should be separate. In the new constitution, the President and Senate have all the executive, and two thirds of the legislative power. In some weighty instances, (as making all kinds of treaties, which are to be laws of the land,) they have the whole legislative and executive powers. They jointly, appoint all officers, civil and military; and they (the Senate) try all impeachments, either of their own members or of the officers appointed by themselves.

Is there not a most formidable combination of power thus created in a few? and can the most critic eye, if a candid one, discover responsibility in this potent corps? or will any sensible man say that great power, without responsibility, can be given to rulers with safety to liberty? It is most clear that the parade of impeachment is nothing to them, or any of them: as little restraint is to be found, I presume, from the fear of offending constituents. The President is for four years' duration; and Virginia (for example) has one vote of thirteen in the choice of him, and this thirteenth vote not of the people, but electors, two removes from the people.[33] The Senate is a body of six years' duration, and, as in the choice of President, the largest state has but a thirteenth vote, so it is in the choice of senators. This latter statement is adduced to show that responsibility is as little to be apprehended from the amenability to constituents, as from the terror of impeachment. You are, therefore, sir, well warranted in saying, either a monarchy or aristocracy will be generated: perhaps the most grievous system of government may arise.

It cannot be denied, with truth, that this new Constitution is, in its first principles, highly and dangerously oligarchic; and it is a point agreed, that a government of the few is, of all governments, the worst.

The only check to be found in favor of the democratic principle, in this system, is the House of Representatives; which, I believe, may

justly be called a mere shred or rag of representation; it being obvious
to the least examination, that smallness of number, and great compar-
ative disparity of power, render that house of little effect, to promote
good or restrain bad government. But what is the power given to this
ill-constructed body? To judge of what may be for the general welfare;
and such judgments, when made the acts of Congress, become the
supreme laws of the land. This seems a power coextensive with every
possible object of human legislation. Yet there is no restraint, in form
of a bill of rights, to secure (what Doctor Blackstone calls) that
residuum of human rights which is not intended to be given up to society, and which, indeed, is not necessary to be given for any social
purpose.[34] The rights of conscience, the freedom of the press, and the
trial by jury, are at mercy. It is there stated that, in criminal cases, the
trial shall be by jury. But how? In the state? What, then, becomes of
the jury of the vicinage, or at least from the county, in the first
instance—the states being from fifty to seven hundred miles in extent?
This mode of trial, even in criminal cases, may be greatly impaired;
and, in civil cases, the inference is strong that it may be altogether
omitted; as the Constitution positively assumes it in criminal, and is
silent about it in civil cases. Nay, it is more strongly discountenanced
in civil cases, by giving the Supreme Court, in appeals, jurisdiction
both as to law and fact.

Judge Blackstone, in his learned Commentaries, art. *Jury Trial*,
says, "It is the most transcendent privilege, which any subject can enjoy or wish for, that he cannot be affected either in his property, his liberty, or his person, but by the unanimous consent of twelve of his
neighbors and equals—a constitution that, I may venture to affirm,
has, under Providence, secured the just liberties of this nation for a
long succession of ages. The impartial administration of justice, which
secures both our persons and our properties, is the great end of civil society. But if that be entirely intrusted to the magistracy,—a select body
of men, and those generally selected, by the prince, of such as enjoy
the highest offices of the state,—these decisions, in spite of their own
natural integrity, will have frequently an involuntary bias towards
those of their own rank and dignity. It is not to be expected from human nature, that the few should always be attentive to the good of the
many." The learned judge further says, that "every tribunal, selected
for the decision of facts, is a step towards establishing aristocracy—the
most oppressive of all governments."

The answer to these objections is, that the new legislature may provide remedies! But as they may, so they may not; and if they did, a succeeding assembly may repeal the provisions. The evil is found resting

upon constitutional bottom; and the remedy, upon the mutable ground of legislation, revocable at any annual meeting. It is the more unfortunate that this great security of human rights—the trial by jury—should be weakened by this system, as power is unnecessarily given in the second section of the third article, to call people from their own country, in all cases of controversy about property between citizens of different states, to be tried in a distant court, where the Congress may sit; for although inferior congressional courts may, for the above purposes, be instituted in the different states, yet this matter altogether is the pleasure of the new legislature; so that, if they please not to institute them, or if they do not regulate the right of appeal reasonably, the people will be exposed to endless oppression, and the necessity of submitting, in multitudes of cases, to pay unjust demands, rather than follow suitors, through great expense, to far-distant tribunals, and to be determined upon there, as it may be, without a jury.

In this congressional legislature, a bare majority of votes can enact commercial laws; so that the representatives of the seven Northern States, as they will have a majority, can, by law, create the most oppressive monopoly upon the five Southern States, whose circumstances and productions are essentially different from those of theirs, although not a single man of these voters are the representatives of, or amenable to, the people of the Southern States.[35] Can such men be, with the least color of truth, called a representative of those they make laws for? It is supposed that the policy of the Northern States will prevent such abuses. But how feeble, sir, is policy, when opposed to interest, among trading people! and what is the restraint arising from policy? Why, that we may be forced, by abuse, to become ship-builders! But how long will it be before a people of agriculture can produce ships sufficient to export such bulky commodities as ours, and of such extent? and if we had the ships, from whence are the seamen to come?—4,000 of whom, at least, will be necessary in Virginia. In questions so liable to abuse, why was not the necessary vote put to two thirds of the members of the legislature?

With the Constitution came, from the Convention, so many members of that body to Congress, and of those, too, who were among the most fiery zealots for their system, that the votes of three states being of them, two states divided by them, and many others mixed with them, it is easy to see that Congress could have little opinion upon the subject.[36]

Some denied our right to make amendments; whilst others, more moderate, agreed to the right, but denied the expediency of amending; but it was plain that a majority was ready to send it on, in terms of approbation. My judgment and conscience forbade the last; and therefore

I moved the amendments that I have the honor to send you enclosed herewith, and demanded the yeas and nays, that they might appear on the Journal.[37]

This seemed to alarm; and, to prevent such appearance in the Journal, it was agreed to transmit the Constitution without a syllable of approbation or disapprobation; so that the term "unanimously" only applied to the transmission, as you will observe by attending to the terms of the resolve for transmitting. Upon the whole, sir, my opinion is, that, as this Constitution abounds with useful regulations, at the same time that it is liable to strong objections, the plan for us to pursue will be to propose the necessary amendments, and to suggest the calling a new convention for the purpose of considering them. To this I see no well-founded objection, but great safety and much good to be the probable result. I am perfectly satisfied that you make such use of this letter as you shall think to be for the public good; and now, after begging your pardon for so great a trespass on your patience, and presenting my best respects to your lady, I will conclude with assuring you that I am, with the sincerest esteem and regard, dear sir, your most affectionate and obedient, humble servant,

RICHARD H. LEE

LETTER FROM ROBERT YATES AND JOHN LANSING, JUNIOR, CONTAINING THEIR REASONS FOR NOT SUBSCRIBING TO THE FEDERAL CONSTITUTION

December 21, 1787

Robert Yates and John Lansing felt ambushed at the Philadelphia convention. Soon after the Virginia Plan was introduced, it became clear to them that most delegates favored exceeding the convention's commission, which was simply to amend the Articles of Confederation. By midconvention, they realized that their hopes to preserve state sovereignty were hopeless. Unlike Elbridge Gerry, who fought to distinguish national power from state power (limiting the former and extending the latter), they left the federal convention. The outcome they wished had already been definitively rejected, the preservation of state sovereignty in a true confederation.[38] Because their main objection to the Constitution was a procedural decision by the convention (and one from which all others flowed), Yates and Lansing do not reference particular clauses or even discuss how the institutions of this new government will be faulty. They concentrate their en-

ergies on the procedural flaw that brought the Constitution to light in the first place. Their flight from the convention and this letter indicate that Yates and Lansing are most concerned with disassociating themselves from a process they think will be a disaster for their state.

This letter was written to New York governor George Clinton on the eve of the meeting of the state legislature that was to consider calling a ratifying convention. The New York Daily Advertiser *printed the letter on January 14, 1788. Its relatively late appearance may indicate that Yates and Lansing may have preferred not to have publicized their views. Their views were widely publicized, however, as this piece was reprinted more than twenty times. New York's politics were sharply divided between an upper-class nationalist faction and a middle-class, state-centric group headed by Clinton. Yates and Lansing were both connected with this latter group. Yates was a longtime justice of New York's Supreme Court, while Lansing was the mayor of Albany.*

Sir: We do ourselves the honor to advise your excellency that, in pursuance to concurrent resolutions of the honorable Senate and Assembly, we have, together with Mr. Hamilton, attended the Convention appointed for revising the Articles of Confederation, and reporting amendments to the same.

It is with the sincerest concern we observe that, in the prosecution of the important objects of our mission, we have been reduced to the disagreeable alternative of either exceeding the powers delegated to us, and giving assent to measures which we conceive destructive to the political happiness of the citizens of the United States, or opposing our opinions to that body of respectable men, to whom those citizens had given the most unequivocal proofs of confidence. Thus circumscribed, under these impressions, to have hesitated would have been to be culpable. We therefore gave the principles of the Constitution, which has received the sanction of a majority of the Convention, our decided and unreserved dissent; but we must candidly confess that we should have been equally opposed to any system, however modified, which had in object the consolidation of the United States into one government.

We beg leave, briefly, to state some cogent reasons, which, among others, influenced us to decide against a consolidation of the states. These are reducible into two heads:—

1st. The limited and well-defined powers under which we acted, and which could not, on any possible construction, embrace an idea of such magnitude as to assent to a general Constitution, in subversion of that of the state.

2nd. A conviction of the impracticability of establishing a general government, pervading every part of the United States, and extending essential benefits to all.

Our powers were explicit, and confined to the sole and express purpose of revising the Articles of Confederation, and reporting such alterations and provisions therein as should render the Federal Constitution adequate to the exigencies of government and the preservation of the Union.

From these expressions, we were led to believe that a system of consolidated government could not, in the remotest degree, have been in contemplation of the legislature of this state; for that so important a trust as the adopting measures which tended to deprive the state government of its most essential rights of sovereignty, and to place it in a dependent situation, could not have been confided by implication; and the circumstance, that the acts of the Convention were to receive a state approbation in the last resort, forcibly corroborated the opinion that our powers could not involve the subversion of a Constitution which, being immediately derived from the people, could only be abolished by their express consent, and not by the legislature possessing authority vested in them for its preservation. Nor could we suppose that, if it had been the intention of the legislature to abrogate the existing Confederation, they would, in such pointed terms, have directed the attention of their delegates to the revision and amendment of it, in total exclusion of every other idea.

Reasoning in this manner, we were of opinion that the leading feature of every amendment ought to be the preservation of the individual states in their uncontrolled constitutional rights; and that, in reserving these, a mode might have been devised of granting to the Confederacy the moneys arising from a general system of revenue, the power of regulating commerce and enforcing the observance of foreign treaties, and other necessary matters of less moment.

Exclusive of our objections originating from the want of power, we entertained an opinion that a general government, however guarded by declarations of rights or cautionary provisions, must unavoidably, in a short time, be productive of the destruction of the civil liberty of such citizens who could be effectually coerced by it, by reason of the extensive territory of the United States, the dispersed situation of its inhabitants, and the insuperable difficulty of controlling or counteracting the views of a set of men (however un-constitutional and oppressive their acts might be) possessed of all the powers of government, and who, from their remoteness from their constituents, and necessary permanency of office, could not be supposed to be uniformly actuated by an attention to their welfare and happiness; that, however wise and energetic the principles of the general government might be, the extremities of the United States could not be kept in due submission and obedience to its laws, at the distance of many hundred miles from the seat of government; that, if the general legislature was composed of so numerous a body of men as to represent the interests of all the inhabitants of the United States, in the usual and true ideas of representation, the expense of supporting it would become intolerably burdensome; and that, if a few only were vested with a power of legislation, the interests of a great majority of the inhabitants of the United States must necessarily be unknown; or, if known, even in the first stages of the operations of the new government, unattended to.

These reasons were, in our opinion, conclusive against any system of consolidated government: to that recommended by the Convention, we suppose most of them very forcibly apply.

It is not our intention to pursue this subject farther than merely to explain our conduct in the discharge of the trust which the honorable legislature reposed in us. Interested, however, as we are in common with our fellow-citizens, in the result, we cannot forbear to declare that we have the strongest apprehensions that a government so organized as that recommended by the Convention cannot afford that security to equal and permanent liberty which we wished to make an invariable object of our pursuit.

We were not present at the completion of the new Constitution; but before we left the Convention, its principles were so well established as to convince us that no alteration was to be expected, to conform it to our ideas of expediency and safety. A persuasion, that our further attendance would be fruitless and unavailing, rendered us less solicitous to return.

We have thus explained our motives for opposing the adoption of the national Constitution, which we conceived it our duty to communicate to your excellency, to be submitted to the consideration of the honorable legislature.

We have the honor to be, with the greatest respect, your excellency's most obedient and very humble servants,

ROBERT YATES
JOHN LANSING, Jun.

NOTES

1. The three items reprinted more than twenty times that do not appear here are the amendments proposed by William Paca in the Maryland convention, an address to constituents of the seceding assemblymen of Pennsylvania, and a letter of Edmund Randolph. Randolph's Antifederalist credentials are dubious, though, leading me not to include his letter. Many of his criticisms of the Constitution mirror those of Mason and Lee (as printed in this chapter). The "Dissent of the Minority" of the Pennsylvania convention reiterates and then extends the observations of the seceding assemblymen; therefore, I did not include the latter document. All the documents in this chapter are printed in their entirety except for the "Dissent of the Minority," which is edited for length. They are presented in the order of their initial public appearance.

2. Not agreeing to abide by the result of the ratification process is a highly unusual stance for Antifederalists, as pointed out in chapter 7.

3. Though Centinel should not be called a conservative, this view of how politics works is reminiscent of a famed conservative thinker, Edmund Burke. In *Reflections on the Revolution in France*, Burke argues that any attempt to radically alter the nature of a society (its constitution, in the broad sense of the word) will fail. The French Revolution was doomed to failure, Burke argued, because it attempted to wipe away France's settled political, social, and religious traditions, which had evolved over centuries. Centinel views the United States in 1787 as Burke viewed France in 1792. The United States was unsettled politically and likely to go awry, but Centinel adds a radical democratic element that is not a part of Burke's philosophy. Burke would recognize that the organic traditions of most states were not democratic; thus, there should not be radical movement toward democracy in them. Centinel believes that democracy is the only legitimate form of government. He fervently hopes that politics becomes "settled," but in a particular way—as a democracy. If the United States develops a democratic tradition, Centinel seems to say, then it will be relatively easy to maintain the democracy. To do so will be an extremely difficult task, he thinks, if the aristocratically tilted Constitution is adopted.

4. These political scientists tend to endorse a Westminster-style parliamentary regime, where a single legislative body headed by a prime minister formulates law. Because the executive and legislative powers are contained in the same institution, this format is not precisely congruent with Centinel's suggestion, in which the executive would be independent of the legislature. Nevertheless, Centinel's reasoning coincides with many political scientists who argue that a more unified government would be more responsive and accountable, since it would be easier to tell who was responsible for public policy. The major works advocating this position are among the most widely recognized in the field. These include Wilson's *Congressional Government* (first published in 1885, where the future president wrote, "as at present constituted, the federal government lacks strength because its powers are divided, lacks promptness because its authorities are multiplied, lacks wieldiness because its processes are roundabout, lacks efficiency because its reponsibility is indistinct and its action without competent di-

rection," [Meridian Books, 1969, p. 206]); "Toward a More Reponsible Party System" (*American Political Science Review*, 44 [September, 1950]), written by the American Political Science Association's Committee on Political Parties; Morris P. Fiorina's article "The Decline of Collective Responsibility in American Politics" (*Daedalus*, 109, no. 3 [Summer 1980]); and *Constitutional Reform and Effective Government* by James L. Sundquist (Brookings, 1986).

5. The two men possessing the highest confidence of Americans that Centinel refers to are George Washington and Ben Franklin. These two were clearly the most widely respected Americans of their time, and any attack on the Constitution had to gingerly explain their endorsement of it.

6. The "unsuspecting goodness" is no doubt Washington's, while the "weakness and indecision attendant on old age" applies to the octogenarian Franklin. Washington had been a military hero, not a political leader, which is why Centinel writes that he is "inexperienced, from his other arduous engagements" in statecraft.

7. Centinel here refers to John Adams' three-volume *Defence of the Constitutions of Government of the United States*, published in 1786–1787. In these volumes, Adams commented on the American state constitutions, arguing that most approximated the British constitution, with its mix (beneficial in Adams' assessment) of democratic, aristocratic, and monarchical powers.

8. Article I, section 8, clause 1.

9. Article III, section 2, clause 1.

10. Article III, section 1.

11. Article VI, clause 2.

12. Article I, section 4, clause 1.

13. Centinel here mixes language contained in two clauses of Article I, section 2. The first portion of the phrase is from clause 1, and the second portion is from clause 3.

14. Article II, section 2, clause 2.

15. Article III, section 2, clause 2.

16. The source of this quote, if not Centinel, is unknown.

17. Gerry carefully avoids objections to the Constitution that are regional in nature or based on the interests of his state. Nevertheless, his views are deeply informed by his position as an elite New Englander. His deep fear of anarchy probably rests on presumptions based on Massachusetts' politics. The tradition of town meetings made the Bay State a site of much populist activism. This activism had turned lawless only the year before, during Shays' Rebellion. Gerry feared that this kind of activity might occur on a national scale.

18. During Gerry's tenure as governor of Massachusetts, the Republican Party redrew electoral districts to favor his prospects for reelection. A cartoon of the districts in question was drawn with a dragon's head and was labeled "The Gerrymander." Legislative redistricting for partisan purposes has ever since been known as "gerrymandering."

19. The fear of anarchy was not widely expressed in Antifederalist tracts, but one reason Antifederalists almost uniformly acquiesced after ratifcation was their unstated fear that if sanctioned law were not abided by, anarchy would result.

20. The legislature did not require a further written statement from Gerry, but the Massachusetts convention asked him to be present when it met. Gerry's presence at the convention developed into something of a personal embarrassment, as he appeared but was not asked to testify.

21. Washington, quoted in Elkins and McKitrick, *The Age of Federalism*, p. 59.

22. Mason was as aware as any slaveholder of the immense contradiction between founding a government based on individual rights and the continuation of slavery. He was among a minority of Virginians who advocated gradual, compensated emancipation. We may judge Mason as we do the far better-remembered Thomas Jefferson, as one whose principles and interests tore him in opposite directions and as one who ultimately chose—probably hypocritically—to privilege interests over principles when it came to slavery. Of course, if a contemporary Virginian would have called for full and immediate emancipation, he would have been a political pariah in the state.

23. Mason also objects to a continuation of the slave trade, which at first blush might seem to be an altruistic stance contrary to Southern interests. But Virginians possessed a surplus of slaves, and many of the slaves sold to the growing plantation culture of the other Southern states were from Virginia. If the slave trade were cut off, Virginia would have less competition for the sale of their surplus slaves, and prices would rise, benefiting the state and its slaveholders.

24. Events of the preceding years are related in the preceding paragraphs, which I omitted. The minority relates that a want of power was not felt until after the war ended but that "all now agreed that it would be advantageous to the union to enlarge the powers of Congress" by allowing it to regulate commerce and collect duties on imports. They also lament that the Pennsylvania legislature decided not to compensate their delegates to the constitutional convention. That stipulation allowed only Philadelphians to serve, the great majority of whom favored a strong national government.

25. The Pennsylvania state constitution was the most democratic of any state. The main reason it was democratic was its unicameral legislature. Those who became Federalists tended to dislike the Pennsylvania constitution because it was so democratic. Thus, the Pennsylvania minority is here acquainting their readers that the majority of the Pennsylvania delegation to the Philadelphia convention feared democracy and wished to curb it.

26. The Federalist petition campaign provoked a countervailing campaign from the Antifederalists. Ultimately, six thousand Pennsylvanians signed a petition asking the legislature not to accept the ratification presented to them by the state convention.

27. Note that the first nine amendments guarantee rights. Many of these suggestions and even some of its specific language were ultimately included in the Bill of Rights written by James Madison and added to the Constitution in 1791. The last five suggested changes alter the structure of the national government. Confident of the beneficial nature of the new regime, Madison and his Federalist colleagues made sure to exclude these kinds of amendments from those transmitted to the states for their approval.

28. Article I, section 8, clause 18.

29. The phrase "general welfare" is contained in the Constitution's Preamble.

30. Article VI, clause 2.

31. In preceding paragraphs, the minority had noted that while "the members of the [state] legislature are taken from among the people, and their interests and welfare are so inseparably connected with those of their constituents, that they can derive no advantage from oppressive laws and taxes," the selection process for members of Congress make it "consist of the lordly and high-minded; of men who will have no congenial feelings with the people, but a perfect indifference for, and contempt of them."

32. At the end of this document were affixed the names of twenty-one delegates to the Pennsylvania ratifying convention who had opposed the Constitution.

33. Here, Lee seems unaware that the number of a state's electors is based primarily on population, meaning that Virginia would have much more clout in picking presidents than, say, Delaware.

34. William Blackstone was the most renowned British jurist. His "Commentaries on the Laws of England," written in 1765 and referenced here, was mandatory reading for any student of the law in Britain or the United States.

35. Lee apparently is not counting Maryland as either a Northern or a Southern state. In making the same objection, most Southerners complain that they will be outvoted eight to five.

36. Lee implies here that it is unsurprising that the Confederation Congress did not object to the Constitution, as so many of its members were at the Philadelphia convention or were like those who were.

37. Lee's suggested amendments are generally not unusual. In addition to advocating personal rights guarantees, he suggests that a privy council be formed to give advice and consent to the president. He reasoned that a privy council would keep executive power distinct from legislative power. Lee's suggested amendments had been made public before his letter to Randolph was printed. For the complete text of his suggested amendments, see *Documentary History of the Ratification of the Constitution,* 14: 370–72.

38. This left arch-nationalist Alexander Hamilton as the sole delegate remaining from New York—but it also left him without voting rights, as solitary members could not speak for their state.

4

Antifederalism of the "Middling Class"

When Alexis de Tocqueville visited the United States in the early 1830s, he was astonished by America's distinctive socioeconomic character. In Europe, there was a stark divide between the many poor peasants and the few who were born to wealth, with not many in between. This division even held in Tocqueville's own postrevolutionary France. In the United States, as in Europe, there were few wealthy individuals. But there were also few poor. The majority of Americans were what we might call "middle class," neither rich nor poor, having to work to make their way in the world, and doing so competently but not luxuriantly.[1] Tocqueville recognized two main reasons why wealth was spread more evenly in the United States than in Europe: first, immigrants brought little with them to the New World, thus starting their lives here on a fairly equal footing. Second, inheritence laws spread wealth among the children of a family rather than passing it exclusively to the eldest male.[2] These leveling factors were at work well before Tocqueville arrived. A large "middling class" thus defined the socioeconomic character of the ratification era as well. Naturally, the attitudes and the trappings of the middle class have changed greatly over the years. For instance, no suburban landscapes existed because most middling Americans in the 1780s were farmers. Nevertheless, this familiar socioeconomic pattern greatly affected the ratification debate.

In the years between 1776 and 1787, middling Americans had significant political opportunities. A few states, like South Carolina and to a lesser extent Virginia, were dominated by their most wealthy citizens, but those states were the exceptions, rather than the norm.[3] In most, the middling class exerted significant control. In fact, in some states, like Pennsylvania and New York, they were dominant. Many middling politicians felt the proposed Constitution would diminish their political power. This phenomenon was of personal interest to them, but it also threatened their ideal of government. Popular government required that the great middling majority, of which they were a part, would make policy. If *(a)* the new national Congress possessed virtually unlimited powers and if *(b)* large electoral districts allowed only the well-known and well-to-do to get elected to the House and if *(c)* state legislatures would only select eminent individuals to the Senate who also happened to be wealthy, then the middling class would have little chance to retain any influence over politics. At stake in the minds of these individuals was whether average people would possess that which was rightfully theirs, political power, or whether the wealthy would predominate in the United States.

The socioeconomic character of each state differed, and with it, each state's politics. Not surprisingly, the middling class objected to the Constitution most vociferously in the states where that group had the most control because it had the most to lose politically there. Thus, many of the quintessential middling Antifederalist writings appeared in New York and Pennsylvania. The "Brutus" essays were first printed in the *New York Journal*, and the writings of "An Old Whig" were serialized in Philadelphia's *Independent Gazetteer*. Though the cities where these two newspapers originated were Federalist strongholds, the small towns and rural areas at some distance from these large cities were home to middling Antifederalists. Melancton Smith, excerpts of whose speeches are printed in this chapter and probably the author of the Brutus series, had lived most of his life in such a place, Poughkeepsie, New York.

With the middling class less numerous and having little political power in South Carolina and Virginia, such protests were less frequent in those states. At the same time, however, middling voices were heard in these states and in every other state where opposition to the Constitution was significant. One of them was Marylander John Francis Mercer, whose letter to the New York and Virginia conventions is included here. At the very least, the middling Antifederalists wanted to see the number of representatives increased, and they wanted further restraints imposed on the national government. In the words of Melancton Smith, increasing the size of the House of Representatives would "open a door for the admission of the substantial yeomanry of our country." In limiting congressional power, states and the middling politicians in them could retain some semblance of control. There are other common Antifederalist themes here, but they are surrounded by a distinctive argument, sometimes explicit and sometimes implied: the middling class rightly controlled the political sphere.

AN OLD WHIG: LETTER I

Philadelphia Independent Gazetteer, October 12, 1787

"An Old Whig" wrote eight essays, with all but one appearing before Pennsylvania's ratification on December 12, 1787. The identity of the author is unkown, but speculation suggests that the series was the result of a collaboration. In a private letter, William Shippen Jr. related that the letters may have been produced by George Bryan, John Smilie, and James Hutchinson, three Pennsylvanians.[4] An Old Whig stresses the need for amendments to the Constitution, particularly to secure rights. This first essay is a logical beginning to those pleas, complaining that the Constitution itself makes amending very difficult. With the great stress Antifederalists placed on amending, one would think this position would be a persistent Antifederalist lament. In fact, it is relatively rare. Most Antifederalists were so busy pointing out the specific substantive defects of the document that they did not note how difficult the document was to amend. And it is very difficult to amend, requiring something approaching a national consensus. If the public doesn't demand amendments now, thinks An Old Whig, then there will be little chance of changing the character of the regime. This letter was reprinted three times.

Mr Printer,

I am one of those who have long wished for a federal government, which should have power to protect our trade and provide for the general security of the United States. Accordingly, when the constitution proposed by the late convention made its appearance, I was disposed to embrace it almost without examination; I was determined not to be offended with trifles or to scan it too critically. "We want something: let us try this; experience is the best teacher; if it does not answer our purpose we can alter it: at all events it will serve for a beginning." Such were my reasonings;—but, upon further reflection, I may say that I am shaken with very considerable doubts and scruples, I want a federal constitution; and yet I am afraid to concur in giving my consent to the establishment of that which is proposed. At the same time I really wish to have my doubts removed, if they are not well founded. I shall therefore take the liberty of laying some of them before the public, through the channel of your paper.

In the first place, it appears to me that I was mistaken in supposing that we could so very easily make trial of this constitution and again change it at our pleasure. The conventions of the several states cannot propose any alterations—they are only to give their *assent* and *ratification*. And after the constitution is once ratified, it must remain fixed until two thirds of both the houses of Congress shall deem it necessary to propose amendments; or the legislatures of two thirds of the several states shall make application to Congress for the calling a convention for proposing amendments, which amendments shall not be valid till they are ratified by the legislatures of three fourths of the several states, or by conventions in three fourths thereof, as one or the other mode of ratification may be proposed by Congress.—This appears to me to be only a cunning way of saying that no alteration shall ever be made; so that whether it is a good constitution or a bad constitution, it will remain forever unamended. Lycurgus, when he promulgated his laws to the Spartans, made them swear that they would make no alterations in them until he should return from a journey which he was then about to undertake.—He chose never to return, and therefore no alterations could be made to his laws. The people were made to believe that they could make trial of his laws for a few months or years, during his absence, and as soon as he returned they could continue to observe them or reject at pleasure. Thus this celebrated Republic was in reality established by a trick.[5] In like manner the proposed constitution holds out a prospect of being subject to be changed if it be found necessary or convenient to change it; but the conditions upon which an alteration can take place, are such as in all probability will never exist. The consequence will be that, when the constitution is once established, it can never be altered or amended without some violent convulsion or civil war.

The conditions, I say, upon which any alterations can take place, appear to me to be such as never will exist—two thirds of both houses of Congress or the legislatures of two thirds of the states, must agree in desiring a convention to be called. This will probably never happen. Then the convention may agree to the amendments or not as they think right; and after all, three fourths of the states must ratify the amendments.—Before all this labyrinth can be traced to a conclusion, ages will revolve, and perhaps the great principles upon which our late glorious revolution was founded, will be totally forgotten. If the principles of liberty are not firmly fixed and established in the present constitution, in vain may we hope for retrieving them hereafter. People once possessed of power are always loath to part with it; and we shall never find two thirds of a Congress voting or proposing any thing which shall derogate from their own authority and importance, or agreeing to give back to the people any part of those privileges which they have once parted with—so far from it that the greatest occasion there may be for a reformation, the less likelihood will there be of accomplishing it. The greater the abuse of power, the more obstinately is it always persisted in. As to any expectation of two thirds of the legislatures concurring in such a request, it is if possible, still more remote. The legislatures of the states will be but forms and shadows, and it will be the height of arrogance and presumption in them, to turn their thoughts to such high subjects. After this constitution is once established, it is too evident that we shall be obliged to fill up the offices of assemblymen and councillors, as we do those of constables, by appointing men to serve whether they will or not, and fining them if they refuse. The members thus appointed, as soon as they can hurry through a law or two for repairing highways or impounding cattle, will conclude the business of their sessions as suddenly as possible; that they may return to their own business.—Their heads will not be perplexed with the great affairs of state—We need not expect two thirds of them ever to interfere in so momentous a question as that of calling a Constitutional convention.—The different legislatures will have no communication with one another from the time of the new constitution being ratified, to the end of the world. Congress will be the great focus of power as well as the great and only medium of communication from one state to another. The great, and the wise, and the mighty will be in possession of places and offices; they will oppose all changes in favor of liberty; they will steadily pursue the acquisition of more and more power to themselves and their adherents. The cause of liberty, if it be forgotten now, will be forgotten forever.—Even the press which has so long been employed in the cause of liberty, and to which perhaps the greatest part of the liberty which exists in the world is owing at this moment;—the press may possibly be restrained of its freedom, and our children may possibly not be suffered to enjoy this most invaluable blessing of a free communication of each others sentiments on political subjects—Such at least appear to be some men's fears, and I cannot find in the proposed constitution any thing expressly calculated to obviate these fears; so that they may or may not be realized according to the principles and dispositions of the men who may happen to govern us hereafter. One thing however is calculated to alarm our fears on this head;—I mean the fashionable language which now prevails so much and is so frequent in the mouths of some who formerly held very different opinions;—THAT

COMMON PEOPLE HAVE NO BUSINESS TO TROUBLE THEM-
SELVES ABOUT GOVERNMENT. If this principle is just, the consequence is plain, that the common people need no information on
the subject of politics. Newspapers, pamphlets and essays are calculated only to mislead and inflame them by holding forth to them
doctrines which they have no business or right to meddle with,
which they ought to leave to their superiors. Should the freedom of
the press be restrained on the subject of politics, there is no doubt
it will soon after be restrained on all other subjects, religious as well
as civil. And if the freedom of the press shall be restrained, it will
be another reason to despair of any amendments being made in favor of liberty, after the proposed constitution shall be once established. Add to this, that under the proposed constitution, it will be
in the power of the Congress to raise and maintain a standing army
for their support, and when they are supported by an army, it will
depend on themselves to say whether any amendments shall be
made in favor of liberty.

If these reflections are just it becomes us to pause, and reflect previously before we establish a system of government which cannot be
amended; which will entail happiness or misery on ourselves and our
children. We ought I say to reflect carefully, we ought not by any
means to be in haste; but rather to suffer a little temporary inconvenience, than by any precipitation to establish a constitution without
knowing whether it is right or wrong, and which if wrong, no length
of time will ever mend. Scarce any people ever deliberately gave up
their liberties; but many instances occur in history of their losing
them forever by a rash and sudden act, to avoid a pressing inconvenience or gratify some violent passion of revenge or fear. It was a celebrated observation of one of our Assemblies before the revolution, during their struggles with the proprietaries, that "those who would give
up essential liberty to purchase a little temporary safety deserve neither liberty nor safety."

For the present I shall conclude with recommending to my
countrymen not to be in haste, to consider carefully what we are doing. It is our own concern; it is our own business; let us give ourselves a little time at least to read the proposed constitution and
know what it contains; for I fear that many, even of those who talk
most about it have not even read it, and many others, who are as
much concerned as any of us, have had no opportunity to read it.
And it is certainly a suspicious circumstance that some people who
are presumed to know most about the new constitution, seem bent
upon forcing it on their countrymen without giving them time to
know what they are doing.

Hereafter I may trouble you further on some parts of this important subject; but I fear this letter is already too long.

Yours.
An Old Whig.

BRUTUS: LETTER I

New York Journal, October 18, 1787

"Brutus" is an intelligent and eloquent critic of the Constitution and is rightly among the best-known Antifederalist essayists. Sixteen letters were written in the series, which ran from October 1787 to April 1788. The philosophical basis for Brutus' objections to the Constitution are contained in his first six letters. The next four letters treat two specific objections, the unlimited power of federal taxation and the possibility of a standing national army. The remaining letters discuss the proposed federal legal system. They do so with greater depth and insight than any other Antifederalist essay. The author clearly has a sharp legal mind and probably possessed either legal training or obtained insight from a legal expert. Brutus' identity is uncertain, but speculation has centered on Melancton Smith. Smith was a merchant, a part-time lawyer, and a one-time Dutchess County judge who coordinated New York's movement against the Constitution. Smith lived in New York City when the essays were written, allowing him easy access to the series' publisher. He also had the legal expertise that is the distinguishing feature of these letters, which few other Antifederalists possessed.

In his first essay, Brutus argues that the national government is "consolidated," by which he means that it is fully sovereign. The proposed government's powers are thus theoretically unlimited. Though the states will still exist, it is likely that the national government will "annihilate" them, "for every body of men, invested with power are ever disposed to increase it, and to acquire a superiority over every thing that stands in their way." This assertion about how psychology interacts with government is worth our consideration, as are some of Brutus' other broad assertions. "In a republic, the manners, sentiments, and interests of the people should be similar," he writes. This view aims at the core of government's character. Brutus does not want us to be connected to other citizens only

by geography and a now-and-then congruence of personal inter-
ests. He asserts that good government can only be achieved
with more solid connections among citizens. Brutus thinks
these connections do exist on the state level, but not between
citizens from the thirteen states. The result of a national gov-
ernment, he fears, will be the loss of the only kind of popular
government that is sustainable and worth having. Brutus' first
letter was reprinted at least four times.

. . . Perhaps this country never saw so critical a period in their political concerns. We have felt the feebleness of the ties by which these
United-States are held together, and the want of sufficient energy in
our present confederation, to manage, in some instances, our general
concerns. . . .

If the constitution, offered to your acceptance, be a wise one, calculated to preserve the invaluable blessings of liberty, to secure the inestimable rights of mankind, and promote human happiness, then, if
you accept it, you will lay a lasting foundation of happiness for millions yet unborn: generations to come will rise up and call you blessed.
. . . if it tends to establish a despotism, or, what is worse, a tyrannic
aristocracy; then, if you adopt it, this only remaining assylum for liberty will be shut up, and posterity will execrate your memory.

Momentous then is the question you have to determine, and you are
called upon by every motive which should influence a noble and virtuous mind, to examine it well, and to make up a wise judgment. It is insisted, indeed, that this constitution must be received, be it ever so imperfect. If it has its defects, it is said, they can be best amended when
they are experienced. But remember, when the people once part with
power, they can seldom or never resume it again but by force. Many instances can be produced in which the people have voluntarily increased
the powers of their rulers; but few, if any, in which rulers have willingly
abridged their authority. This is a sufficient reason to induce you to be
careful, in the first instance, how you deposit the powers of government.

With these few introductory remarks, I shall proceed to a consideration of this constitution:

The first question that presents itself on the subject is, whether a
confederated government be the best for the United States or not? Or
in other words, whether the thirteen United States should be reduced
to one great republic, governed by one legislature, and under the direction of one executive and judicial; or whether they should continue
thirteen confederated republics, under the direction and controul of a
supreme federal head for certain and defined national purposes only?

This enquiry is important, because, although the government reported by the convention does not go to a perfect and entire consolidation, yet it approaches so near to it, that it must, if executed, certainly and infallibly terminate in it.

This government is to possess absolute and uncontroulable power, legislative, executive and judicial, with respect to every object to which it extends, for by the last clause of section 8th, article 1st, it is declared "that the Congress shall have power to make all laws which shall be necessary and proper for carrying into execution the foregoing powers, and all other powers vested by this constitution, in the government of the United States; or in any department or office[r] thereof."[6] And by the 6th article, it is declared "that this constitution, and the laws of the United States, which shall be made, under authority of the United States, shall be bound thereby, any thing in the constitution, or law of any state to the contrary notwithstanding."[7] It appears from these articles that there is no need of any intervention of the state governments, between the Congress and the people, to execute any one power vested in the general government, and that the constitution and laws of every state are nullified and declared void, so far as they are or shall be inconsistent with this constitution, or the laws made in pursuance of it, or with treaties made under the authority of the United States.—The government then, so far as it extends, is a complete one, and not a confederation. It is as much one complete government as that of New-York or Massachusetts, has as absolute and perfect powers to make and execute all laws, to appoint officers, institute courts, declare offences, and annex penalties, with respect to every object to which it extends, as any other in the world. So far therefore as its powers reach, all ideas of confederation are given up and lost. It is true this government is limited to certain objects, or to speak more properly, some small degree of power is still left to the states, but a little attention to the powers vested in the general government, will convince every candid man, that if it is capable of being executed, all that is reserved for the individual states must very soon be annihilated, except so far as they are barely necessary to the organization of the general government. The powers of the general legislature extend to every case that is of the least importance—there is nothing valuable to human nature, nothing dear to freemen, but what is within its power. It has authority to make laws which will affect the lives, liberty, and property of every man in the United States; nor can the constitution or laws of any state, in any way prevent or impede the full and complete execution of every power given. The legislative power is competent to lay taxes, duties, imposts, and excises:—there is no limitation to this power, unless it be said that the clause which directs the use to which those taxes, and duties shall be applied, may be said to be a limitation; but this is no restriction of the power at all, for by this clause they are to be applied to pay the debts and provide for the common defence and general welfare of the United States; but the legislature have authority to contract debts at their discretion; they are the sole judges of what is necessary to provide for the common defence, and they only are to determine what is for the general welfare; this power therefore is neither more nor less, than a power to lay and collect taxes, imposts, and excises, at their pleasure; not only [is] the power to lay taxes unlimited, as to the amount they may require, but it is perfect and absolute to raise them in any mode they please. No state legislature, or any power in the state governments, have any more to do in carrying this into effect, than the authority of one state has to do with that of another. In the business therefore of laying and collecting taxes, the idea of confederation is totally lost, and that of one entire republic is embraced. It is proper here to remark, that the authority to lay and collect taxes is the most important of any power that can be granted; it connects with it almost all other powers, or at least will in process of time draw all others after it; it is the great mean of protection, security, and defence, in a good government, and the great engine of oppression and tyranny in a bad one. This cannot fail of being the case, if we consider the contracted limits which are set by this constitution, to the late governments, on this article of raising money. No state can emit paper money—lay any duties, or imposts, on imports, or exports, but by consent of the Congress; and then the net produce shall be for the benefit of the United States: the only means therefore left, for any state to support its government and discharge its debts, is by direct taxation; and the United States have also power to lay and collect taxes, in any way they please. Every one who has thought on the subject, must be convinced that but small sums of money can be collected in any country, by direct taxes, when the foederal government begins to exercise the right of taxation in all its parts, the legislatures of the several states will find it impossible to raise monies to support their governments. Without money they cannot be supported, and they must dwindle away, and, as before observed, their powers absorbed in that of the general government.

. . . the legislature of the United States are vested with the great and uncontroulable powers, of laying and collecting taxes, duties, imposts, and excises; of regulating trade, raising and supporting armies, organizing, arming, and disciplining the militia, instituting courts, and other general powers. And are by this clause invested with the power of making all laws, proper and necessary, for carrying all these into execution; and they may so exercise this power as entirely to annihilate all the state governments, and reduce this country to one single government. And if they may do it, it is pretty certain they will; for it will be found that the power retained by individual states, small as it is, will be a clog upon the wheels of the government of the United States; the latter therefore will be naturally inclined to remove it out of the way. Besides, it is a truth confirmed by the unerring experience of the ages, that every man, and every body of men, invested with power are ever disposed to increase it, and to acquire a superiority over every thing that stands in their way. This disposition, which is implanted in human nature, will operate in the federal legislature to lessen and ultimately to subvert the state authority, and having such advantages, will most certainly succeed, if the federal government succeeds at all. It must be very evident then, that what this constitution wants of being a complete consolidation of the several parts of the union into one complete government, possessed of perfect legislative, judicial, and executive powers, to all intents and purposes, it will necessarily acquire in its exercise and operation.

Let us now proceed to enquire, as I at first proposed, whether it be best the thirteen United States should be reduced to one great republic, or not? It is here taken for granted that all agree in this, that whatever government we adopt, it ought to be a free one; that it should be so framed as to secure the liberty of the citizens of America, and such an one as to admit of a full, fair, and equal representation of the people. The question then will be, whether a government thus constituted, and founded on such principles, is practicable, and can be exercised over the whole United States, reduced into one state?

If respect is to be paid to the opinion of the greatest and wisest men who have ever thought or wrote on the science of government, we shall be constrained to conclude, that a free republic cannot succeed over a country of such immense extent, containing such a number of inhabitants, and these encreasing in such rapid progression as that of the whole United States. Among the many illustrious authorities which might be produced to this point, I shall content myself with quoting only two. The one is the baron de Montesquieu, spirit of the laws, chap. xvi, vol. I, "It is natural to a republic to have only a small territory, otherwise it cannot long subsist. In a large republic there are men of large fortunes, and consequently of less moderation; there are trusts too great to be placed in any single subject; he has interests of his own; he soon begins to think that he may be happy, great and glorious, by oppressing his fellow citizens; and that he may raise himself to grandeur on the ruins of his country. In a large republic, the public good is sacrificed to a thousand views; it is subordinate to expectations, and depends on accidents. In a small one, the interest of the public is easier perceived, better understood, and more within the reach of every citizen; abuses are of less extent, and of course are less protected." Of the same opinion is the marquis Beccarari.[8]

History furnishes no example of a free republic, any thing like the extent of the United States. The Grecian republics were of small extent; so also was that of the Romans. Both of these, it is true, in process of time, extended their conquests over large territories of country; and the consequence was, that their governments were changed from that of free governments to those of the most tyrannical that ever existed in the world.

Not only the opinion of the greatest men, and the experience of mankind, are against the idea of an extensive republic, but a variety of reasons may be drawn from the reason and nature of things, against it. In every government, the will of the sovereign is law. In despotic governments, the supreme authority being lodged in one, his will is law, and can be as easily expressed to a large extensive territory as to a small one. In a pure democracy the people are the sovereign, and their will is declared by themselves; for this purpose they must all come together to deliberate, and decide. This kind of government cannot be exercised, therefore, over a country of any considerable extent; it must be confined to a single city, or at least limited to such bounds as that the people can conveniently assemble, be able to debate, understand the subject submitted to them, and declare their opinion concerning it.[9]

In a free republic, although all laws are derived from the consent of the people, yet the people do not declare their consent by themselves in person, but by representatives, chosen by them, who are supposed to know the minds of their constituents, and to be possessed of integrity to declare this mind.

In every free government, the people must give their assent to the laws by which they are governed. This is the true criterion between a free government and an arbitrary one. The former are ruled by the will of the whole, expressed in any manner they may agree upon; the latter by the will of one, or a few. If the people are to give their assent to the laws, by persons chosen and appointed by them, the manner of the choice and the number chosen, must be such, as to possess, be disposed, and consequently qualified to declare the sentiments of the people; for if they do not know, or are not disposed to speak the sentiments of the people, the people do not govern, but the sovereignty is in a few. Now, in a large extended country, it is impossible to have a representation, possessing the sentiments, and of integrity, to declare the minds of the people, without having it so numerous and so unwieldy, as to be subject in great measure to the inconveniency of a democratic government.

The territory of the United States is of vast extent; it now contains near three millions of souls, and is capable of containing much more than ten times that number. Is it practicable for a country, so large and so numerous as they will soon become, to elect a representation, that will speak their sentiments, without their becoming so numerous as to be incapable of transacting public business? It certainly is not.

In a republic, the manners, sentiments, and interests of the people should be similar. If this be not the case, there will be a constant clashing of opinions; and the representatives of one part will be continually striving against those of the other. This will retard the operations of good government, and prevent such conclusions as will promote the public good. If we apply this remark to the condition of the United States, we shall be convinced that it forbids that we should be one government. . . .

. . . the people will not be likely to have such confidence in their rulers, in a republic so extensive as the United States, as necessary for these purposes. The confidence which the people have in their rulers, in a free republic, arises from their knowing them, from their being responsible to them for their conduct, and from the power they have of displacing them when they misbehave: but in a republic of the extent of this continent, the people in general would be acquainted with very few of their rulers: the people at large would know little of their proceedings, and it would be extremely difficult to change them. The people in Georgia and New-Hampshire could not know one another's mind, and therefore could not act in concert to enable them to effect a general change of representatives. The different parts of so extensive a country could not possibly be made acquainted with the conduct of their representatives, nor be informed of the reasons upon which measures were founded. The consequence will be, they will have no confidence in their legislature, suspect them of ambitious views, be jealous of every measure they adopt, and will not support the laws they pass. Hence the government will be nerveless and inefficient, and no way will be left to render it otherwise, but by establishing an armed force to execute the laws at the point of the bayonet—a government of all others the most to be dreaded.

In a republic of such vast extent as the United-States, the legislature cannot attend to the various concerns and wants of its different parts. It cannot be sufficiently numerous to be acquainted with the local condition and wants of the different districts, and if it could, it is impossible it should have sufficient time to attend to and provide for all the variety of cases of this nature, that would be continually arising.

In so extensive a republic, the great officers of government would soon become above the controul of the people, and abuse their power to the purpose of aggrandizing themselves, and oppressing them. . . .

These are some of the reasons by which it appears, that a free republic cannot long subsist over a country of the great extent of these states. If then this new constitution is calculated to consolidate the thirteen states into one, as it evidently is, it ought not to be adopted.

. . . There are many objections, of small moment, of which I shall take no notice—perfection is not to be expected in any thing that is the production of man—and if I did not in my conscience believe that this scheme was defective in the fundamental principles—in the foundation upon which a free and equal government must rest—I would hold my peace.

Brutus.

AN OLD WHIG: LETTER VII

Philadelphia Independent Gazetteer, November 28, 1787

An Old Whig's seventh letter was issued while Pennsylvania's ratification convention was in session. As in his first offering (printed at the beginning of the chapter), An Old Whig argues in favor of amending the Constitution. He suggests a second convention be held to do so. Federalists argued that holding a second convention would produce confusion and threaten to reverse the progress already made toward a viable centralized government. This essay is notable for its counterargument to those Federalists. Instead of yielding confusion and uncertainty, such a convention would likely "harmonize" the states. An Old Whig noted that the Antifederalist objections in the various states were similar. If properly addressed by a second convention, the whole nation could come together to support the Constitution. This essay was reprinted in at least four additional newspapers.

Mr. Printer,
    Many people seem to be convinced that the proposed constitution is liable to a number of important objections; that there are defects in it which ought to be supplied, and errors which ought to be amended;

but they apprehend that we must either receive this constitution in its present form, or be left without any continental government whatsoever. To be sure, if this were the case, it would be most prudent for us, like a man who is wedded to a bad wife, to submit to our misfortune with patience, and make the best of a bad bargain. But if we will summon up resolution sufficient to examine into our true circumstances, we shall find that we are not in so deplorable a situation as people have been taught to believe, from the suggestions of interested men, who wish to force down the proposed plan of government without delay, for the purpose of providing offices for themselves and their friends. We shall find, that, with a little wisdom and patience, we have it yet in our power, not only to establish a federal constitution, but to establish a good one.

It is true that the continental convention has directed their proposed constitution to be laid before a convention of delegates to be chosen in each state, "for their assent and ratification," which seems to preclude the idea of any power in the several conventions, of proposing any alterations, or indeed of even rejecting the plan proposed, if they should disapprove of it. Still, however, the question recurs, what authority the late convention had to bind the people of the United States, to any particular form of government, or to forbid them to adopt such form of government as they should think fit. I know it is a language frequent in the mouths of some heaven-born PHAETONS amongst us, who like the son of Apollo think themselves entitled to guide the chariot of the sun; the common people have no right to judge of the affairs of government; that they are not fit for it; that they should leave these matters to their superiors. This however, is not the language of men of real understanding, even among the advoctes for the proposed constitution; but these still recognize the authority of the people, and will admit, at least in words, that the people have a right to be consulted. Then I ask, if the people in the different states have a right to be consulted, in the new form of continental government, what authority could the late convention have to preclude them from proposing amendments to the plan they should offer? Had the convention any right to bind the people to the form of government they should propose? Let us consider this matter.

The late convention were chosen by the general assembly of each state; they had the sanction of Congress;—for what? To consider what alterations were necessary to be made in the articles of confederation. What have they done? They have made a new Constitution for the United States. I will not say, that in doing so, they have exceeded their authority; but on the other hand, I trust that no man of understanding amongst them will pretend to say, that any thing they did or could do, was of the least avail to lessen the rights of the people to judge for themselves in the last resort. This right, is perhaps, unalienable, but at all events, there is no pretence for saying that this right was ever meant to be surrendered up into the hands of the late continental convention.

The people have an undoubted right to judge of every part of the government which is offered to them: No power on earth has a right to preclude them; and they may exercise this choice either by themselves or their delegates legally chosen to represent them in the State-Convention.—I venture to say that no man, reasoning upon *revolution* principles, can possibly controvert this right.

Indeed very few go so far as to controvert the right of the people to propose amendments; but we are told that the thing is impracticable; that if we begin to propose amendments there will be no end to them; that the several states will never agree in their amendments; that we shall never unite in any plan; that if we reject this we shall either have a worse or none at all; that we ought therefore to adopt this *at once*, without alteration or amendment.—Now these are very kind gentlemen, who insist upon doing so much good for us, whether we will or not. Idiots and maniacs ought certainly to be restrained from doing themselves mischief, and should be compelled to that which is for their own good. Whether the people of America are to be considered in this light, and treated accordingly, is a question which deserves, perhaps more consideration than it has yet received. A contest between the patients and their doctors, which are mad or which are fools, might possibly be a very unhappy one. I hope at least that we shall be able to settle this important business without so preposterous a dispute. What then would you have us do, it may be asked? Would you have us adopt the proposed Constitution or reject it? I answer that I would neither wish the one nor the other. Though I would be far from pretending to dictate to the representatives of the people what steps ought to be pursued, yet a method seems to present itself so simple, so perfectly calculated to obviate all difficulties, to reconcile us with one another, and establish unanimity and harmony among the people of this country, that I cannot forbear to suggest it. I hope that most of my readers have already anticipated me in what I am about to propose. Whether they have or not, I shall venture to state it, in the humble expectations that it may have some tendency to reconcile honest men of all parties with one another.

The method I would propose is this—

1st. Let the Conventions of each state, as they meet, after considering the proposed Constitution, state their objections and propose their amendments.

So far from these objections and amendments clashing with each other in irreconcilable discord, as it has been too often suggested they would do, it appears that from what has been hitherto published in the different states in opposition to the proposed Constitution, we have a right to expect that they will harmonize in a very great degree. The reason I say so, is, that about the same time, in very different parts of the continent, the very same objections have been made, and the very same alterations proposed by different writers, who I verily believe, know nothing at all of each other, and were very far from acting in a premeditated concert, and that others who have not appeared as writers in the newspapers, in the different states, have appeared to act and speak in perfect unison with those objections and amendments, particularly in the article of a Bill of Rights. That in short, the very same sentiments seem to have been echoed from the different parts of the continent by the opposers of the proposed Constitution; and these sentiments have been very little contradicted by its friends, otherwise than by suggesting their fears, that by opposing the Constitution at present proposed, we might be disappointed of any federal government or receive a worse one than the present.—It would be a most delightful surprize to find ourselves all of one opinion at last; and I cannot forbear hoping that when we come fairly to compare our sentiments, we shall find ourselves much more nearly agreed than in the hurry and surprize in which we have been involved on this subject, we ever suffered ourselves to imagine.

2d. When the Conventions have stated these objections and amendments, let them transmit them to Congress and adjourn, praying that Congress will direct another Convention to be called from the different states, to consider of these objections and amendments, and pledging themselves to abide by whatever decision shall be made by such future Convention on the subject; whether it be to amend the proposed Constitution or to reject any alteration and ratify it as it stands.

3d. If a new Convention of the United States should meet, and revise the proposed Constitution, let us agree to abide by their decision.—It is past a doubt that every good citizen of America pants for an efficient federal government—I have no doubt we shall concur at last in some plan of continental government, even if many people could imagine exceptions to it; but if the exceptions which are made at present, shall be maturely considered and even be pronounced by our future representatives as of no importance; (which I trust they will not) even in that case, I have no doubt that almost every man, will give up his own private opinion and concur in that decision.

4th. If by any means another Continental Convention should fail to meet, then let the Conventions of the several states again assemble and at last decide the great solemn question whether we shall adopt the Constitution now proposed, or reject it? And, whenever it becomes necessary to decide upon this point, one at least who from the beginning has been invariably anxious for the liberty and independence of his country, will concur in adopting and supporting this Constitution, rather than none;—though I confess I could easily imagine some other form of confederation, which I should think better entitled to my hearty approbation;—and indeed I am not afraid of a worse.

I am, &c.
An Old Whig.

LETTER OF MARYLAND'S JOHN FRANCIS MERCER TO MEMBERS OF THE NEW YORK AND VIRGINIA CONVENTIONS

May 1788

"Momentum" is critical in politics. A few well-timed advances can make the difference between a candidate's election or defeat, between enacting legislation or having it rejected. The power of momentum was also at work during the ratification process. Maryland was the seventh state to ratify. It did so by an overwhelming margin (sixty-three to eleven) and without recommending amendments. Maryland's actions were important for the Federalists because some observers had predicted that the state would not ratify.[10] The convention's balloting on April 26, 1788, proved them wrong. It also put the Constitution within two votes of being legally sanctioned. This strong Federalist showing may have influenced some delegates in South Carolina, New Hampshire, New York, and Virginia, which were all likely to vote on ratification in the next two months. John Francis Mercer did not want the outcome in Maryland to have such an effect. Mercer thus wrote the following letter to help maintain Antifederalist strength in Virginia and New York. If those states could hold

firm against ratification, amendments might be obtained before the new government was implemented. Mercer had been one of the eleven Marylanders to vote against the Constitution. He also attended the Philadelphia convention (see chapter 2) and previously served in the Confederation Congress.[11] He was later elected to the House of Representatives and served as Maryland's governor. Mercer's comments were sent directly to the New York and Virginia conventions and were not printed in newspapers.

Gentlemen

The galling Chains of Despotizm under the oppressive weight of which nine tenths of our Fellow Mortals groan—the Tortures which unfeeling Tyranny has invented and fearlessly practiced in every Age and every Clime, are melancholy and terrifying proofs of the Incapacity of the *many* to defend those rights, which God and Nature gave them, from the artful and unceasing usurpations of the *Few*:—and they are frightful Lessons to teach us a watchful Jealousy of great and unnecessary Grants of Power and of Changes in a State of Society which we know to be mild and free—Still there are moments of national Languor and Lethargy which the Ambitious, ever enterprizing, mark with Alacrity and use with Success.—The People long unaccustomed in a good and guarded Government, to bold and selfish Designs in their Rulers, look up with an unsuspicious Confidence, to any alteration, which those entrusted with Power may propose—however unconstitutional the changes, if recommended by men used to govern them, they seem to come forward under the Sanction of legal authority—if prepared in Secrecy—the public mind taken by surprise, and every Engine previously set in Motion—the unconcerted and unconnected Defence of Individuals is branded with the opprobrious Epithet of *Opposition* and overwhelmed in the directed Tide of popular Clamour— a clamour which a Number of wealthy Men may at all Times command at a small Expence from the most indigent of the Populace.

We forbear to remark on the Manner in which the Constitution proposed for the United States came forward—as the Circumstances are known to you, your own Feelings will render any Observations unnecessary.

The Object of our present Address is to prevent your forming unjust Conclusions from the Adoption of the Constitution in the State of Maryland by so large a Majority of the Convention and the subsequent dissolution of that Body, without proposing any Amendments.—

Permit us to assure You that the Torrent which burst forth at the Birth of the Constitution had but little Effect on the Minds of many of us—and altho' it might prevent our having that weight with our

Countrymen, in the first Paroxisms of Phrenzy which forever accompany great and sudden Revolutions in Government—we were yet determined not to be wanting in our Duty to the Republic, at that Moment when Reason should resume her Empire over the unagitated Minds of our fellow Citizens—from many Circumstances we despaired of this in Maryland untill the adoption of the Constitution— At that Period, when our Efforts could not be subjected to Calumniating Misrepresentation,—we expected that an Appeal to the reflection of our Countrymen, would be listened to with attention and produce those Effects which unanswered and unanswerable Reasons ought to command—All opposition being thus postponed and every necessary Step to inform the minds of our Citizens on one Side neglected—while unremitting Exertions by a number of wealthy and respectable Characters were continued on the other—it cannot be surprizing that the Elections were generally favorable to the Constitution—In a very few of the Counties did any Candidates propose themselves against it—very few voted and even in those Counties where the opposition succeeded by such a decided Majority— those Gentlemen's offering was merely accidental. They had refused every Solicitation of the people and had actually determined not to serve in Convention until within 6 Days before the Election—[12]

That the People of the State would have made alterations and amendments a Condition of Adoption, is a Question which from the above Circumstances it is impossible to decide—but that four fifths of the people of Maryland are now in favor of considerable Alterations and Amendments, and will insist on them,—we don't hesitate to declare (as our Opinion) to You and the world.—The difference between amending *before* or *after* adoption (provided it is amended) is certainly not worth a Distinction.—

We are persuaded that the People of so large a Continent, so different in Interests, so distinct in Habits, cannot in all cases legislate in one Body by themselves or their Representatives—By themselves it is obviously impracticable—By their Representatives it will be found on Investigation equally so—for if these representatives are to pursue the general Interest without Constitutional checks and restraints—it must be done by a mutual Sacrifice of the Interests, wishes and prejudices of the parts they represent—and then they cannot be said to represent those Parts, but to misrepresent them.[13]—Besides as their Constituents cannot judge of their Conduct by their own Sense of what is right and proper—and as a representative can always in this view screen his abuse of Trust under the Cloak of Compromize, we do not see what check can remain in the hands of the Constituents—for they cannot Know how far the Compromise was necessary, and the representative wrong—and to turn out and disgrace a Man when they cannot prove him wrong, and when he will have of Course the voice of the Body he is a Member of in his Favor, would in the Event be found subversive of the Principles of good Government.—

Thus then the pursuit of the general Interest produces an unchecked Misrepresentation—but if Representatives are to pursue the partial Interests of the Districts they represent (which to recommend themselves to their Constituents it is most probably they will do) then the Majority must ruin the Minority, for the Majority will be found interested to throw the Burthens of Government upon that Minority which in these States present a fair Opening by difference of *Cultivation—Importation* and *property*—In such extensive Territories governed by one Legislature, the Experience of Mankind tells us that if not by Preference of the People will at least be led gradually to confide the legislative Power to the Hands of one Man and his Family— who alone can represent the whole, without partial Interests and this is or leads to unlimited Despotizm—

We have not that permanent and fixed distinction of rank or orders of Men among us, which unalterably seperating the interests and views, produces that division in pursuits, which is the great security of the mixed Government we seperated from, and which we now seem so anxiously to copy; —if the New Senate of the United States will be really opposite in their pursuits and views from the Representatives, have they not a most dangerous power, of interesting foreign Nations by Treaty to support *their* views?—for instance the relinquishment of the navigation of Missisippi—And yet these Treaties are expressly declared paramount to the Constitutions of the several States and Being the *Supreme Law*, must of course control the national legislature, if not supercede the Constitution of the United States itself—the check of the President over a Body, with which he must act in concert, or his influence and power be almost annihilated, can prove no great Constitutional security; And even the Representative body itself—and much more the Senate—are not sufficiently numerous to secure them from corruption—for all Governments tend to corruption, in proportion as power concentrating in the hands of the *few*, renders them objects of corruption to Foreign Nations and among themselves—

For these and many other reasons we are for preserving the Rights of the State Governments, where they must not be necessarily relinquished for the welfare of the Union—and where so relinquished the line should be definitely drawn. If under the proposed Constitution the States exercise any Power, it would seem to be at the mercy of the General

Government—for it is remarkable that the clause securing to them those rights not expressly relinquished in the old Confoederation, is left out in the new Constitution; And we conceive that there is not Power which Congress may *think* necessary to exercise for the *general welfare*, which they may not assume under this Constitution—and this *Constitution* and the Laws made under it are declared paramount even to the unalienable rights, which have heretofore been assured to the Citizens of these States by their Constitutional compacts.—

Altho' this new Constitution can boast indeed of a bill of Rights of seven Articles—yet of what Nature is that Bill of Rights? to hold out such a security to the rights of property as might lead very wealthy and influential Men and Families into a blind compliance and adoption—whilst the Rights that are essential to the great body of Yeomanry of America are entirely disregarded.—[14]

Moreover those very powers, which are to be expressly vested in the new Congress, are of a nature most liable to abuse—They are those which tempt the avarice and ambition of Men to a violation of the rights of their fellow Citizens, and they will be screend under the sanction of an undefined and unlimited authority—Against the *abuse* and *improper* exercise of these special powers, the People have a right to be secured by a sacred Declaration, defining the rights of the Individual and limiting by them, the extent of the exercise—The People were secured against the abuse of those Powers by fundamental Laws and a Bill of Rights, under the Government of Britain and under their own Constitutions—That Government which permits the abuse of Power, recommends it; and will deservedly experience the tyranny which it authorizes; for the history of Mankind establishes the truth of this political adage—*that in Government what may be done will be done.*

The most blind admirer of this Constitution must in his heart confess that it is as far inferior to the British Constitution, of which it is an imperfect imitation as darkness is to light—In the British Constitution, the rights of Men, the primary objects of the social Compact—are fixed on an immoveable foundation and clearly defined and ascertained by their Magna Charta, their Petition of Rights and Bill of Rights and their Effective administration by ostensible Ministers, secures Responsibility—In this new Constitution—a complicated System sets responsibility at defiance and the Rights of Men, neglected and undefined are left alone at the mercy of events; We vainly plume ourselves on the safeguard alone of Representation, forgetting that it will be a Representation on principles inconsistent with true and just Representation—that it is but a delusive shadow of Representation proffering in theory what can never be fairly reduced to practice;—And after all Government by Representation (unless confirmed in its views and conduct by the constant inspection, immediate superintendance, and frequent interference and control of the People themselves on one side, or an hereditary nobility on the other, both of which orders have fixed and permanent views) is really only a scene of perpetual rapine and confusion.—and even with the best checks it has failed in all the Governments of Europe, of which it was once the basis, except that of England.—

When We turn our Eyes back to the scenes of blood and desolation which we have waded through to separate from Great Britain—we behold with manly indignation that our blood and treasure have been wasted to establish a Government in which the Interest of the *few* is preferred to the Rights *of the Many*—When We see a Government so every way inferior to that we were born under, proposed as the reward of our sufferings in an eight years calamitous war—our astonishment is only equalled by our resentment—On the conduct of Virginia and New York, two important States, the preservation of Liberty in great measure depends—the chief security of a Confoederacy of Republics was boldly disregarded and the old Cofoederation violated by requiring Nine instead of 13 voices to alter the Constitution.—but still the resistance of either of these States, in the present temper of America (for the late conduct of the Party here must open the eyes of the People in Massachusetts with respect to the fate of their amendments) will secure all that we mean to contend for—*The natural and unalienable Rights of Men* in a constitutional manner—At the distant appearance of danger to these, We took up arms in the late Revolution—and may we never have cause to look back with regret on that period when connected with the Empire of Great Britain, We were *happy, secure,* and *free.*

SPEECHES BY MELANCTON SMITH
IN NEW YORK'S STATE CONVENTION

June 1788

Smith was a merchant and part-time lawyer who had moved from Poughkeepsie to New York City in 1785. He was a rising star in New York politics and was closely connected with long-time governor George Clinton. Smith coordinated Antifederalist electioneering efforts for the New York convention. He did his job well, as two-thirds of the delegates elected opposed the Constitution. In fact, he may have done his job too well. New York's convention began as the New Hampshire and Virginia conven-

tions were meeting. During New York's deliberations, both these states ratified the Constitution. New Hampshire was the ninth state to do so, and although nine ratifications were required to give the Constitution legal status, they were not enough to ensure the Constitution's success. The approval by Virginia, the largest and wealthiest state, virtually assured that the Constitution would be successfully implemented. Suddenly, New York— the site of the Confederation's capital and the temporarily assigned capital for the new federal government under the Constitution—did not want to be left behind by the new government. So it fell to Antifederalists, and Smith in particular, to engineer acceptance of the Constitution. When it came time to vote on ratification, several Antifederalists did not show up. Because the Antifederalist majority was so large, some Antifederalists also had to vote in favor of ratification, which is precisely what Smith and a few of his colleagues did. The contradiction between Smith's very public opposition to the Constitution and his vote in favor of ratification was too blatant to hide. After ratification, these "ratifying Antifederalists" were not only ostracized by their own political party, but they also were not embraced by the Federalists. Thus, Smith's political career ended. In these speeches, Smith shows the same kind of attention to detail and depth of argument characteristic of Brutus, the series of letters he is suspected to have written. His speeches are one of the best justifications of why "representatives . . . should be a true picture of the people."

Smith's speech of June 20 is not written in the first person (Smith is referred to as "he" and "him"), but the speech of June 21 is written as if being delivered by Smith.

June 20, 1788

. . . When we were colonies, our representation was better than any that was then known: since the revolution, we had advanced still nearer to perfection. He [Smith] considered it as an object, of all others the most important, to have it fixed on its true principle; yet he was convinced that it was impracticable to have such a representation in a consolidated government. However, said he, we may approach a great way towards perfection by increasing the representation and limiting the powers of Congress. He considered that the great interests and liberties of the people could only be secured by the state governments. He admitted that, if the new government was only confined to great national objects, it would be less exceptionable; but it extended to everything dear to human nature. That this was the case, would be proved without any long chain of reasoning; for that power which had both the purse and the sword had the government of the whole country, and might extend its powers to any and every object. He had already observed that, by the true doctrine of representation, this principle was established—that the representative[s] must be chosen by the free will of the majority of his constituents. It therefore followed that the representative[s] should be chosen from small districts. This being admitted, he would ask, Could 65 men for 3,000,000, or 1 for 30,000 be chosen in this manner? Would they be possessed of the requisite information to make happy the great number of souls that were spread over this extensive country? There was another objection to the clause: if great affairs of government were trusted to few men, they would be more liable to corruption. Corruption, he knew, was unfashionable amongst us, but he supposed that Americans were like other men; and though they had hitherto displayed such great virtues, still they were men; and therefore such steps should be taken as to prevent the possibility of corruption. We were now taken in that stage of society in which we could deliberate with freedom; how long it might continue, God only knew! Twenty years hence, perhaps, these maxims might become unfashionable. We already hear, said he, in all parts of the country, gentlemen ridiculing that spirit of patriotism, and love of liberty, which carried us through all our difficulties in times of danger. When patriotism was already nearly hooted out of society, ought we not to take some precautions against the progress of corruption?

He had one more observation to make, to show that the representation was insufficient. Government, he said, must rest, for its execution, on the good opinion of the people; for, if it was made heaven, and had not the confidence of the people, it could not be executed; that this was proved by the example given by the gentleman of the Jewish theocracy. It must have a good setting out, or the instant it takes place, there is an end of liberty. He believed that the inefficacy of the old Confederation had arisen from that want of confidence; and this caused, in a great degree, by the continual declamation of gentlemen of importance against it from one end of the continent to the other, who had frequently compared it to a rope of sand. It had pervaded every class of citizens; and their misfortunes, the consequences of idleness and extravagance, were attributed to the defects of that system. At the close of the war, our country had been left in distress; and it was impossible that any government on earth could immediately retrieve it; it must be time and industry alone that could effect it. He said, he would pursue these observations no further at present,—and concluded with making the following motion:—

"*Resolved*, That it is proper that the number of representatives be fixed at the rate of one for every twenty thousand inhabitants, to be ascertained on the principles mentioned in the 2d section of the 1st article of the Constitution, until they amount to three hundred; after which they shall be apportioned among the states, in proportion to the number of inhabitants of the states respectively; and that, before the first enumeration be made, the several states shall be entitled to choose double the number of representatives, for that purpose mentioned in the Constitution."

June 21, 1788

It has been observed, by an honorable member, that the Eastern States insisted upon a small representation, on the principles of economy. This argument must have no weight in the mind of a considerate person. The difference of expense, between supporting a House of Representatives sufficiently numerous, and the present proposed one, would be twenty or thirty thousand dollars per annum. The man who would seriously object to this expense, to secure his liberties, does not deserve to enjoy them. Besides, by increasing the number of representatives, we open a door for the admission of the substantial yeomanry of our country, who, being possessed of the habits of economy, will be cautious of imprudent expenditures, by which means a greater saving will be made of public money than is sufficient to support them.[15] A reduction of the numbers of the state legislatures might also be made, by which means there might be a saving of expense much more than sufficient for the purpose of supporting the general legislature; for as, under this system, all the powers of legislation relating to our general concerns, are vested in the general government, the powers of the state legislatures will be so curtailed as to render it less necessary to have them so numerous as they now are.

But an honorable gentleman has observed, that it is a problem that cannot be solved, what the proper number is which ought to compose the House of Representatives, and calls upon me to fix the number.[16] I admit that this is a question that will not admit of a solution with mathematical certainty; few political questions will; yet we may determine with certainty that certain numbers are too small or too large. We may be sure that ten is too small, and a thousand too large a number. Every one will allow that the first number is too small to possess the sentiments, be influenced by the interests of the people, or secure against corruption; a thousand would be too numerous to be capable of deliberating.

To determine whether the number of representatives proposed by this Constitution is sufficient, it is proper to examine the qualifications which this house ought to possess, in order to exercise their power discreetly for the happiness of the people. The idea that naturally suggests itself to our minds, when we speak of representatives, is, that they resemble those they represent. They should be a true picture of the people, possess a knowledge of their circumstances and their wants, sympathize in all their distresses, and be disposed to seek their true interests. The knowledge necessary for the representative of a free people not only comprehends extensive political and commercial information, such as is acquired by men of refined education, who have leisure to attain to high degrees of improvement, but it should also comprehend that kind of acquaintance with the common concerns and occupations of the people, which men of the middling class of life are, in general, more competent to than those of a superior class. To understand the true commercial interests of a country, not only requires just ideas of the general commerce of the world, but also, and principally, a knowledge of the productions of your own country, and their value, what your soil is capable of producing, the nature of your manufactures, and the capacity of the country to increase both. To exercise the power of laying taxes, duties, and excises, with discretion, requires something more than an acquaintance with the abstruse parts of the system of finance. It calls for a knowledge of the circumstances and ability of the people in general—a discernment how the burdens imposed will bear upon the different classes.

From these observations results this conclusion—that the number of representatives should be so large, as that, while it embraces the men of the first class, it should admit those of the middling class of life. I am convinced that this government is so constituted that the representatives will generally be composed of the first class in the community, which I shall distinguish by the name of the *natural aristocracy* of the country. I do not mean to give offence by using this term. I am sensible this idea is treated by many gentlemen as chimerical. I shall be asked what is meant by the *natural aristocracy*, and told that no such distinction among classes of men exists among us. It is true, it is our singular felicity that we have no legal or hereditary distinctions of this kind; but still there are real differences. Every society naturally divides itself into classes. The Author of nature has bestowed on some greater capacities than others; birth, education, talents, and wealth, create distinctions among men as visible, and of as much influence, as titles, stars, and garters. In every society, men of this class will command a superior degree of respect; and if the government is so constituted as to admit but few to exercise the powers of it, it will, according to the natural course of things, be in their hands. Men in the middling class, who are qualified as representatives, will not be so anxious to be chosen as those of the first. When the number is so small, the office will be highly elevated and distinguished; the style in which the members live will probably be high; circumstances of this kind will render the place of a representative not a desirable one to sensible, substantial men, who have been used to walk in the plain and frugal paths of life.

Besides, the influence of the great will generally enable them to succeed in elections. It will be difficult to combine a district of country containing thirty or forty thousand inhabitants,—frame your election laws as you please,—in any other character, unless it be in one of conspicuous military, popular, civil, or legal talents. The great easily form associations; the poor and middling class form them with difficulty. If the elections be by plurality,—as probably will be the case in this state,—it is almost certain none but the great will be chosen, for they easily unite their interests: the common people will divide, and their divisions will be promoted by others. There will be scarcely a chance of their uniting in any other but some great man, unless in some popular demagogue, who will probably be destitute of principle. A substantial yeoman, of sense and discernment, will hardly ever be chosen. From these remarks, it appears that the government will fall into the hands of the few and the great. This will be a government of oppression. I do not mean to declaim against the great, and charge them indiscriminately with want of principle and honesty. The same passions and prejudices govern all men. The circumstances in which men are placed in a great measure give a cast to the human character. Those in middling circumstances have less temptation; they are inclined by habit, and the company with whom they associate, to set bounds to their passions and appetites. If this is not sufficient, the want of means to gratify them will be a restraint: they are obliged to employ their time in their respective callings; hence the substantial yeomanry of the country are more temperate, of better morals, and less ambition, than the great. The latter do not feel for the poor and middling class; the reasons are obvious—they are not obliged to use the same pains and labor to procure property as the other. They feel not the inconveniences arising from the payment of small sums. The great consider themselves above the common people, entitled to more respect, do not associate with them; they fancy themselves to have a right of preeminence in every thing. In short, they possess the same feelings, are under the influence of the same motives, as an hereditary nobility. I know the idea that such a distinction exists in this country is ridiculed by some; but I am not the less apprehensive of danger from their influence on this account. Such distinctions exist all the world over, have been taken notice of by all writers on free government, and are founded in the nature of things. It has been the principal care of free government to guard against the encroachments of the great. Common observation and experience prove the existence of such distinctions. Will any one say that there does not exist in this country the pride of family, of wealth, of talents, and that they do not command influence and respect among the common people? Congress, in their address to the inhabitants of the province of Quebec, in 1775, state this distinction in the following forcible words, quoted from the Marquis Beccaria: "In every human society there is an essay continually tending to confer on one part the height of power and happiness and to reduce the other to the extreme of weakness and misery. The intent of good laws is to oppose this effort, and to diffuse their influence univerally and equally."[17] We ought to guard against the government being placed in the hands of this class. They cannot have sympathy with their constituents which is necessary to connect them closely to their interests. Being in the habit of profuse living, they will be profuse in the public expenses. They find no difficulty in paying their taxes, and therefore do not feel public burdens. Besides, if they govern, they will enjoy the emoluments of the government. The middling class, from their frugal habits, and feeling themselves the public burdens, will be careful how they increase them.

But I may be asked, Would you exclude the first class in the community from any share in legislation? I answer, By no means. They would be factious, discontented, and constantly disturbing the government. It would also be unjust. They have their liberties to protect, as well as others, and the largest share of property. But my idea is, that the Constitution should be so framed as to admit this class, together with a sufficient number of the middling class to control them. You will then combine the abilities and honesty of the community, a proper degree of information, and a disposition to pursue the public good. A representative body, composed principally of respectable yeomanry, is the best possible security to liberty. When the interest of this part of the community is pursued, the public good is pursued, because the body of every nation consists of this class, and because the interest of both the rich and the poor are involved in that of the middling class. No burden can be laid on the poor but what will sensibly affect the middling class. Any law rendering property insecure would be injurious to them. When, therefore, this class in society pursue their own interest, they promote that of the public, for it is involved in it.

In so small a number of representatives, there is great danger from corruption and combination. A great politician has said that every man has his price. I hope this is not true in all its extent; but I ask the gentleman to inform me what government there is in which it has not been practised. Notwithstanding all that has been said of the defects in the constitution of the ancient confederacies in the Grecian republics, their destruction is to be imputed more to this cause than to any imperfection in their forms of government. This was the deadly poison that effected their dissolution. This is an extensive country, increasing in population and growing in consequence. Very many lucrative offices will be in the grant of the government, which will be objects of avarice and ambition. How easy will it be to gain over a sufficient number, in the bestowment of offices, to promote the views and the purposes of those who grant them! Foreign corruption is also to be guarded against. A system of corruption is known to be the system of government in Europe. It is practised without blushing; and we may lay it to our account, it will be attempted among us. The most effectual as well as natural security against this is a strong democratic branch in the legislature, frequently chosen, including in it a number of the substantial, sensible yeomanry of the country. Does the House of Representatives answer this description? I confess, to me they hardly wear the complexion of a democratic branch; they appear the mere shadow of representation. The whole number, in both houses, amounts to ninety-one; of these forty-six make a quorum; and twenty-four of those, being secured, may carry any point. Can the liberties of three millions of people be securely trusted in the hands of twenty-four men? Is it prudent to commit to so small a number the decision of the great questions which will come before them? Reason revolts at the idea.

The honorable gentleman from New York has said, that sixty-five members of the House of Representatives are sufficient for the present situation of the country; and, taking it for granted that they will increase as one for thirty thousand, in twenty-five years they will amount to two hundred.[18] It is admitted, by this observation, that the number fixed in the Constitution is not sufficient without it is augmented. It is not declared that an increase shall be made, but is left at the discretion of the legislature, by the gentleman's own concession; therefore the Constitution is imperfect. We certainly ought to fix, in the Constitution, those things which are essential to liberty. If any thing falls under this description, it is the number of the legislature. To say, as this gentleman does, that our security is to depend upon the spirit of the people, who will be watchful of their liberties, and not suffer them to be infringed, is absurd. It would equally prove that we might adopt any form of government. I believe, were we to create a despot, he would not immediately dare to act the tyrant; but it would not be long before he would destroy the spirit of the people, or the people would destroy him. If our people have a high sense of liberty, the government should be congenial to this spirit, calculated to cherish the love of liberty, while yet it had sufficient force to restrain licentiousness. Government operates on the spirit of the people, as well as the spirit of the people operates upon it; and if they are not conformable to each other, the one or the other will prevail. In a less time than twenty-five years, the government will receive its tone. What the spirit of the country may be at the end of that period, it is impossible to foretell. Our duty is to frame a government friendly to liberty and the rights of mankind, which will tend to cherish and cultivate a love of liberty among our citizens. If this government becomes oppressive, it will be by degrees: it will aim at its end by disseminating sentiments of government opposite to republicanism, and proceed from step to step in depriving the people of a share in the government. A recollection of the change that has taken place in the minds of many in this country in the course of a few years, ought to put us on our guard. Many, who are ardent advocates for the new system, reprobate republican principles as chimerical, and such as ought to be expelled from society. Who would have thought, ten years ago, that the very men who risked their lives and fortunes in support of republican principles, would now treat them as the fictions of fancy? A few years ago, we fought for liberty; we framed a general government on free principles; we placed the state legislatures, in whom the people have a full and a fair representation, between Congress and the people. We were then, it is true, too cautious, and too much restricted the powers of the general government. But now it is proposed to go into the contrary, and a more dangerous extreme—to remove all barriers, to give the new government free access to our pockets, and ample command of our persons, and that without providing for a genuine and fair representation of the people. No one can say what the progress of the change of sentiment may be in twenty-five years. The same men who now cry up the necessity of an energetic government, to induce a compliance with this system, may, in much less time, reprobate this in as severe terms as they now do the Confederation, and may as strongly urge the necessity of going as far beyond this as this is beyond the Confederation. Men of this class are increasing: they have influence, talents, and industry. It is time to form a barrier against them. And while we are willing to establish a government adequate to the purposes of the Union, let us be careful to establish it on the broad basis of equal liberty.

NOTES

1. The specific phrase "middle class" was not generally in the vocabulary of those who participated in the ratification debate. Nevertheless, many authors, like Brutus, did refer to "the middling class" to describe the great majority of Americans who were neither rich nor poor, a phrase that I employ in this introduction. A word frequently used to describe the small farmers who made up the bulk of the population in most states who were neither rich nor poor was the "yeomanry." Ratification debate participants also referred to "mechanics," laborers who practiced trades other than farming. Together, the yeomanry and the mechanics made up the middling class.

2. *Democracy in America*, part 1, chapter 2. The widespread availability of land was also a "levelling" factor, as was the relative scarcity of labor.

3. The prevalence of slavery was the foremost factor leading to a more aristocratic brand of politics in these states. The climate and the laws of these states combined to allow families to possess vast plantations powered by slave labor. These families were able to parlay their material advantages into political advantages in a way that could not be done in other states. The prevalence of slavery in these states also contributed to politics resembling European politics more than in other states, as slaves resembled the landless peasants who toiled for little reward.

4. *DHRC*, vol. 2, p. 288.

5. Contrary to the implication of this passage, Lycurgus was generally celebrated for his actions. Lycurgus's intent was to set up something timeless, not easily altered. Many of the Constitution's authors were trying to do the same. James Madison, for instance, believed that a Constitution that was difficult to amend would more quickly and surely be treated reverentially. When a constitution was treated with reverence, it would be heeded. If that constitution were well written, it would yield good government and promote stability. A candid Federalist might respond to An Old Whig's argument by saying that corners may have been cut in formulating the Constitution, but that was done to institute a good government.

6. Article I, section 8, clause 18.

7. Article VI, clause 2.

8. One of the best-known works of the Enlightenment was Cesare Beccaria's *On Crimes and Punishments*. Beccaria argued that to attain justice, laws needed to be clear. Clarity in the law was much more likely to be provided by citizen legislators than monarchs or aristocrats, much of whose power flowed from the ease with which they manipulated obscure laws. Unlike Montesquieu, Beccaria did not extensively analyze geographical size as a determinant of regime type. He agreed with Montesquieu that a republic should re-

main small in size, but he did so simply because Montesquieu's argument was convincing to him. Thus, Brutus's treatment of Beccaria is suitably brief.

9. Note that Brutus calls a government where all citizens assemble and make decisions a "pure democracy." In contrast, look to James Madison's treatment of this kind of government in "Federalist #10." Madison simply calls this arrangement "democracy," and he argues that it inevitably fails because majorities tyrannize over minorities.

10. For example, Mercy Otis Warren in "A Columbian Patriot."

11. Mercer was elected to that body at the age of twenty-three and served three years as a delegate from Virginia before being rotated out of office. Mercer moved from Virginia to Maryland in 1785.

12. Here Mercer claims that Maryland's politicians who opposed the Constitution muted their opposition because of its popularity in the state. Few of them stood for election to the state convention for fear of facing public ridicule. After ratification, Mercer claims, these same Antifederalists will voice their opposition. In the next paragraph, he also claims that the great majority of Marylanders will also favor amendments.

13. As I noted in chapter 1, this paragraph bears a striking similarity to Madison's argument in "Federalist #10." The states are different and will have to compromise with each other to formulate public policy. A key difference keeps Madison and Mercer on opposite sides of the ratification debate: Madison thinks that this compromising will have a beneficial moderating effect on the nation's politics, while Mercer thinks that there will be so much compromising that the people of no state will be properly represented.

14. The "bill of Rights of seven Articles" that Mercer refers to is contained in Article I, section 9, of the Constitution. This section prevents the national government from doing such things as suspending habeas corpus (except in national emergencies), passing ex post facto laws, and granting titles of nobility. The reason Mercer thinks this section is of benefit to property holders is that one of the clauses ensures free and open commerce among the states, something bound to be of benefit to the nation's wealthy individuals.

15. The term "yeomanry" seems to be used here by Smith to describe the middle class in general, not just small farmers.

16. Smith's main Federalist opponent at the convention was Alexander Hamilton, to whom he refers here.

17. The work quoted is Beccaria's *On Crimes and Punishments*, published in 1770, which applied Enlightenment principles to the law (see note 8).

18. Smith is again referring to Alexander Hamilton.

5

Virulent Antifederalism

The middling Antifederalists were quite sure that the Constitution would allow the national government to predominate over the states. They were generally unwilling, however, to attribute this troubling development to a conspiracy. There were Antifederalists who had no such qualms. A vocal minority of the Constitution's critics complained vociferously about the sinister designs of the document's framers and believed that the populace might have to throw off the threatened despotism of these "well-born conspirators." I call these individuals "virulent Antifederalists," and a sampling of their writings is contained in this chapter.

The virulent strain of Antifederalism made more sense in some locations than it did in others. This brand of criticism was most prevalent in Pennsylvania and more generally in the so-called backcountry areas closer to the frontier than to the Atlantic coast. Pennsylvania's ratification process had been particularly contentious. Those who disliked the Constitution walked out of Pennsylvania's assembly in late September 1787 to deprive those who favored the Constitution the quorum necessary for calling a state convention. But a Philadelphia mob that was favorable to the Constitution physically dragged two Antifederalists back to the chamber to produce a quorum. In the ensuing convention, Federalists rushed the document to ratification without a full discussion of its provisions; they failed to entertain the possibility of amendments; and they did not include the minority's views in its official proceedings. All this occurred before the end of 1787, leaving the Pennsylvania Antifederalists embittered and searching for creative ways to put a damper on the Federalist movement.

Many in the backcountry had already become disillusioned by postrevolutionary politics. Shays' Rebellion in Massachusetts, for instance, was indicative of a major regional rift between coastal interests and the agrarian interior. Those in the Connecticut River Valley, many of whom had to borrow to keep their farms operating, were frustrated by state policies that reflected the interests of lenders. Instead of allowing farm foreclosures to proceed at a rapid pace in 1786, they disrupted court proceedings. Though no other state experienced the level of lawlessness that Massachusetts did, this coastal-versus-interior rift existed to some degree in almost every state. Backcountry observers viewed delegates to the Philadelphia convention with suspicion because they were generally coastal politicians who were known to defend interests averse to their own. The Philadelphia convention was thus not viewed as a godsend by these individuals but a nightmare: it collected the most prominent coastal politicians throughout the nation who had an interest in maintaining coastal dominance. With the delegates meeting behind closed doors and exceeding their commission by scrapping the Articles of Confederation, the fears of those in the backcountry were exacerbated. The proposed national government would allow these same slick coastal politicians to dominate the backcountry more efficiently, completely, and ruthlessly.

One of the ways that Pennsylvania Antifederalists continued their fight after ratification was through a petition campaign. Petitions calling on the Pennsylvania assembly to nullify the state's ratification were circulated through the western counties of the state and netted more than six thousand signatures, an incredible number for the time.[1] The Pennsylvania Antifederalists also published their own dissent to remedy the silence imposed on them at the ratification convention. (The dissent to the Pennsylvania convention's ratification is contained in chapter 3; see "Dissent of the Pennsylvania Minority.") The most unusual events between Pennsylvania's ratification and the end of the ratification fight occurred in Carlisle. Federalists in that city planned a parade on the evening of December 26 to celebrate the state's ratification. Local Antifederalists who were upset at the Federalists' tactics formed a counterdemonstration. The parade ground to a halt when the Antifederalists confronted the Federalists. The Federalists escalated tensions by telling the counterdemonstrators to disband, threatening those who stood in their way with physical harm. The Antifederalists, who easily outnumbered the Federalists, did not take kindly to these threats and a riot erupted in which several Federalists were hurt, including at least one mortally. At noon the next day, the Federalists assembled again, planning to resume their parade. Antifederalist counterdemonstrators turned out with effigies of Pennsylvania chief justice Thomas McKean and Philadelphia convention delegate James Wilson. After these straw figures were paraded around the town, they were ceremonially hanged and then burned.

The incidents of Carlisle were unusual, but the tension that underlay them was real. The essays by the Pennsylvania writer Centinel indicate that virulent attacks on the Federalists resonated in many parts of the state. The frequency with which his arguments were reprinted show that these tensions were much more widespread than a single riot in a small Pennsylvania town might indicate. Eight of Centinel's essays were reprinted at least five times. Centinel's first letter, contained in chapter 3, was reprinted at least twenty-seven times.[2] Centinel also achieved prominence because Federalists wished to portray their opposition as so radical that it was unrealistic. Centinel's harsh rhetoric led Federalists to point to him as an exemplar of Antifederalism, even though his views are quite unusual. Nevertheless, there were other significant virulent Antifederalists. "The Scourge" disputes the Federalist account of the events at Carlisle, even writing lyrics ridiculing his opponents. "Republicus," meanwhile, takes a more general view. He lays out a theory of government in order to attack the specific government proposed in the Constitution. Finally, the North Carolina ratification convention speeches of Joseph McDowell are included as well. McDowell's objections lead him to proclaim that he "will never agree to a government that tends to the destruction of the liberty of the people."

CENTINEL: LETTER III

Philadelphia Independent Gazetteer, November 8, 1787

This letter is typical of Centinel's style. The author employs sharp, accusatory rhetoric without engaging in much logical argument that might lead readers to his conclusion that the Constitution is, in fact, the result of a conspiracy. The major intellectual thrust of this essay is that even though reform movements may be necessary and even though most of the participants may be well intentioned, they are often co-opted by the ambitious and self-serving few. Centinel believed that such a dynamic was at work in the United States. The Articles of Confederation were defective and in need of alterations, but the amending process had been taken over by designing men. They had even convinced a few eminent figures to champion their cause (Centinel is probably referring to Benjamin Franklin and

*George Washington, though he doesn't refer to them by name).
The guiding lights behind the Federalist movement were self-
serving, like the "corrupt politician Machiavel," who counseled
retaining the form of popular government without its substance.
This essay was reprinted at least seven times.*

TO THE PEOPLE OF PENNSYLVANIA

John 3d, verse 20th—"*For every one that doeth evil, hateth
the light, neither cometh to light, lest his deeds should be
reproved.*" But "*there is nothing covered that shall not be
revealed; neither hid that shall not be known. Therefore
whatever ye have spoken in darkness, shall be heard in the
light: and that which ye have spoken in the ear in closets,
shall be proclaimed on the housetops.*" St. Luke, chap. xii,
2d and 3d verses.[3]

Friends, Countrymen, and Fellow Citizens! The formation of a good government, is the greatest effort of human wisdom, actuated by disinterested patriotism; but such is the cursed nature of ambition, so prevalent
among men, that it would sacrifice every thing to its selfish gratification;
hence the fairest opportunities of advancing the happiness of humanity,
are so far from being properly improved, that they are too often converted
to the votaries of power and domination, into the means of obtaining
their nefarious ends. It will be the misfortune of America of adding to the
number of examples of this kind, if the proposed plan of government
should be adopted; but I trust, short as the time allowed you for consideration is, you will be so fully convinced of the truth of this, as to escape
the impending danger: it is only necessary to strip the monster of its assumed garb, and to exhibit it in its native colours, to excite the universal
abhorrence and rejection of every virtuous and patriotic mind.

For the sake of my dear country, for the honor of human nature, I
hope and am persuaded, that the good sense of the people will enable
them to rise superior to the most formidable conspiracy against the
liberties of a free and enlightened nation, that the world has ever witnessed. How glorious would be the triumph! How it would immortal-
ize the present generation in the annals of freedom! . . .

In many of the states, particularly in this and the northern states,
there are aristocratic junto's of the *well-born few*, who had been zealously endeavouring since the establishment of their constitutions, to
humble that offensive *upstart, equal liberty*; but all their efforts were
unavailing, the *ill-bred churl* obstinately kept his assumed station.

However, that which could not be accomplished in the several states, is now attempted through the medium of the future Congress.—Experience having shewn great defects in the present confederation, particularly in the regulation of commerce and marritime affairs; it became the universal wish of America to grant further powers, so as to make the federal government adequate to the ends of its institution. The anxiety on this head was greatly encreased, from the impoverishment and distress occasioned by the excessive importation of foreign merchandise and luxuries and consequent drain of specie, since the peace: thus the people were in the disposition of a drowning man, eager to catch at any thing that promised relief, however delusory. Such an opportunity for the acquisition of *undue* power, has never been viewed with indifference by the ambitious and designing in any age or nation, and it has accordingly been too successfully improved by such men among us. The deputies from this state (with the exception of two) and most of those from the other states in the union, were unfortunately of this complexion, and many of them of such superior endowments, that in an *exparte* discussion of the subject by specious glosses, they have gained the concurrence of some well-disposed men, in whom their country has great confidence, which has given a great sanction to their scheme of power.[4]

A comparison of the authority under which the convention acted, and their form of government will shew that they have despised their delegated power, and assumed sovereignty; that they have entirely annihilated the old confederation, and the particular government of the several states, and instead thereof have established one general government that is to pervade the union; constituted on the most *unequal* principles, destitute of accountability to its constituents, and as despotic in its nature, as the Venetian aristocracy; a government that will give full scope to the magnificent designs of the *well-born*; a government where tyranny may glut its vengeance on the *low-born*, unchecked by *an odious bill of rights*: as has been fully illustrated in my two preceding numbers; and yet as a blind upon the understandings of the people, they have continued the forms of the particular government, and termed the whole a confederation of the United States, pursuant to the sentiments of that profound, but corrupt politician Machiavel, who advises any one who would change the constitution of a state, to keep as much as possible to the old forms; for then the people seeing the same officers, the same formalities, courts of justice and other outward appearances, are insensible of the alteration, and believe themselves in possession of their old government.[5] Thus Caesar, when he seized the Roman liberties, caused himself to be chosen dictator (which was an ancient office) continued the senate, the consuls, the tribunes, the censors, and all other offices and forms of the common-wealth; and yet changed Rome from the most free, to the most tyrannical government in the world.

The convention, after vesting all the great and efficient powers of sovereignty in general government, insidiously declare by section 4th of article 4th, "that the United States shall guarantee to every state in this union a republican *form* of government;" but of what avail will be the *form*, without the *reality* of freedom. . . .

The authors and advocates of the new plan, conscious that its establishment can only be obtained from the ignorance of the people of its true nature, and their unbounded confidence in some of the men concurring; have hurried on its adoption with a precipitation that betrays their design: before many had seen the new plan, and before any had time to examine it; they by their ready minions, attended by some well-disposed but mistaken persons, obtained the subscriptions of the people to papers expressing their entire approbation of, and their wish to have it established; thus precluding them from any consideration: but lest the people should discover the juggle, the elections of the state conventions, are urged on at very early days. . . . In order to put the matter beyond all recal, they have proceeded a step further, they have made the deputies nominated for the state convention for this city and elsewhere pledge their sacred honor, previous to their election, that they would implicitly adopt the proposed government in toto; thus short as the period is before the final fiat is to be given, consideration is rendered nugatory, and conviction of its dangers or impropriety unavailable.[6] A good cause does not stand in need of such means; it scorns all indirect advantages and borrowed helps, and trusts alone to its own native merit and intrinsic strength: the lion is never known to make use of cunning, nor can a good cause suffer by a free and thorough examination—It is knavery that seeks disguise. . . .

My fellow citizens, as a lover of my country, as the friend to mankind, whilst it is yet safe to write, and whilst it is yet in your power to avoid it, I warn you of the impending danger. To this remote quarter of the world, has liberty fled—Other countries now subject to slavery, were once as free as we yet are; therefore for your own sakes, for the sake of your posterity, as well as for that of the oppressed of all nations, cherish this remaining asylum of liberty.

CENTINEL: LETTER XI

Philadelphia Independent Gazetteer, January 16, 1788

This is a curious essay, even for the incendiary Centinel. Here he takes positions that no other writer of any stature, Federalist or

Antifederalist, took. He defends anarchy as less problematic than despotism. Anarchy, writes Centinel, is a temporary state. Whenever it exists, there is great incentive to restore order and to found a functional government. Despotism, on the other hand, is more permanent and thus a more miserable state. This reasoning may be sound, but it shows that Centinel has something of a tin ear. In the post–Shays' Rebellion climate, anarchy was the political evil in the forefront of Americans' minds. Centinel does not defend anarchy, but his argument could be easily twisted, as it was by his political opponents, to make it appear as if he did. This essay gave certain Federalists the idea to write a Centinel letter themselves, in which anarchy itself would be defended (see "Centinel XV" in appendix 1) to amuse political sophisticates and disgust those who were not so knowledgeable.

Centinel also downplays the negative results of the Union's dissolution. His reasoning on this point is similar to his reasoning about anarchy. It is worth temporarily dissolving the Union to make sure that despotism does not take hold. Centinel even notes that "occasional wars" would be preferable to the long-lasting despotism that might be brought by the Constitution. This argument also has some merit, but it understandably scared many and was easily manipulated by the Federalists to their advantage. This essay appeared as news of the Carlisle riot was spreading through the country, an event that made Centinel's language all the more problematic. This essay was reprinted three times.

TO THE PEOPLE OF PENNSYLVANIA

Fellow-Citizens, The arguments upon which the advocates of the new constitution the most dwell, are the distresses of the community, the evils of anarchy, and the horrible consequences that would ensue from the dissolution of the union of the states, and the institution of separate confederacies or republics: The unanimity of the federal convention, and the sanction of great names, can be no further urged as an argument after the exposition made by the attorney-general of Maryland, who was a member of that convention; he has opened such a scene of discord and accommodation of republicanism to despotism as excite the most serious apprehensions in every patriotic mind.[7] The first argument has been noticed in the preceeding essays; wherein it is shewn that this is not the criterion whereby to determine the merits of the new constitution; that notwithstanding the reality of the distresses of the people, the new constitution may not only be inadequate as a remedy, but destructive of liberty, and the completion of misery: The remaining two arguments will be discussed in this number;[8] their futility elucidated; and thus the medium of deception being dissipated, the public attention, with undiverted, undiminished force, will be directed to the proper object, will be confined to the consideration of the nature and construction of the plan of government itself, the question will then be, Whether this plan be calculated for our welfare, or misery; whether it is the temple of liberty, or the structure of despotism? and as the former, or the latter, shall appear to be the case, to adopt or reject it accordingly, otherwise to banish the demon of domination by suitable amendments and qualifications.

The evils of anarchy have been portrayed with all the imagery of language, in the glowing colours of eloquence; the affrighted mind is thence led to clasp the new constitution as the instrument of deliverance, as the only avenue to safety and happiness: To avoid the possible and transitory evils of one extreme, it is seduced into the certain and permanent misery necessarily attendant on the other. A state of anarchy from its very nature, can never be of long continuance; the greater its violence, the shorter the duration;[9] order and security are immediately sought by the distracted people beneath the shelter of equal laws, and the salutary restraints of regular government; and if this be not attainable, absolute power is assumed by the *one*, or the *few*, who shall be the most enterprising and successful. If anarchy, therefore, were the inevitable consequence of rejecting the new constitution, it would be infinitely better to incur it; for even then there would be at least the chance of a good government rising out of licentiousness;[10] but to rush at once into despotism, because there is a bare possibility of anarchy ensuing from the rejection, or from what is yet more visionary, the small delay that would be occasioned by a revision and correction of the proposed system of government, is so superlatively weak, so fatally blind, that it is astonishing any person of common understanding should suffer such an imposition to have the least influence on his judgment; still more astonishing, that so flimsy and deceptive a doctrine should make converts among the enlightened freemen of America, who have so long enjoyed the blessings of liberty; but when I view among such converts, men otherwise *pre-eminent*, it raises a blush for the weakness of humanity, that these her brightest ornaments should be so dim-sighted to what is self-evident to most men, that such imbecility of judgement should appear where so much perfection was looked for; this ought to teach us to depend more on our own judgment and the nature of the case, than upon the opinions of the greatest and best of men, who, from *constitutional* infirmities, or *particu-*

lar situations may sometimes view an object through a delusive medium;[11] but the opinions of great men are much more frequently the dictates of ambition, or private interest.

The source of the apprehensions of this so much dreaded anarchy would upon investigation be found to arise from the artful suggestions of designing men, and not from a rational possibility grounded on the actual state of affairs; the least reflection is sufficient to detect the fallacy to shew that there is no one circumstance to justify the production of such an event: On the contrary, a short time will evince to the utter dismay and confusion of the conspirators, that a perseverance in cramming down their scheme of power upon the freemen of this state, will inevitably produce an anarchy destructive of their darling domination, and *may* kindle a flame prejudicial to their safety; they should be cautious not to trespass too far on the forbearance of freemen, when wresting their dearest concerns; but prudently retreat from the gathering storm.

The other spectre that has been raised to terrify and alarm the people out of the exercise of their judgment on this great occasion, is the dread of our splitting into separate confederacies or republics, that might become rival powers and consequently liable to mutual wars from the usual motives of contention. This is an event still more improbable than the foregoing; it is a presumption unwarrantable, either by the situation of affairs, or the sentiments of the people; no disposition leading to it exists; the advocates of the new constitution seem to view such a separation with horror, and its opponents are strenuously contending for a confederation that shall embrace all America under its comprehensive and salutary protection. This hobgoblin appears to have sprung from the deranged brain of Publius, a New-York writer, who, mistaking sound for argument, has with Herculean labour accumulated myriads of unmeaning sentences, and *mechanically* endeavored to force conviction by a torrent of misplaced words; he might have spared his readers the fatigue of wading through his long-winded disquisitions on the direful effects of the contentions of inimical states, as totally inapplicable to the subject he was *professedly* treating; this writer has devoted much time, and wasted more paper in combating chimeras of his own creation:[12] However, for the sake of argument, I will admit, that the necessary consequence of rejecting, or delaying the establishment of the new constitution, would be the dissolution of the union, and the institution of even rival and inimical republics; yet ought such an apprehension, if well founded, to drive us into the fangs of despotism: Infinitely preferable would be occasional wars to such an event; the former, although a severe scourge, is transient in its continuance, and in its operation partial, but a small proportion of the community are exposed to its greatest horrors, and yet fewer experience its greatest evils; the latter is permanent and universal misery, without remission or exemption: as passing clouds obscure for a time the splendour of the sun, so do wars interrupt the welfare of mankind; but despotism is a settled gloom that totally extinguishes happiness, not a ray of comfort can penetrate to cheer the dejected mind; the goad of power with unabating rigor insists upon the utmost exaction, like a merciless task master, is continually inflicting the task, and is never satiated with the feast of unfeeling domination, or the most abject servility.

The celebrated Lord Kains whose disquisitions on human nature evidence extraordinary strength of judgement and depth of investigation, says that a continual *civil* war, which is the most destructive and horrible scene of human discord, is preferable to the uniformity of wretchedness and misery attendant upon despotism;—of all *possible* evils, as I observed in my first number, *this* is the worst and the most to be *dreaded*.[13]

I congratulate my fellow-citizens that a good government, the greatest earthly blessing, may be so easily obtained, that our circumstances are so favorable that nothing but the folly of the conspirators can produce anarchy or civil war, which would presently terminate in their destruction and the permanent harmony of the state alone, interrupted by their ambitious machinations.

In a former number I stated a charge of a very heinous nature, and highly prejudicial to the public welfare, and at this great crisis peculiarly alarming and threatening to liberty; I mean the suppression of the circulation of the newspapers from state to state by the of-c-rs of the P-t-O-ce,[14] who in violation of their duty and integrity have prostituted their of-ces to forward the nefarious design of enslaving their countrymen, by thus cutting off all communication by the usual vehicle between the patriots of America;—I find that notwithstanding that public appeal, they persevere in this villainous and daring practice. The newspapers of the other states that contain any useful information, are still withheld from the printers of this state, and I see by the annunciation of the Editor of Mr. Greenleaf's patriotic New-York paper, that the printers of that place are still treated in like manner; this informs his readers that but two southern papers have come to hand, and that they contain no information, which he affects to ascribe to the negligence of the p-t boy, not caring to quarrel with the p-t m-t-r g—-l.[15]

THE SCOURGE

Carlisle Gazette, **January 23, 1788**

> *This piece was written nearly a month after the rioting in Carlisle, probably by William Petrikin, one of those arrested for disrupting the Federalist parade. The Carlisle Gazette had carried several commentaries on the incidents of late December 1787. The first, by "An Old Man," excoriated the Antifederalists for their mob-like behavior. "One of the People," also likely written by Petrikin, responded by disputing "An Old Man's" version of the incidents. The Federalist essay "Another of the People" attacked "One of the People" in turn, and "The Scourge" is a response to that attack. Petrikin was jailed on February 25 for his part in the riot. As a matter of principle, he and five other prisoners refused to post bail, even though it was well within their means. Militiamen from several counties marched on Carlisle with the intent of freeing these prisoners. Once these militiamen got to the town, their representatives negotiated a compromise: they would return home if charges against the prisoners were dropped. On March 1, the prisoners, including Petrikin, were set free.*
>
> *The newspaper in which this essay appeared had frustrated area Antifederalists, as it printed mainly Federalist material. Petrikin himself complained to a friend in a letter that "we are at a great loss here for Intelligence."[16] The essay itself is distinguished for several reasons: foremost is its virulence—"The Scourge" has no qualms about calling the Carlisle Federalists liars; second, it provides a partisan's account of the events that happened in Carlisle; finally, it employs multiple literary genres. The Scourge concludes with an original satirical poem, designed to be both funny and pointed. There is no account of this essay being reprinted.*

> JUDGES. 3, Chap. 21, v.—And Ehud put forth his left hand and took the dagger from his right thigh and thrust it into his belly, verse 22, and the dirt came out—My father chastised you with whips but I will chastise you with scorpions. First Kings. 19th Chap. 11th V.[17]

The various and repeated defeats which that party who arrogates to themselves the appellation of federalists has received from the friends of liberty in Carlisle has almost tortured their souls to distraction; many schemes of revenge have been devised which have proved unsuccessful—Immediately after their last attempt to rejoice was baffled, they betook themselves to law for revenge; as this was their native region (some of the principal partizans being attornies)[18] they assured themselves of an easy victory, and solaced their ravenous souls with an ample and speedy glut of revenge; threats, menaces and awful denounciations was now issued out; nothing less than gaols, dungeons, chains and fetters, were to be the portion of their adversaries, but their bravadoes were all visionary, their dastardly souls shrunk back into their own native cowardice, and their sanguinary hopes of vengeance was again disappointed. They then betook themselves to scribbling professions on their side, and by the help of their invention they fabricated a system of falsehood and misrepresentations, and procured An Old Man whom they before employed as a spy to father them, which they published in the *Carlisle Gazette*;[19] this provoked One of the People to draw forth the dagger of truth and thrust it into their bellies, which had the very effect he expected, and which naturally results from such causes, viz. the dirt came out.[20] I don't undertake the disagreeable task of wading through such heaps of putrid matter from any design to point forth their nauseous qualities to the public; to suppose they needed this, would be an insult upon their understanding, but I am a passionate friend of liberty which makes me delight in tormenting tyrants; I must therefore give the dagger another thrust, for there is more dirt yet. The authors of the piece signed, Another of the People, conscious that reason and truth detested their cause like the rest of their new federal brethren, betake themselves to personal slander, defamation and detraction, in order to vent their spleen and emit their disappointed malice. . . . [21]

Perhaps the authors of the old man's adopted brat may be very pious men for ought I know, but if they are, they have certainly sworn to conceal it from the rest of mankind, but men differ in opinion about religious as well as civil matters, perhaps they account it divine precepts and moral duties, to print falshoods, threaten the lives of their neighbours, go to church once or twice of a Sunday to hear a solemn lecture on politics, blended with geography and astronomy, and interspersed with a few religious hints, and spend the remainder of the day in sacrificing to Bacchus; but it is evident this pious parade is not so much intended to embellish their own character as it is to defame another man's, but as his character is established in Pennsylvania infinitely above the reach of their malicious insinuations, and as Cumberland county hath already given demonstration to the world that they esteem him a better man than any of their fraternity; I shall therefore leave the public indignation to be their scourge. . . .[22]

They talk of a well dressed man wrestling with a chimney sweep; this is the comparison they draw between themselves and the people. Candid public: these are the men who endeavour by fraud and force, to cram down your throats a constitution which would immediately create them your rulers; they here present you with a small specimen of what treatment you may expect when the constitution becomes "the supreme law of the land." The most contemptuous and degrading epithets, is given to all such as are not of their faction; no better named than "rabble, mob, chimney sweeps, ragamuffins, vile, contemptible, senseless, ignorant, suited only by nature to a state of insignificance and contempt," is conferred on such citizens as oppose the ambitious views of this imperious junto—Rouse then my fellow citizens before it is too late; act with a spirit becoming freemen; convince the world and your adversaries too, who wish to become tyrants—That you are not insensible of the invaluable blessings of liberty—That you esteem life and property, but secondary objects; when your liberty comes to be attacked.

Teach these domineering despots who wish to rejoice, because they have a prospect of rioting on your spoils; that you perceive their designs, that you can both read and understand their constitution, & spurn it with contempt. . . .

It is denied by them that the rejoicers had muskets, bayonets and bludgeons at the time of their rout, I know not what they had at the time of their rout, perhaps they threw them away that they might not incumber them in their flight; but that they had them immediately before their rout is a fact given in testimony, where no party riden lawyers were admitted as inquisitors, nor was the truth partly heard and partly stifled, but the truth, the whole truth, and nothing but the truth was required and stated with the utmost precision; neither was self-accusation extorted from the simple and ignorant, by terror and menace, so that any person who may be solicitous to ascertain a true state of facts, may have information from other depositions besides those in the "upright magistrates" inquisition; upright indeed! rather the dupe and creature of a domineering faction.[23] They affirm "the drum of the mob was their own drum," but if they mean the people's drum it is a palpable falsehood; it can be proven by more than fifty witnesses, that the people's drum beat around two squares before they (the federalists) left the ground.[24]—They seem to be mightily chagrined at calling the intended rejoicers a mob, but why so much offended, they were only acting in unison with their new federal brethren in the city, whose conduct they cordially approved [and] chearfully recognized the authority of the mob in Philadelphia, who broke open private houses, and dragged two of the members through the streets to the State-House, and then guarded the Assembly while they were passing the resolutions for calling the state convention.

The midnight mob headed by Jemey the Caledonian,[25] who attacked the lodgings of the western members of Assembly and Council, on the night of the elections for convention men, was an upright, orderly association, and highly serviceable to the federal junto. The mob who insulted the western members, when advocating the rights of the people in convention, was of great utility, as they served to keep the members who were advocates for the proposed constitution, &c. in countenance when reason and argument had deserted them—In a word were it not for the mob the new constitution would not yet have been adopted in Pennsylvania; and our Carlisle rejoicers would have wanted this cause "to be pleased," and to assemble in a mobocratical manner, to express that pleasure. They further say "one of the captains had not slept off his night's drunkenness;" what more dirt yet, will the fluxion never cease. It is notoriously known that the person here alluded to, maintains a character very averse of what they represent; and that his opposition to the rejoicing proceeded from the love of freedom which stimulated him, to expose himself to the perils and dangers, during the late struggle for American independence; when their old man, and other ringleaders of these pretended federalists, basely sculked behind the curtain. . . .

They say "the threat in the concluding paragraph is the most despicable; they knew or might have known the authors by applying to the printers."[26] What! is it granted that the old man was not the author, then it seems, one of the people was right in his conjecture, that the piece was a bastard, and the old man only adopting father, or rather grand-father.—Gentlemen, apply your own proverb, "lyers should have good memories," applying to the printers for the authors names we detest. We know it is the practice of our despotic opponents; but we contend for a free press, and abhor every thing that has the least tendency to shackle it. Neither do we employ pimps and spies to catch what intelligence they can, by obtruding themselves upon companies, where their presence is as disagreeable and surfeiting as the fluxion of dirt which is emitted by the authors of another of the people.

Thus I have so far dissected this putrid carcase, were I to take notice of all the dirt which it contains, I must transcribe the whole; but this is a task by far too laborious, disagreeable and nauseous.—Other persons pointed at will therefore excuse me, if I omit saying any thing in their behalf; it greatly accelerated our business in this affair, that we have the good-will, faith, and credit of the country on our side. . . .

The FEDERAL JOY, to the tune of
Alexander, hated thinking.

I. AWAKE my muse in copious numbers,
    Sing the federal joy compleat,

The loud huzzas the cannon thunders
        Announce their triumphs to be great.
II.   Behold they march with curls flying,
        Weary steps, and powdered heads,
Soften'd hands, with eyes espying
        Crowds of whigs assembled.[27]
III.   But see they halt, & now are forming
        Regular as veteran bands,
Breathing defiance, scoffing, scorning,
        The low opposers of their plans.
IV.   But now a crew for constitution,
        Harshly then began to treat them,
Despising federal institution,
        Nor aw'd by powder or pomatum.
V. From words to blows, those vile aggressors,
        Rudely drove our harmless band,
Despoil'd the work of their hair-dressers,
        Daring assumed the chief command.
VI.   Now helter skelter in disorder,
        Flew our heroes to their homes,
Happy their legs were in good order,
        To save from geting broken bones.
VII.   Lawyers, doctors and store-keepers,
        Forsook their general in his need.
And from their windows began peeping
        Viewing their valliant hero bleed.
VIII.   But lie veterans in the morning,
        Appear'd in arms bright array,
Revenge, Revenge, they cry'd when forming
        We ne'er again will run away.
IX.   Full thirteen rounds for federal honor
        Shall thunder loud, tho' hell oppose;
Display our new terrific banner,
        To intimidate our scurvy foes.
X.   Undauntedly three rounds they fir'd,
        When lo a drum, most dreadful sound
Awak'd new fears, courage retir'd,
        Paleness in every face was found.
XI.   Again their shanks were put in motion,
        With rapid strides they homewards stretches,
Or to avoid another portion,
        Or s - - t a second pair of breeches.[28]
XII.   And now the pannic being over,
        When not afraid of club or rope,
Descends to law for to recover
        Money for to purchase soap.
XIII.   But not a souse for all their swearing,
        Tho' shirt and breeches both were foul'd;

Liberties sons are persevering,
    Nor will by fed'rals be controul'd.
XIV.   And if those harpies seek preferment
    Thro' their countries streaming blood,
They'll dig graves for their interment,
    Or smother in the purple flood.

REPUBLICUS: LETTER I

Lexington Kentucky Gazette, February 16, 1788

This piece by Republicus is unusual for a virulent Antifederalist because of its theoretical bent. The essay was printed in Lexington, where the westernmost newspaper was published in the United States, the Kentucky Gazette. This area was decidedly the backcountry, having only been opened for settlement after the Revolution. Kentucky was still a district of Virginia at this point, not a separate state, and some of the preferences Republicus displays are distinctively Virginian, like a preference for representation by population in the Senate. At the same time, there are positions here that would not be endorsed by most Virginians east of the Appalachians: universal male suffrage and a single-chambered legislature, for instance. The author of this essay is unknown. His contribution to the ratification debate is nevertheless of interest because it shows that even settlers close to the frontier could intelligently weigh in on the proposed Constitution. Lexington was deep into the backcountry—so deep that it is unlikely that this letter received much notice outside of sparsely populated Kentucky. There is no evidence that the essay was reprinted by any other newspaper.

    pierce my vein,
    Take of the crimson stream meandering there,
    And chatechize it well, Apply your glass.
    Search more and probe it, if it be not blood
    Congenial with thine own.

                          Cowper

So soon after the close of a bloody and distressing war, which we have sustained in defence of the liberties and indefeasible rights of mankind; during which those rights have been investigated with the utmost precision: it may, to some, seem a little extraordinary to resume so trite a subject; but as there is a prospect of an aera near approaching, big with events highly, very highly interesting to these western districts; and as it seems, that some, even of our leading characters, have been too much hurried to have given those subjects so much of their attention as they seem to have merited; or may have forgotten some of the features peculiar to the picture of liberty; I beg leave to hold up to public view, some of the outlines of the charming portrait, in order to attach my fellow citizens to the original form from whence they are taken: and add a few very plain observations on civil government . . . as universal observation assures us, that mankind are more generally actuated by their passions and appetites, than by their reason; something is necessary to restrain, countroul, or at least to counteract those passions: hence the necessity of civil government; and on that necessity it originates: the lust of power, or of property, would stimulate the strong, or the artful, to seize the persons, or properties of the weak, or the simple, and appropriate them to their own use, in contempt of the sacred law of nature. Hence, mankind found it necessary to enter into solemn compacts of mutual defence, and security, and in those compacts, to establish certain rules, founded upon, or at least agreeable to, the universal reason of mankind, (the common law of nature) to which they should all be equally subject; as they rightfully, and originally were in their unconnected state, to that original law; and this only to secure to themselves that liberty, and those rights to which they as said above are all naturally, equally, and unalienably entitled. Thus it appears how civil government becomes a substitute for moral virtue: and that instead of infringing the rightful liberties of mankind, it tends to secure them: and by this criterion may every government be tried: that government which tends not to secure the lives, liberties and properties of every individual of the community, as far as the law of reason would have done, is unjust and iniquitous and merits not the name of civil government. I said above that civil government originates in necessity: I now add it originates with the people under that necessity. They form the compact, they prescribe the rules and they also enact them or delegate others to do it for them; who are indiscriminately, and in the proper sense of the word *their servants* and accountable to them and to them only how they execute those trusts. . . . It is not only necessary that government should be formed on principles of equal right; but also that those principles should be precisely delineated and guaranteed by the most solemn sanctions. This if you please we will call a constitution. There should also be woven into the very texture of that constitution certain antidotes or preservatives against corruption or degeneracy, and care should be taken by every member of the community, that those antidotes be duly administered. Otherwise tho they may begin their career on a very fair plain, yet, it may at last terminate in a precipice, which they may never discover till it be too late to retract.

And first the constitution should provide for a fair and equal representation. That is that every member of the union have a freedom of suffrage and that every equal number of people have an equal number of representatives; for if the preceding sentiments are just, no one deprived of suffrage, ought (unless he voluntarily adopt it at least implicitly) to be under the controul or direction of such constitution, or any law made in consequence of it: it is not law to him he is in respect of it, still in a state of nature: and without equality of numbers it would be unjust; for it is incontestable that if every man has an equal natural right to governing power, he has an equal right to every thing that represents it; and if we suppose for instance that one district to contain one hundred inhabitants, and another a thousand: each entitled to send two representatives if we suppose the former to be only duly represented, then there will be nine hundred in the latter not represented at all; But this is so plain a case that it is only strange that it should ever have been controverted.[29]

But again it should provide against their holding those trusts for long terms. This would call into public service a greater variety of estimable characters; would beget an emulation who should serve their country the most essentially; and make it perhaps as fashionable a virtue to serve the interest of the public, as it has been formerly a vice to serve the private interest of some favorite family or worthless dependent. Besides, this is a security which the people owe to themselves, for the fidelity of their servants; and perhaps the only good security they can have: add to this temporary intervals of ineligibility, that they may in a private capacity feel all the good and evil effects resulting from their administration; and be prevented from acquiring any influence, dangerous to the liberty of the community. Who ever doubts the utility of this provisionary measure let him just recur to the state of the British government under the triennial and septennial parliaments: and he will soon be satisfied.

But it should also provide for its own stability and permanency: and that no law may ever come into existence the foundation of which is not found in those primary principles: as the constitution comes immediately from the people; so ought the laws to flow immediately from the constitution; it should like a circle circumscribe all legislative power as the legislative ought to circumscribe the executive, and both take their form from the people as the great centre of all; it should with all the authority becoming the majesty of a free people from whence it proceeds command; hitherto shalt thou come but no further; for if it suffers itself to be broken in one instance, why not in a thousand; it becomes like a bubble, its existence is no more and the issue may be fatal.

But lastly, and above all it should provide that no man or set of men whatsoever from within or without, should even possess a power of controul, suspension, or negation, either permanent, or temporary, on or over any resolves, acts, procedures, or laws made by the people themselves, or their representatives duly chosen as above, for whenever this happens, their liberty expires, they are under the direction of a will different from, and superior to their own: and though they may still have the privilege of nominating those who possess that power, it is only the poor and degrading privilege of pointing out, among many tyrannical masters, whose lash they will choose to feel. In short they are slaves.

It has been disputed whether one house, or rather power of legislature be more eligible, or rather to be chose than two. I shall hazard a few random thoughts on the subject. And first, if an institution answers all the ends designed by the institution, as well as any other institution, or plan could have done, or can do, there remain no possibility of its doing more; it is therefore perfect, if anything is added it becomes a redundancy, consequently an imperfection. I hope twill not be denied, that a single legislative body, is capable of making laws, the perfection of those laws depend on the wisdom, virtue, and integrity of the legislature, but does it appear, that the more wisdom, virtue, and integrity, will, or can possibly be found in two houses than in one, provided they consist of the same number, but more particularly of the same identical person? No man will affirm this. But it may be said that a second house or senate, being generally fewer in number, do by their separation acquire an influence which would have been lost, had the whole been incorporated in one house, I answer, perhaps it might not have been lost; it would no doubt sometimes so happen, that they, in conjunction with the minority of the other house would be able to set aside some bills, which for want of their assistance there, have passed, this would have been a shorter, and easier way; and attended besides, with much less expence of time and money; and excepting in some such instances, all such influence ought to be lost; for in no instance ought the minority to govern the majority. Again, it is more simple: and it is a well known maxim that the simpler a machine is, it is the more perfect; the reason on which it is grounded is obvious: viz. because it is the less liable to disorder, the disorder more easily discovered, and when discovered, more easily repaired and in no instance is this maxim more applicable than in the great machine of government. But say they there ought to be two houses because there are two separate interests. I answer by denying that any community can possibly have any but one common public interest, that is, the greatest good of the whole and of every individual part of that whole: but if it be private interest that is meant, I confess that there are not only two, but twenty and it may be more private interests in every government, and the same argument would prove that there ought to be twenty or indeed five hundred houses of legislature in each government: and by proving too much falls to the ground. But the grand argument of all, is that by being separate they have a power of checking some bills which would otherwise pass into laws and might be detrimental to society. Had not this argument been produced on the other side, I should certainly have produced it in favour of one house: however I ask is a minority in one house, properly entitled to over rule a majority in the other? Are they not as likely to check a good bill as a bad one? and has it not in fact often happened? Is it not as probable that the second house lay some of their checks on a good bill which perhaps they had little considered as that the first, should pass a bad one, where it had originated and perhaps thoroughly considered? But let us turn the argument over and take a view of the other side of it. The inconsistencies that attend the idea of two houses are innumerable. Take one, supposing them both our representatives (tho it will be hard to prove them so). It makes their constituents to say in many instances by their representatives in one house, 'this shall be a law,' by their representatives in the other with respect to the same bill; 'This shall not be a law.' It impowers one body of men to enact statutes; and another to forbid their being carried into execution. It resembles a man putting forth his right hand to do some important business and then stretching forth his left hand to prevent it; but supposing them not our representatives at all, they have no business there, and all their mighty power of checking, is a mere farce.

. . . In the above hints, I have spoken my sentiments but their authority comes from their being the sentiments of a Locke, a Sidney and of all the great and good names who have favoured the world with the observations on this important subject:[30] but what gives them the highest possible dignity with me; I believe them to be the sentiments of reason itself: and while I remain under the conviction should a government arise, flowing from any other source and running in another channel; though I shall always submit to the laws of my country, with as much cheerfulness as I can; yet the voice of the united world shall never persuade me to say it is right.

Republicus

REPUBLICUS: LETTER II

Lexington Kentucky Gazette, March 1, 1788

*In his second essay, Republicus turns from a theoretical treat-
ment of government to a commentary on constitutional clauses
he finds offensive. Of particular interest is his passionate objection to clauses that protect the slave trade. Virginians generally
opposed the slave trade because of their surplus of slaves. If the
slave trade were prohibited, Virginia would benefit because
other states would then "import" slaves from the "Old Dominion." At the same time, the slaveholding culture had not taken
hold in the district of Kentucky as it had in Virginia proper, and
Republicus attempted to sway his fellow citizens by arguing
that it should not be allowed to take hold. As with Republicus'
first letter, there is no evidence this letter was reprinted.*

> True Liberty
> . . . Always with right reason dwells
> Twinn'd, and from her hath no dividual being.
>
> Milton

There is but one source of political happiness, viz. liberty; our liberty
is founded on our reason, which is the gift of heaven: this proves its excellence; but many sources of unhappiness, and slavery: every one of
which, owes its existence to the abuse of some passion or appetite of
mankind. Ambitious persons, already raised to a pitch of eminence
disgraceful to human nature; not contented with the vassalage of thousands, who have given themselves up to the vilest subjection, even to
be bought or sold like asses or swine; too often, merely to gratify a
wanton lust of domination, employ those very wretches, in the infernal business of subjecting others, before happy and free; this consti-
tutes external slavery; of such an attempt we had a recent trial; but
there is another sort of slavery which from the modesty of its appearance, and gentleness of its approaches, is not so alarming, and therefore the more dangerous; of which we ought continually to beware:
viz. internal, that is, when a people already free, implicitly intrust, or
permit, any set of men to form constitutions of government or enact
laws for them; without inquiring, whether such constitutions, have for
their basis, the true principles of liberty, and equal right. . . .

Article I. Section I. "All legislative power herein granted, shall be
vested in a Congress of the united states; which shall consist of a senate
and a house of representatives."

The absurdity of two houses of legislature has formerly been touched upon on the supposition of their being both our representatives; but that observation becomes here unnecessary: this appears without a mask: they (the senate) are not even the supposed representatives of any body; but distinguished from them, in as express terms as english words can do it; how then is this a Congress of the united States; when such meeting, does neither consist of the whole people of these states, nor wholly of the representatives of those people? but not to dispute about words let us consider the election, the proportional numbers, and the powers of this senatorial body. And first, they are to be chosen by the legislative bodies of the several states respectively: what numeral proportion these legislative bodies may bear to their constituents, or the people at large, is to me uncertain; but I will suppose it as one to two hundred; it is plain, that if they represent any body at all, it can be only those who have elected them, viz. one two-hundredth part of the people: bodies, having been chosen only for legislative purposes, and election, and legislation, being powers wholly different, and indeed too important to be both committed to the same set of men, at the same time; that choice can invest them with no right to delegate representatives for any body but themselves; but I confess this argument is superfluous, this constitution having in so many words, separated the very idea or character of a senator from that of a representative. Again, as to their numbers, there are to be two senators from each state; is not this visibly subversive of the great original right to equality? does it not tend to obliterate the very idea? To demonstrate this, requires only that we compare the representation of the state of Rhode-Island and Providence plantations with that of Virginia; the former from their numbers, are intitled to have only one representative in Congress; the latter, on the same principle, and for the same reason, are to have ten. If Virginia, from her numbers, has a right to ten times the influence of Rhode-Island in the lower house of Congress, why not in the senate?[31] I see no reasonable answer to this, but that the lower house consists of the representatives of the people, consequently are a regular, well proportioned body, the senate an unmeaning and arbitrary [delegation?] of the different legislatures; and of consequence a body irregular, deformed, and disproportionate.

But again, if we consider this power, it contains a very considerable and essential share of the elective, legislative, executive, and judiciary department, and in all these, they are independent of the people, not in any instance responsible to them: from whence can their right to such power arise? It was never delegated to them from the people, who alone were justly possessed of it; no exterior power had

authority to confer it; it appears therefore a mere non entity; or rather
a complicated usurpation of power without right: and therefore to be
rejected: and yet, extraordinary as it may seem, this senatorial dignity, is to continue in the same hands six years, and even at the end
of that term, they are again eligible, and so on a third, a fourth, a seventh time, to perpetuity. But I long to have them off my hands, as I
would any other useless or dangerous commodity, and can only consider their institution, as a servile and ill-judg'd imitation of the
house of lords in the British parliament, where (though there appears
now and then a virtuous character) dissipation, venality, and corruption, are alternately, and incessantly breeding and growing, and tri-
umphing; have often distracted the kingdom, and in some degree, in-
slaved the nation. I go now to Art. 2, Sec. I which vest the supreme
continental executive power in a president: in order to the choice of
whom, the legislative body of each state, is empowered to point out
to their constituents, some mode of choice, or (to save trouble) may
choose themselves, a certain number of electors, who shall meet in
their respective states, and vote by ballot, for two persons, one of
whom, at least shall not be an inhabitant of the same state with
themselves.[32] Or in other words, they shall vote for two, one or both
of whom they know nothing of. An extraordinary refinement this, on
the plain simple business of election; and of which the grand convention have certainly the honour of being the first investors; and that for
an officer too, of so much importance as a president; invested with
legislative and executive powers—who is to be commander in chief of
the army, navy, militia, etc. grant reprieves and pardons, have a temporary negative on all bills and resolves, convene and adjourn both
houses of congress, be supreme conservator of the laws, commission
all officers, make treaties, etc. etc. and who is to continue for four
years, and is only removable on conviction of treason or bribery and
trial be only by the senate, who are to be his own council whose interest in every instance runs parallel with his own; and who are neither the officers of the people, nor accountable to them. Is it then become necessary, that a free people, should first resign their right of
suffrage into other hands besides their own, and then, secondly, that
they to whom they resign it, should be compelled to choose men,
whose persons, characters, manners, or principles they know nothing
of; and after all, (excepting some such change as is not likely to happen twice in the same century) to intrust Congress with the final decision at last? Is it necessary, is it rational that the sacred rights of
mankind should thus dwindle down to Electors, of electors, and those
again electors of other electors; this seems to be degrading them, even

below the prophetical curse denounced by the good old patriarch, on the offspring of the degenerate son; "servant of servants."

Art. I Sect. 4. "The times, places and manner of holding elections for senators, and representatives, shall be prescribed in each State, by the legislature thereof; but the Congress may, at any time by law, make or alter such regulations, except as to the place of chusing senators."[33] Whether this clause gives Congress a power to call the people of Georgia to chuse their representatives in the city of Boston, and on the twentieth of December, and so of every other State, I leave to be determined by better judges of language than myself; however, I believe I shall not be amiss in assertion, that it invests them with power to appoint the time of choosing senators, at the greatest possible distance from the usual, and perhaps constitutionally appointed time of meeting for the purpose of legislation: This latter in large States, or newly settled countries amounts to little less than a peremptory exclusion of all members of legislatures, in extensive districts; who from their situation, are less liable to corruption: the former, if true, would put it into the power of a few, a very few! to appoint representatives for the whole continent: and both together, tend to perpetuate the authority, not only of the same men, but also of their heirs for ever. Again, I would ask (considering how prone mankind are to engross power, and then abuse it) is it not probable, at least possible, that the president who is to be vested with all this demi-omnipotence, who is not chosen by the community, and who consequently as to them, is irresponsible, and independent; that he, I say, by a few, artful and dependent emissaries in congress, may not only perpetuate his own personal administration, but also make it hereditary: that be the same means, he may render his suspensive power over the law, as operative, and permanent, as that of [King] G[eorge]. the 3d over the acts of the British parliament: and under the modest title of president, may exercise the combined authority of legislation, and execution, in a latitude not yet unthought of: or, that upon his being invested with those powers a second, or third time, he may acquire such enormous influence, as, added to his uncontroulable power over the army, navy, and militia; together with his private interest in the officers, of all these different departments, who are all to be appointed by himself, and so his creatures, in the true political sense of the word; and more especially when added to all this, he has the power of forming treaties and alliances, and calling them to his assistance; that he may, I say, under all these advantages, and almost irresistable temptations, on some pretended pique, haughtily, and contemptuously, turn our poor lower house, (the only shadow of liberty we shall have left) out of doors, and give us law at the bayonets point; or may not the senate, who are nearly in the same situation, with respect to the people from similar motives, and by similar means, erect themselves easily into an oligarchy, towards which they have already attempted so large a stride; to one of which channels, or rather to a confluence of both, we seem to be fast gliding away; and the moment we arrive at it—farewell liberty. This leads me to Art. I Sect. 9. "The migration or importation of such persons, as any of the States now existing, shall think proper to admit, shall not be prohibited by the Congress prior to the year 1808; (twenty years hence) but a tax, or duty may be imposed on such importation, not exceeding ten dollars for each person."[34] An excellent clause this, in an Algerian constitution: but not so well calculated (I hope) for the latitude of America. It is not to be disguised that by "such persons," slaves are principally, if not wholly intended: and shall this be found among the principles of a free people, and making a radical part of the grand base on which they would erect an edifice sacred to liberty. "Tell it not in Gath!"[35] O that no envious surge might ever roll it to the eastern side of the Atlantic! Unhappy africans! What have they done? Have they murdered our citizens or burnt our settlements? Have they butchered, scalped, and exhausted every device of torture, on our defenceless women, and innocent children; as the savage meserians [mercenaries?] of our own country have done? No, no![36] Then, why deprive them of the greatest of all blessings, liberty, "without which," says Dr. Price man is a beast, and life a curse, while coward-like, we court, caress, and cringe to our murderers.[37] Ignorant, and comparatively innocent, till we taught them the diabolical arts of destruction, captivity, and death; and provided them with the infernal means of carrying them into practice: and all this to furnish ourselves with slaves, at the guilty expence oftimes, of the blood of, ten times the number of those thus enslaved, who lost their lives in the gallant and virtuous defence of themselves, and families. Has this guilt ever been attoned? and do we boast of being advocates of liberty? shocking absurdity! More absurd still that a license for such an execrable trade, should be radically woven into, and become an essential part of our national constitution—a constitution formed by a chosen assembly of our most eminent and respectable citizens: and where a personage presided, second to no individual of the human family.

> The boast of America.—The wonder of Europe
> O liberty! O virtue! O my country.

Tell us, ye who can that, cooly, reduce the impious principle of slavery, to a constitutional system: ye professed violators of liberties of mankind: where will ye stop? what security can you give, that, when there shall remain no more black people, ye will not enslave others, white as yourselves? when Africa is exhausted, will ye spare America? and is not twenty years (taking into account the slain with the more unhappy captives, victims to perpetual slavery) sufficient to depopulate her inmost forest? Or is this only an ill boding prelude, sounded in the ears, and designedly introductory to the fate of these (yet unhappy) states, who gave you existence; and who even now, while you are thus ungratefully soaring toward the summit of *Aristocracy*, are honouring you with their confidence? I shudder at the catastrophe! awake my fellow citizens! and let this infamous clause, together with the principle which gave it birth, be not only expunged out of your constitution but countermanded, eradicated, torn from your heart forever.

To conclude, I can think of but one source of right to government, or any branch of it; and that is *the people*. They, and only they, have a right to determine whether they will make laws, or execute them, or do both in a collective body, or by a delegated authority. Delegation is a positive actual investiture. Therefore if any people are subjected to an authority which they have not thus actually chosen; even though they may have tamely submitted to it, yet it is not their legitimate government: they are wholly passive, and as far as they are so, are in a state of slavery. Thank heaven we are not yet arrived at that state; and while we continue to have sense enough to discover and detect, and virtue enough to detest and oppose every attempt, either of *force* or *fraud*, either from *without* or *within*, to bring us into it, we never will.

Let us therefore continue united in the cause of rational liberty. Let unity and liberty be our mark as well as our motto: for only such an union can secure our freedom; and division will inevitably destroy it. Thus a mountain of sand may peace meal be removed by the feeble hands of a child: but if consolidated to a rock, it mocks the united efforts of mankind, and can only fall in a general wreck of nature.

Republicus

SPEECHES OF JOSEPH McDOWELL IN NORTH CAROLINA'S RATIFICATION CONVENTION

July and August 1788

Few virulent Antifederalist speeches from state conventions are recorded. Most of these Antifederalists came from the backcountry. They were less educated than their coastal counterparts and thus less well-equipped, both in terms of knowledge and confidence, to engage in formal debate with the Federalists. Strenuous objections were also more likely to be left out of the official proceedings of state conventions. But North Carolina was overwhelmingly Antifederalist, and thus the objections of Joseph McDowell were preserved. McDowell sat in the first North Carolina convention, at Hillsborough, which met from July 21 to August 4, 1788. Delegates at this convention, including McDowell, voted not to ratify the Constitution by a wide margin (193–75). A second convention, held at Fayetteville in November 1789 after the new government was already operational, ratified the document. Joseph McDowell was later elected to the U.S. House of Representatives, serving a single term from 1797 to 1799.

Mr Chairman, this is a power [the power of direct taxation] that I will never agree to give up from the hands of the people of this country. We know that the amount of the imposts will be trifling, and that the expenses of this government will be very great; consequently the taxes will be very high. The tax-gatherers will be sent, and our property will be wrested out of our hands. The Senate is most dangerously constructed. Our only security is the House of Representatives. They may be continued at Congress eight or ten years. At such a distance from their homes, and for so long a time, they will have no feeling for, nor any knowledge of, the situation of the people. If elected from the seaports, they will not know the western part of the country and vice versa. Two cooperative powers cannot exist together. One must submit. The inferior must give up to the superior. While I am up, I will say something to what has been said by the gentleman to ridicule the General Assembly.[38] He represents the legislature in a very opprobrious light. It is very astonishing that the people should choose men of such characters to represent them. If the people be virtuous, why should they put confidence in men of a contrary disposition? As to paper money, it was the result of necessity. We were involved in a great war. What money had been in the country was sent to other parts of the world. What would have been the consequence if paper money had not been made? We must have been undone. Our political existence must have been destroyed. The extreme scarcity of specie, with other good causes, particularly the solicitation of the officers to receive it at its nominal value, for their pay, produced subsequent emissions. He tells us that all the people wish this power to be given—that the mode of payment need only be pointed out, and that they will willingly pay. How are they to raise the money? Have they it in their chests? Suppose, for instance, there be a tax of two shillings per hundred laid on land; where is the money to pay for it? We have it not. I am acquainted with the people. I know of their situation. They have no money. Requisitions may yet be complied with.[39] Industry and frugality may enable the people to pay moderate taxes, if laid by those who have a knowledge of their situation and a feeling for them. If the tax-gatherers come upon us, they will, like the locusts of old, destroy us. They will have pretty high salaries, and exert themselves to oppress us. When we consider these things, we should be cautious. They will be weighed, I trust, by the House. Nothing said by the gentlemen on the other side has obviated my objections.

Mr Chairman, the objections to this part of the Constitution [on the federal judiciary] have not been answered to my satisfaction yet. We know that the trial by a jury of the vicinage is one of the greatest securities for property. If causes are to be decided at such a great distance, the poor will be oppressed; in land affairs, particularly, the wealthy suitor will prevail. A poor man, who has just claim on a piece of land, has not substance to stand it. Can it be supposed that any man, of common circumstances, can stand the expense and trouble of going from Georgia to Philadelphia, there to have a suit tried? And can it be justly determined without the benefit of a trial by jury? These are things which have justly alarmed the people. What made the people revolt from Great Britain? The trial by jury, that great safeguard of liberty, was taken away, and a stamp duty was laid upon them. This alarmed them, and led them to fear that greater oppressions would take place. We then resisted. It involved us in a war, and caused us to relinquish a government which made us happy in every thing else. The war was very bloody, but we got our independence. We are not giving away our dear-bought rights. We ought to consider what we are about to do before we determine.

Mr. Chairman, instead of reasons and authorities to convince me, assertions are made. Many respectable gentlemen are satisfied that the taxes will be higher. By what authority does the gentleman say that the impost will be productive, when our trade is come to nothing? Sir, borrowing money is detrimental and ruinous to nations. The interest is lost money. We have been obliged to borrow money to pay interest! We have no way of paying additional and extraordinary sums. The people cannot stand them. I should be extremely sorry to live under a government which the people could not understand, and which it would require the greatest abilities to understand. It ought to be plain and easy to the meanest capacity. What would be the consequence of ambiguity? It may raise animosity and revolutions, and involve us in bloodshed. It becomes us to be extremely cautious.

Mr. Chairman, I was in hopes that amendments would have been brought forward to the Constitution before the idea of adopting it had been thought of or proposed. From the best information, there is a great proportion of the people in the adopting states averse to it as it stands. I collect my information from respectable authority. I know the necessity of a federal government. I therefore wish this was one in which our liberties and privileges were secured; for I consider the Union as the rock of our political salvation. I am for the strongest federal government.[40] A bill of rights ought to have been inserted, to ascertain our most valuable and unalienable rights.

The 1st clause of the 4th section gives Congress an unlimited power over elections. This matter was not cleared up to my satisfaction. They have full power to alter it from one time of the year to another, so as that it shall be impossible for the people to attend. They may fix the time in winter, and the place at Edenton, when the weather will be so bad that the people cannot attend. The state governments will be mere boards of election. The clause of elections gives the Congress power over the time and manner of choosing the Senate. I wish to know why reservation was made of the place of choosing senators, and not also of electing representatives. It points to the time when the states shall be all consolidated into one empire. Trial by jury is not secured. The objections against this want of security have not been cleared up in a satisfactory manner. It is neither secured in civil nor criminal cases. The federal appellate cognizance of law and fact puts it in the power of the wealthy to recover unjustly of the poor man, who is not able to attend at such extreme distance, and bear such enormous expense as it must produce. It ought to be limited so as to prevent such oppressions.

I say the trial by jury is not sufficiently secured in criminal cases. The very intention of the trial by jury is, that the accused may be tried as persons who come from the vicinage or neighborhood, who may be acquainted with his character. The substance, therefore, of this privilege is taken away.

By the power of taxation, every article capable of being taxed may be so heavily taxed that the people cannot bear the taxes necessary to be raised for the support of their state governments. Whatever law we may make, may be repealed by their laws. All these things, with others, tend to make us one general empire. Such a government cannot be well regulated. When we are connected with the Northern

States, who have a majority in their favor, laws may be made which will answer their convenience, but will be oppressive to the last degree upon the Southern States. They differ in climate, soil, customs, manners &c. A large majority of the people of this country [North Carolina] are against this Constitution, because they think it replete with dangerous defects. They ought to be satisfied with it before it is adopted; otherwise it cannot operate happily. Without the affections of the people, it will not have sufficient energy. To enforce its execution, recourse must be had to arms and bloodshed. How much better it would be if the people were satisfied with it! From all these considerations, I now rise to oppose its adoption; for I never will agree to a government that tends to the destruction of the liberty of the people.

NOTES

1. *The Documentary History of the Ratification of the Constitution (DHRC)*, vol. 2, pp. 710–11, 720–21.

2. Cornell, *The Other Founders*, pp. 309–12.

3. These are quotations from the King James version of the Bible.

4. The "well-disposed men, in whom their country has great confidence" are likely George Washington and Benjamin Franklin. The ardent Federalism of these two presented difficulties for many Antifederalists, but particularly for the virulent Antifederalists. They had to explain why the nation's two most respected men favored the Constitution. They wisely chose not to attack their characters. Instead, like Centinel does here, they usually claim that Washington and Franklin were duped by the other Federalists.

5. That "profound, but corrupt politician Machiavel" was Niccolo Machiavelli, the Florentine civil servant who lived from 1469 to 1527 and wrote *The Prince* and *The Discourses*. Centinel may be alluding to book 1, chapter 25 of *The Discourses*, which is titled "He who proposes to change an Old-established Form of Government in a Free City should retain at least the Shadow of its Ancient Customs."

6. Some of Pennsylvania's prominent Federalists, sensing that they could seize the advantage by being aggressive, publicly pledged to support the Constitution unconditionally if elected to the state ratification convention. This tactic was not unsuccessful. Even though Pennsylvania's two factions had roughly even strength in the state assembly, two-thirds of those elected to the ratification convention were Federalists.

7. Luther Martin was Maryland's attorney general. See his "Genuine Information," printed in chapter 2.

8. The two subjects he promises to treat are anarchy and the possibility of the Union's dissolution.

9. This position is reminiscent of the English political theorist of the seventeenth century, Thomas Hobbes, who argued that a fear of anarchy ("a war

of all against all") impelled individuals to form a social contract and agree to live under government that might provide safety.

10. Here Centinel's views widely diverge from Thomas Hobbes' (see previous note). Hobbes believed that anarchy, which he called the state of nature, was the worst possible state of political affairs. *Any* government was superior to none. However, certain governments were much better at stifling the natural human impulse to engage in a war of all against all—Hobbes thought a single all-powerful ruler or "absolute sovereign" was best at limiting debilitating conflict among human beings. Thus, it was the best form of government to Hobbes, and all other forms, especially governments that sanctioned significant popular input, were far inferior. Centinel clearly hopes for a government with meaningful popular input.

11. Centinel is probably alluding to George Washington and Ben Franklin. The "constitutional infirmity" is likely meant to apply specifically to Franklin, who was eighty-one years old.

12. In "Federalist #1," Alexander Hamilton as "Publius" raised the possibility of the Union's dissolving into separate republics and argued in favor of the Constitution on that basis. Centinel is correct in pointing out that Hamilton's argument in this regard was spurious. None wanted dissolution of the Union. Centinel's diatribe against Publius here, a formidable opponent not easily dismissed, threatens to obscure Centinel's own more reasonable position on the durability of the Union.

13. Centinel is apparently referring to Lord Kames, a thinker of the Scottish Enlightenment who was best known for his *Historical Law Tracts* (1758).

14. In potentially libelous writing, it was a common practice to omit selected letters of key words. Here Centinel is accusing officers of the U.S. Post Office of tampering with the mail and not allowing Antifederalist writings to circulate. These were accusations of criminal behavior, and excising a few key letters was thought to provide some insulation against prosecution.

15. Once again, Centinel or his editor eliminated letters of key words to avoid possibility of prosecution, here from "post" boy and "post master general." Thomas Greenleaf was the printer of the *New York Journal*, a New York City paper. Greenleaf was an avowed Antifederalist in an area that was dominated by Federalists. At one point during the ratification debate, Greenleaf's printing shop was ransacked by Federalists (Cornell, 112).

16. Petrikin to John Nicholson, February 24, 1788, *DHRC*, vol. 2, 694.

17. These verses are from the King James version of the Bible. The first verses are correctly cited, but the reference to 1st Kings 19:11 should actually be 1st Kings 12:11.

18. Lawyers were targets of scorn in the 1780s, as they are today. They were a particularly easy target in areas like Carlisle, where most citizens were day laborers or farmers.

19. *DHRC*, vol. 2, 670–73.

20. *DHRC*, vol. 2, 674–78. It should be noted that "dirt" is a synonym for excrement, and following the biblical passage cited (Judges 3:21–22), The Scourge is using that sense of the word. In modern jargon, The Scourge is calling the Federalist version of incidents at Carlisle bullshit, and he thinks his own writing exposes their argument for what it is.

21. *DHRC*, vol. 2, 679–84.

22. In this paragraph, The Scourge is apparently defending John Jordan, one of the Antifederalist "rioters" who was also presiding judge of the Cumberland County Court of Common Pleas.

23. The deposition The Scourge refers to was in reality an arrest warrant issued by the Pennsylvania Supreme Court to the sheriff of Cumberland County, Charles Leeper. It directed Leeper to apprehend twenty-one named individuals who "in a riotous, routous, and unlawful manner did assault, beat, and wound James Armstrong Wilson . . . and divers others of the citizens and inhabitants of the said commonwealth" (*DHRC*, vol. 2, 684–85).

24. At issue in this entire paragraph is whether it was the Antifederalists or the Federalists who acted in a disorderly and riotous manner. The Antifederalist counterdemonstrators had brought a drum to the town square. By writing "the people's drum beat around two squares before they . . . left the ground," The Scourge is simply indicating that the Antifederalists were engaged in an orderly procession around the town square, not the riotous behavior the Pennsylvania Supreme Court's arrest warrant charges them with. That both sides actively charge their opponents with mob behavior indicates how stigmatized lawless action was in the wake of Shays' Rebellion.

25. James (or Jemey) the Caledonian was a derisive nickname for James Wilson, who had been born in Scotland. Wilson was a leading proponent of the Constitution in Pennsylvania (see chapter 1).

26. When individuals were anonymously insulted in the press, they could ask the printer to divulge the author's name so that they could confront their accuser. The printer could refuse to divulge his source, but if he did and if the insult was sufficiently grave, a duel could result. The ratification-era norm of concealing an author's identity was at odds with (but usually trumped) this chivalrous norm of an earlier era.

27. In this poem, The Scourge pretends to be a Federalist but does so to ridicule Federalist dress, manners, and habits. He also recounts the events of December 26 and 27, 1787. The Carlisle Federalists, with their fine, powdered wigs and soft hands, ran from their two confrontations with the Antifederalists, soiling their breeches in the process.

28. The Scourge's excrement references continue with an allusion to how scared the Carlisle Federalists were when confronted by their opposition. They were so frightened they s—t their pants.

29. The phrases "state of nature" and "natural right" were popularized by John Locke, the late seventeenth-century British political philosopher. Locke's *Second Treatise of Government* is the greatest and most influential defense of equal rights ever written. To Locke (and to Thomas Hobbes before him), the "state of nature" described times where there was no constituted government. It was Locke's claim that in a state of nature, all had equal, natural rights, and from this equality stemmed civic equality once government was formed. Locke did not explicitly argue that equal rights dictated that all (or even all males) should possess equal political power, but it is an argument that is easily made from the widely accepted Lockeian principles about the equality of rights.

30. Algernon Sidney was a contemporary of John Locke's and a fellow opponent of monarchism. Perhaps one reason Republicus chose not to cite Locke, Sidney, or other political theorists in the text of his letter is that their thoughts only loosely resemble Republicus' points.

31. With Kentucky still a part of Virginia and ripe for a population explosion, this argument made perfect sense for Republicus, not just from principle, but also to protect the interests of his area.

32. Article II, section 1, clause 3.

33. Article I, section 4, clause 1.

34. Article I, section 9, clause 1.

35. This is a biblical reference from 2 Samuel 1:20, where the newly anointed King David hopes that other people will not hear of King Saul's death lest they rejoice. By analogy, Republicus does not want word of the Constitution's countenance of slavery to travel to other lands. The contradiction of slavery's existence in a state founded on ideals of equality and freedom could be pointed out in Kentucky without alienating readers. This is a strong indication that at least in 1788, most Kentuckians were against slavery. It was not uncommon for Virginians east of the Appalachians to argue against protection of the slave trade, but their motives were selfish. Many Virginians who held slaves did not wish to see an extension of the practice, but they also had a "surplus" of slave labor. Virginia's slaves were reproducing at a rapid enough rate that slaves became an export of the state. The fewer slaves brought to America by the slave trade, the more lucrative this export would be for Virginia masters. Republicus' antislavery seems to go well beyond that position to an outright condemnation of the practice itself.

36. Though well disposed toward the "unhappy Africans," Republicus shows himself not so well disposed toward Native Americans. Republicus' geographical location helps prefigure his view. Few west of the Appalachians held slaves, but they felt threatened by Indian raids.

37. Richard Price was an English pamphleteer who gained prominence in the 1770s for his fear that the English people were losing their liberties.

38. Here McDowell refers to a previous speech by William Hill, a Federalist who opposed the issuance of paper money by the state and felt that the North Carolina legislature and the Confederation Congress should be less deferential to the populace (*Elliot's Debates*, vol. 4, pp. 85–86).

39. Requisitions were requests for revenue from the states by the Confederation. The Confederation Congress could not tax individuals directly; it had to requisition money from the states. It would be up to the states to determine how to raise the revenue. The Constitution granted the power of direct taxation to the national government, but McDowell wants to see the practice of requisitions continued.

40. In saying that he is "for the strongest federal government," McDowell means federal as it was used in his day; that is, he was for the strongest *confederation* possible, or the most powerful centralized government that would not threaten state sovereignty.

6

Elite Antifederalism

Most wealthy and prominent Americans supported the Constitution. They had good reason to. Merchants and producers of goods expected economic conditions to improve with ratification, and prominent politicians looked forward to holding positions of real power at the national level. The elites who opposed the Constitution did not look past these potential advantages. Their objections did not result from their elite status, but despite it.

Because the elite Antifederalists discerned many of the same advantages as other prominent and wealthy individuals, their opposition tended to be mild. There are no denunciations of the "conspirators" of Philadelphia, as there are in the writings of virulent Antifederalists. There are also few blanket condemnations of the system engineered there. Rather, most elite Antifederalists said that they would be satisfied with a few key alterations to the system. The two most prominent alterations they desired were a bill of rights and a larger House of Representatives.

This second objection helps reveal their distinct perspective. They hoped the new government would balance aristocratic and democratic interests. The American legislature, they believed, should be similar to Britain's, which balanced these interests in an aristocratic House of Lords and a more democratic House of Commons. The Senate would approximate the House of Lords. Instead of a hereditary aristocracy as in Britain, the upper branch would be populated by highly accomplished individuals selected by the state legislatures. In contrast to the more aristocratic Senate, the House would represent the people. Both the democratic "estate" and aristocratic "estate" would thus be represented in Congress, and they would have to agree to form laws, thus approximating a common good. One of the biggest problems with the Constitution according to the elite Antifederalists was that the House of Representatives was not sufficiently democratic. If the House was populated by the wealthy and prominent, then there would be no democratic counterbalance to the Senate. Increasing the number of representatives was proposed to enhance democratic representation in the House. Elite Antifederalists always believed that prominent men like themselves should hold more political power than their raw numbers dictated, but they understood that their power—like all power—needed to be checked.

Though they did not view the Federalist movement as a conspiracy, elite Antifederalists worried about the designs of certain proponents of the Constitution. Some wanted all democratic influences on the national government eliminated. Federal Farmer chides these Federalists by writing "I am not among those men who think a democratic branch a nuisance." The Federal Farmer's choice of words is revealing. He wants a democratic *branch* of government, not a democratic government. And there is a great deal of difference between the two. These Antifederalists felt that democratic government, where all institutions reflected the will of the masses, would be just as problematic as a purely aristocratic government. Only a government that combined aristocracy and democracy could be successful. They understood that both of these groups would try to get their way on every point—in so doing, the groups were simply arguing for their interests. But if either group were actually to dominate, the nation would likely be thrown into civil war, as either a majority of its people or those who controlled its wealth would be greatly discontented. In the assessment of the elite Antifederalists, the Constitution threatened the legitimate aspirations of the democratic element of society. Had the Constitution been overly democratic in nature, one can easily imagine their sticking up for the legitimate aspirations of the nation's aristocracy.

The elite Antifederalists were the smallest contingent of the Constitution's critics. What they lacked in numbers, they made up in prominence. Their elite perspective did not necessarily resonate with the public, who were committed to a more popular government. Thus, fewer essayists write from this perspective than they do from the "middling" view and perhaps from the "virulent" view as well. Nevertheless, the prominence of these individuals gave them important platforms to express themselves. Three future critics of the Constitution were delegates to the Philadelphia convention: George Mason, Elbridge Gerry, and Edmund Randolph, each of whom voiced "elite" objections to the document being formulated. Many of those elected to state ratification conventions possessed such beliefs. One of them, William Grayson from Virginia, is featured here. Despite relatively few elite essayists, one of the finest examples of Antifederalist argument does fall into this category, that of the Federal Farmer. Several of his essays are excerpted here as well.

EXCERPTS OF SPEECHES FROM THE PHILADELPHIA CONVENTION

Many delegates at the Philadelphia convention feared democracy. This fear was more common among Federalists than Antifederalists. Even so, several of the future Antifederalists' speeches expressed this fear. Particularly early in the convention, George Mason, Elbridge Gerry, and Edmund Randolph pointed out that the states suffered from an excess of democracy. They hoped to reintroduce an element of aristocracy into the government to temper democracy. At some point during the convention, however, these three realized that other delegates were so convinced of the dangers of democracy that they were willing to formulate a government almost wholly aristocratic in nature. At that point Mason, Gerry, and Randolph felt they needed to argue in favor of a democratic element in the national government and the reservation of powers to the states. This new tack was spurred by the changing context around them and is a quite dramatic shift. At the same time, these three never lost their fear for governments where common citizens would dominate. The excerpts here, except when noted in parentheses at the end of the quote, are from James Madison's convention notes. They reveal that certain key Antifederalists were hardly champions of popular government. Nevertheless, to their credit (and despite their own position among the nation's governing elite), they argued that the inclusion of democratic views was crucial to the new regime's success. Because these men each wrote letters explaining their objections to the Constitution, their views weren't exactly secret (see chapter 3 for Gerry's and Mason's public letters explaining their positions). Nevertheless, the convention's agreement to not publicize their proceedings allowed them to speak with greater candor than in their publicly stated reasons for objecting to the Constitution.

May 31, 1787

Mr. Gerry. The evils we experience flow from the excess of democracy. The people do not want [i.e., lack] virtue; but are the dupes of pretended patriots. In Massts. it has been fully confirmed by experience that they are daily misled into the most baneful measures and opinions by the false reports circulated by designing men, and which no one on the spot can refute. One principal evil arises from the want of due provision for those employed in the administration of Governnt. It would seem to be a maxim of democracy to starve the public servants. He mentioned the popular clamor in Massts. for the reduction of salaries and the attack made on that of the Govr. though secured by the spirit of the Constitution itself. He had he said been too republican heretofore: he was still republican, but had been taught by experience the danger of the levelling spirit.

Mr. Gerry did not like the election [of the first branch of the legislature] by the people. The maxims taken from the British constitution were often fallacious when applied to our situation which was extremely different.[1] Experience he said had shewn that the State Legislatures drawn immediately from the people did not always possess their confidence. He had no objection however to an election by the people if it were so qualified that men of honor & character might not be unwilling to be joined in the appointments. He seemed to think the people might nominate a certain number out of which the State legislatures be bound to choose.

Mr. Randf. observed that he had at the time of offering his propositions stated his ideas as far as the nature of general propositions required; that details made no part of the plan, and could not perhaps with propriety have been introduced. If he was to give an opinion as to the number of the second branch [the Senate], he should say that it ought to be much smaller than that of the first; so small as to be exempt from the passionate proceedings to which numerous assemblies are liable. He observed that the general object was to provide a cure for the evils under which the U.S. laboured; that in tracing these evils to their origin every man had found it in the turbulence and follies of democracy: that some check therefore was to be sought for agst. this tendency of our Governments: and that a good Senate seemed most likely to answer the purpose.

June 5

Mr Gerry. Observed that in the Eastern States the Confedn. had been sanctioned by the people themselves. He seemed afraid of referring the new system to them. The people in that quarter have, at this time, the wildest ideas of Government in the world. They were for abolishing the Senate in Massts. and giving all the other powers of Govt. to the other branch of the Legislature.

June 7

Mr. Gerry insisted that the commercial & monied interest wd. be more secure in the hands of the State Legislatures, than of the people at large. The former have more sense of character, and will be restrained by that from injustice. The people are for paper money when the Legislatures are agst. it.[2] In Massts. the County Conventions had declared a wish for a depreciating paper that wd. sink itself. Besides, in some States there are two Branches in the Legislature, one of which is somewhat aristocratic. There wd. therefore be so far a better chance of refinement in the choice.

June 13

Mr. Gerry. If we dislike the British government for the oppressive measures by them carried on against us, yet he hoped we would not be so far prejudiced as to make ours in every thing opposite to theirs. (Yates)

June 26

Mr. Gerry wished we could be united in our ideas concerning a permanent Govt. All aim at the same end, but there are great differences as to the means. One circumstance He thought should be carefully attended to. There were not 1/1000 part of our fellow citizens who were not agst. every approach towards Monarchy. Will they ever agree to a plan which seems to make such an approach? The Convention ought to be extremely cautious in what they hold out to the people. Whatever plan may be proposed will be espoused with warmth by many out of respect to the quarter it proceeds from as well as from an approbation of the plan itself. And if the plan should be of such a nature as to rouse a violent opposition, it is easy to foresee that discord & confusion will ensue, and it is even possible that we may become a prey to foreign powers. He did not deny the position of Mr. Madison that the majority will generally violate justice when they have an interest in so doing; But did not think there was any such temptation in this Country. Our situation was different from that of G. Britain: and the great body of lands yet to be parcelled out & settled would very much prolong the difference. Notwithstanding the symtoms of injustice which had marked many of our public Councils, thay had not proceeded so far as to not to leave hopes, that there would be a sufficient sense of justice & virtue for the purpose of Govt. He admitted the evils arising from a frequency of elections: and would agree to give the Senate a duration of four or five years. A longer term would defeat itself. It never would be adopted by the people.

Col. Mason. He did not rise to make any motion, but to hint at an idea which seemed to be proper for consideration. One important object in constituting the Senate was to secure the rights of property. To give them weight & firmness for this purpose, a considerable duration in office was thought necessary. But a longer term than 6 years, would be of no avail in this respect, if needy persons should be appointed. He suggested therefore the propriety of annexing to the office a qualification of property. He thought this would be very practicable; as the rules of taxation would supply a scale for measuring the degree of wealth possessed by every man.

July 2

Mr. Gerry. The world at large expect something from us. If we do nothing, it appears to me we must have war and confusion—for the old confederation would be at an end. Let us see if no concession can be made. Accommodation is absolutely necessary, and defects may be amended by a future convention. (Yates)

July 17

Col. Mason. . . . a Government which is to last ought at least to be practicable. Would this be the case if the proposed election [of the president] should be left to the people at large? He conceived it would be as unnatural to refer the choice of a proper character for chief Magistrate to the people, as it would, to refer a trial of colours to a blind man. The extent of the Country renders it impossible that the people can have the requisite capacity to judge of the respective pretensions of the Candidates.

July 19

Mr. Gerry. If the Executive is to be elected by the Legislature he certainly ought not to be re-eligible. This would make him absolutely dependent. He was agst. a popular election. The people are uninformed, and would be misled by a few designing men. He urged the expediency of an appointment of the Executive by Electors to be chosen by the State Executives. The people of the States will then choose the 1st. branch: The legislatures of the States the 2nd. branch of the National Legislature, and the Executives of the States, the National Executive— This he thought would form a strong attachmt. in the States to the National System. The popular mode of electing the chief Magistrate would certainly be the worst of all. If he should be so elected & should do his duty, he will be turned out for it like Govr Bowdoin in Massts & President Sullivan in N. Hampshire.[3]

July 23

Mr. Gerry . . . —Great confusion he was confident would result from a recurrence to the people [for approval of amendments]. They would never agree on any thing. He could not see any ground to suppose that the people will do what their rulers will not. The rulers will either conform to, or influence the sense of the people.

July 26

Mr. Gerry. If the argumts. used to day were to prevail, we might have a Legislature composed of public debtors, pensioners, placemen, & contractors. He thought the proposed qualifications would be pleasing to the people. They will be considered as a security agst unnecessary or undue burdens being imposed on them. He moved to add "pensioners" to the disqualified characters which was negatived.

August 7

Col. Mason. The force of habit is certainly not attended to by those gentlemen who wish for innovations on this point [requiring a property qualification for voters in federal elections]. Eight or nine States have extended the right of suffrage beyond the freeholders.[4] What will the people there say, if they should be disfranchised. A power to alter the qualifications would be a dangerous power in the hands of the Legislature.

August 8

Mr. Mason. . . . thought it a defect in the plan that the Representatives would be too few to bring with them all the local knowledge necessary.

Col. Mason was unwilling to travel over this ground again. To strike out the section [granting the House exclusive power to originate "money bills"], was to unhinge the compromise of which it made a part. The duration of the Senate made it improper. He does not object to that duration. On the Contrary he approved it. But joined with the smallness of the number, it was an argument against adding to the other great powers vested in that body. His idea of an Aristocracy was that it was the governt of the few over the many. An aristocratic body, like the screw in mechanics, workig. its way by slow degrees, and holding fast whatever it gains, should ever be suspected of an encroaching tendency—The purse strings should never be put in its hands.[5]

August 13

Mr. Randolph regarded this point [on the ability of the House to originate money bills] as of such consequence, that as he valued the peace of his Country, he would press the adoption of it. We had numerous & monstrous difficulties to combat. Surely we ought not to increase them. When the people behold in the Senate, the countenance of an aristocracy; and in the president, the form at least of a little monarch, will not their alarms be sufficiently raised without taking from their immediate representatives, a right which has been so long appropriated to them?

August 14

Col. Mason ironically[6] proposed to strike out the whole section [requiring federal representatives to rotate out of office], as a more effectual expedient for encouraging that exotic corruption which might not otherwise thrive so well in the American Soil—for compleating that Aristocracy which was probably in the contemplation of some among us. . . .

August 23

Mr. Gerry. . . . Will any man say that liberty will be as safe in the hands of eighty or a hundred men taken from the whole continent, as in the hands of two or three hundred taken from a single State?

Mr. Gerry. Let us at once destroy the State Govts have an Executive for life or hereditary, and a proper Senate, and then there would be some consistency in giving full powers to the Genl Govt. but as the States are not to be abolished, he wondered at the attempts that were made to give powers inconsistent with their existence. He warned the Convention agst pushing the experiment too far. Some people will support a plan of vigorous Government at every risk. Others of a more democratic cast will oppose it with equal determination. And a Civil war may be produced by the conflict.[7]

September 5

Mr. Randolph. We have in some revolutions of this plan made a bold stroke for Monarchy.[8] We are now doing the same for an aristocracy. He dwelt on the tendency of such an influence in the Senate over the election of the President in addition to its other powers, to convert that body into a real & dangerous Aristocracy—

Col. Mason. As the mode of appointment is now regulated, he could not forbear expressing his opinion that it is utterly inadmissable. He would prefer the Government of Prussia to one which will put all power into the hands of seven or eight men, and fix an Aristocracy worse than absolute monarchy.[9]

September 15

Mason: In the House of Representatives there is not the substance but the shadow only of representation; which can never produce proper information in the legislature, or inspire confidence in the people; the laws will therefore be made by men little concerned in, and unacquainted with their effects and consequences. This objection has been in some degree lessened by an amendment, often before refused and at last made by an erasure, after the engrossment upon parchment of the word *forty* and inserting *thirty*, in the third clause of the second section of the first article.[10]

The Senate have the power of altering all the money bills, and of originating appropriations of money, and the salaries of the officers in their own appointment, in conjunction with the president of the United States, although they are not the representatives of the people or amenable to them.

These with their other great powers, viz.: their power in the appointment of ambassadors and all public officers, in making treaties, and in trying all impeachments, their influence upon and connection with the supreme Executive from these causes, their duration of office and their being a constantly existing body, almost continually sitting, joined with their being one complete branch of the legislature, will destroy any balance in the government, and enable them to accomplish what usurpations they please upon the rights and liberties of the people [Mason wrote these comments on his copy of the draft of the Constitution circulated on September 12].

FEDERAL FARMER'S LETTERS TO THE REPUBLICAN

November 1787 and May 1788

The Federal Farmer is perhaps the most well-respected Antifederalist essayist. His high reputation can be attributed to the temperate and learned nature of his commentary. In "Federalist #68," Alexander Hamilton, writing as "Publius," called these essays the "most plausible" of the Antifederalist arguments to appear in print. More frequently, however, the Federal Farmer's arguments were ignored by Federalist essayists, as it was easier to attack less reasonable and less polished commentaries. The Federal Farmer's letters were addressed to "the Republican," probably a reference to New York Governor George Clinton. They were written as a series of eighteen letters, but issued as two pamphlets. The first pamphlet included five letters, and it was first advertised for sale in New York City in early November 1787. Several thousand copies of this pamphlet were sold, and it received wide readership and distribution. A second pamphlet containing the remaining letters appeared in May 1788.

The author of the Federal Farmer essays is unknown. A contemporary Federalist author, "New England," attributed the letters to Virginian Richard Henry Lee. There is, in fact, no evidence that Richard Henry Lee wrote the essays, and there is considerable reason to doubt that he did. New England's purpose for saying that Lee wrote the works was likely partisan. Lee was known to dislike George Washington, and the character of any man who disliked Washington was suspected. By extension, his arguments about the Constitution would be suspected as well. Additionally, several statements in the work indicate that the author is a Northerner rather than a Southerner. Nevertheless, the attribution to Lee was accepted without question for more than a century. No consensus has emerged as to the author's true identity, but many have been convinced by a recent journal article that suggests that Melancton Smith wrote the es-

says.[11] In my view, this claim is suspect for two reasons. First, Smith's "middling" view clashes with the elite perspective subtly displayed in these essays. Second, the Federal Farmer favors dual sovereignty, a perspective not openly espoused by Smith or his New York colleagues. They argued that states should retain sovereignty and that the national government should be a confederation, not a sovereign entity of itself.

Typical of one who views politics as an epic struggle between the aristocratic and democratic elements of society, Federal Farmer thinks the ratification fight might turn violent. He urges restraint and moderation despite the immoderate temper of some on both sides. Just as he thinks government should balance aristocratic and democratic interests, he also thinks powers should be balanced between states and the nation. As an advocate of dual sovereignty, Federal Farmer complains that the states will be annihilated by the national government. With the national government so dangerously tilted toward aristocracy, an oppressive regime would likely result, perhaps precipitating a civil war. To forestall that possibility, the Federal Farmer suggests amending the Constitution to guarantee individual rights, to protect the prerogatives of states, and to broaden representation in the House.

I have included excerpts from Letter I, Letter III, Letter V, and Letter VIII. In addition to being one of the most thoughtful of the Antifederalist essayists, Federal Farmer was among the most widely read. The entire first series of letters was reprinted at least nine times, both in newspapers and separately as a pamphlet. The second set of letters did not circulate so widely, but it too was reprinted and circulated in pamphlet form.

Letter I

Dear Sir, My letters to you last winter, on the subject of a well-balanced national government for the United States, were the result of free enquiry;[12] when I passed from that subject to enquiries relative to our commerce, revenues, past administration, &c. I anticipated the anxieties I feel, on carefully examining the plan of government proposed by the convention. It appears to be a plan retaining some federal features; but to be the first important step, and to aim strongly to one consolidated government of the United States. It leaves the powers of government, and the representation of the people, so unnaturally divided between the general and state government, that the operations of our system must be very uncertain. My uniform federal attachments, and the interest I have in the protection of property, and a steady execution of the laws, will convince you, that, if I am under any biass at all, it is in favor of any general system which shall promise those advantages. The instability of our laws increase my wishes for firm and steady government; but then, I can consent to no government, which, in my opinion, is not calculated equally to preserve the rights of all orders of men in the community. . . . I know our situation is critical, and it behoves us to make the best of it. A federal government of some sort is necessary. We have suffered the present to languish; and whether the confederation was capable or not originally of answering any valuable purposes, it is now but of little importance. I will pass by the men, and states, who have been particularly instrumental in preparing the way for a change, and, perhaps, for governments not very favourable to the people at large. A constitution is now presented, which we may reject, or which we may accept, with or without amendments; and to which point we ought to direct our exertions, is the question. To determine this question, with propriety, we must attentively examine the system itself, and the probable consequences of either step. This I shall endeavour to do, so far as I am able, with candour and fairness; and leave you to decide upon the propriety of my opinions, the weight of my reasons, and how far my conclusions are well drawn. Whatever may be the conduct of others, on the present occasion, I do not mean, hastily and positively to decide on the merits of the constitution proposed. I shall be open to conviction, and always disposed to adopt that which, all things considered, shall appear to me to be most for the happiness of the community. It must be granted, that if men hastily and blindly adopt a system of government, they will as hastily and as blindly be led to alter or abolish it; and changes must ensue, one after another, till the peaceable and better part of the community will grow weary with changes, tumults and disorders, and be disposed to accept any government, however despotic, that shall promise stability and firmness.

The first principal question that occurs, is, whether, considering our situation, we ought to precipitate the adoption of the proposed constitution? If we remain cool and temperate, we are in no immediate danger of any commotions; we are in a state of perfect peace, and in no danger of invasions; the state governments are in the full exercise of their powers; and our governments answer all present exigencies, except the regulation of trade, securing credit, in some cases, and providing for the interest, in some instances, of the public debts; and whether we adopt a change, three or nine months hence, can make but little odds with the private circumstances of

individuals; their happiness and prosperity, after all, depend principally upon their own exertions. We are hardly recovered from a long
and distressing war: The farmers, fishermen, &c. have not yet fully
repaired the waste made by it. Industry and frugality are again as-
suming their proper station. Private debts are lessened, and public
debts incurred by the war, have been, by various ways diminished;
and the public lands have now become a productive source for di-
minishing them much more. I know uneasy men, who wish very
much to [be] precipitate, do not admit all these facts; but they are
facts well known to all men who are thoroughly informed in the affairs of this country. It must, however, be admitted, that our federal
system is defective, and that some of the state governments are not
well administered; but, then, we impute to the defects in our governments, many evils and embarrassments which are most clearly
the result of the late war. We must allow men to conduct on the
present occasion, as on all similar one's. They will urge a thousand
pretences to answer their purposes on both sides. When we want a
man to change his condition, we describe it as miserable, wretched,
and despised; and draw a pleasing picture of that which we would
have him assume. And when we wish the contrary, we reverse our
descriptions. Whenever a clamor is raised, and idle men get to work,
it is highly necessary to examine facts carefully, and without unreasonably suspecting men of falsehood, to examine, and enquire attentively, under what impressions they act. It is too often the case
in political concerns, that men state facts not as they are, but as
they wish them to be; and almost every man, by calling to mind past
scenes, will find this to be true.

Nothing but the passions of ambitious, impatient, or disorderly
men, I conceive, will plunge us into commotions, if time should be
taken fully to examine and consider the system proposed. Men who
feel easy in their circumstances, and such as are not sanguine in their
expectations relative to the consequences of the proposed change, will
remain quiet under the existing governments. Many commercial and
monied men, who are uneasy, not without just cause, ought to be respected; and, by no means, unreasonably disappointed in their expectations and hopes; but as to those who expect employments under the
new constitution; as to those weak and ardent men who always expect
to be gainers by revolutions, and whose lot it generally is to get out of
one difficulty into another, they are very little to be regarded: and as
to those who designedly avail themselves of this weakness and ardor,
they are to be despised. It is natural for men, who wish to hasten the
adoption of a measure, to tell us, now is the crisis-now is the critical

moment which must be seized, or all will be lost: and to shut the door against free enquiry, whenever conscious the thing presented has defects in it, which time and investigation will probably discover. This has been the custom of tyrants and their dependents in all ages. If it is true, what has been so often said, that the people of this country cannot change their condition for the worse, I presume it still behooves them to endeavour deliberately to change it for the better. The fickle and ardent, in any community, are the proper tools for establishing despotic government. But it is deliberate and thinking men, who must establish and secure governments on free principles. Before they decide on the plan proposed, they will enquire whether it will probably be a blessing or a curse to this people.

The present moment discovers a new face in our affairs. Our object has been all along, to reform our federal system, and to strengthen our governments-to establish peace, order and justice in the community-but a new object now presents. The plan of government now proposed, is evidently calculated totally to change, in time, our condition as a people. Instead of being thirteen republics, under a federal head, it is clearly designed to make us one consolidated government. Of this, I think, I shall fully convince you, in my following letters on this subject. This consolidation of the states has been the object of several men in this country for some time past. Whether such a change can ever be effected in any manner; whether it can be effected without convulsions and civil wars; whether such a change will not totally destroy the liberties of this country-time only can determine. . . .

I shall premise, that the plan proposed, is a plan of accommodation-and that it is in this way only, and by giving up a part of our opinions, that we can ever expect to obtain a government founded in freedom and compact. This circumstance candid men will always keep in view, in the discussion of the subject.

The plan proposed appears to be partly federal, but principally however, calculated ultimately to make the states one consolidated government.

The first interesting question, therefore, suggested, is, how far the states can be consolidated into one entire government on free principles. In considering this question extensive objects are to be taken into view, and important changes in the forms of government to be carefully attended to in all their consequences. The happiness of the people at large must be the great object with every honest statesman, and he will direct every movement to this point. If we are so situated as a people, as not to be able to enjoy equal happiness and advantages under one government, the consolidation of the states cannot be admitted.

There are three different forms of free government under which the United States may exist as one nation; and now is, perhaps, the time to determine to which we will direct our views. 1. Distinct republics connected under a foederal head. In this case the respective state governments must be the principal guardians of the peoples rights, and exclusively regulate their internal police; in them must rest the balance of government. The congress of the states, or federal head, must consist of delegates amenable to, and removeable by the respective states: This congress must have general directing powers; powers to require men and monies of the states; to make treaties; peace and war; to direct the operations of armies &c. Under this federal modification of government, the powers of congress would be rather advisory or recommendatory than coercive. 2. We may do away with the several state governments, and form or consolidate all the states into one entire government, with one executive, one judiciary, and one legislature, consisting of senators and representatives collected from all parts of the union: In this case there would be a compleat consolidation of the states. 3. We may consolidate the states as to certain national objects, and leave them severally distinct independent republics, as to internal police generally. Let the general government consist of an executive, a judiciary and balanced legislature, and its powers extend exclusively to all foreign concerns, causes arising on the seas, to commerce, imports, armies, navies, Indian affairs, peace and war, and to a few internal concerns of the community; to the coin, post-offices, weights and measures, a general plan for the militia, to naturalization, *and, perhaps to bankruptcies,* leaving the internal police of the community, in other respects, exclusively to the state governments; as the administration of justice in all causes arising internally, the laying and collecting of internal taxes, and the forming of the militia according to a general plan prescribed. In this case there would be a compleat consolidation quoad certain objects only.

Touching the first, or federal plan, I do not think much can be said in its favor: The sovereignty of the nation, without coercive and efficient powers to collect the strength of it, cannot always be depended on to answer the purposes of government; and in a congress of representatives of foreign states, there must necessarily be an unreasonable mixture of powers in the same hands.

As to the second, or compleat consolidating plan, it deserves to be carefully considered at this time by every American: If it be impracticable, it is a fatal error to model our governments, directing our views ultimately to it.

The third plan, or partial consolidation, is, in my opinion, the only one that can secure the freedom and happiness of this people. I once had some general ideas that the second plan was practicable, but from long attention, and the proceedings of the convention, I am fully satisfied, that this third plan is the only one we can with safety and propriety proceed upon. Making this the standard to point out, with candour and fairness, the parts of the new constitution which appear to be improper, is my object. The convention appears to have proposed the partial consolidation evidently with a view to collect all powers ultimately, in the United States into one entire government; and from its views in this respect, and from the tenacity, of the small states to have an equal vote in the senate, probably originated the greatest defects in the proposed plan.

Independent of the opinions of many great authors, that a free elective government cannot be extended over large territories, a few reflections must evince, that one government and general legislation alone never can extend equal benefits to all parts of the United States: Different laws, customs, and opinions exist in the different states, which by a uniform system of laws would be unreasonably invaded. The United States contain about a million of square miles, and in half a century will, probably, contain ten millions of people; and from the center to the extremes is about 800 miles.

Before we do away [with] the state governments, or adopt measures that will tend to abolish them, and to consolidate the states into one entire government several principles should be considered and facts ascertained:-These, and my examination into the essential parts of the proposed plan, I shall pursue in my next.[13]

Letter III

. . . It is not my object to multiply objections, or to contend about inconsiderable powers or amendments. I wish the system adopted with a few alterations; but those, in my mind, are essential ones; if adopted without, every good citizen will acquiesce, though I shall consider the duration of our governments, and the liberties of this people, very much dependent on the administration of the general government. A wise and honest administration, may make the people happy under any government; but necessity only can justify even our leaving open avenues to the abuse of power, by wicked, unthinking, or ambitious men. . . .

As to the organization-the house of representatives, the democrative branch, as it is called, is to consist of 65 members; that is, about one representative for fifty thousand inhabitants, to be chosen biennially-the federal legislature may increase this number to one for every thirty thousand inhabitants, abating fractional numbers in each state.-Thirty-three representatives will make a quorum for doing business, and a majority of those present determine the sense of the house.-I have no idea that the interests, feelings, and opinions of three or four millions of people, especially touching internal taxation, can be collected in such a house.-In the nature of things, nine times in ten, men of elevated classes in the community only can be chosen-Connecticut, for instance, will have five representatives-not one man in a hundred of those who form the democratic branch in the state legislature, will on a fair computation, be one of the five-The people of this country, in one sense, may all be democratic; but if we make the proper distinction between the few men of wealth and abilities, and consider them, as we ought, as the natural aristocracy of the country, and the great body of the people, the middle and lower classes, as the democracy, this federal representative branch will have but very little democracy in it. . . .

In considering the practicability of having a full and equal representation of the people from all parts of the union, not only distances and different opinions, customs, and views, common in extensive tracts of country, are to be taken into view, but many differences peculiar to Eastern, Middle, and Southern States. These differences are not so perceivable among the members of congress, and men who would properly form the democratic branch. The Eastern states are very democratic, and composed chiefly of moderate freeholders:[14] they have but few rich men and no slaves; the Southern states are composed chiefly of rich planters and slaves; they have but few moderate freeholders, and the prevailing influence, in them, is generally a dissipated aristocracy: The Middle states partake partly of the Eastern, and partly of the Southern character.

Perhaps, nothing could be more disjointed, unweildy and incompetent to doing business with harmony and dispatch, than a federal house of representatives properly numerous for the great objects of taxation, &c. collected from the several states; whether such men would ever act in concert; whether they would not worry along a few years, and then be the means of separating the parts of the union, is very problematical-View this system in whatever form we can, propriety brings us still to this point, a federal government possessed of general and complete powers, as to those national objects which cannot well come under the cognizance of the internal laws of the respective states, and this federal government, accordingly, consisting of branches not very numerous.

The house of representatives is on the plan of consolidation, but the senate is entirely on the federal plan; and Delaware will have as much constitutional influence in the senate, as the largest state in the union; and in this senate are lodged legislative, executive and judicial powers: Ten states in this union urge that they are small states, nine of which were present in the convention.[15]-They were interested in collecting large powers into the hands of the senate, in which each state still will have its equal share of power.[16] I suppose it was impracticable for the three large states, as they were called, to get the senate formed on any other principles:-But this only proves, that we cannot form one general government on equal and just principles-and proves, that we ought not to lodge in it such extensive powers before we are convinced of the practicability of organizing it on just and equal principles. The senate will consist of two members from each state, chosen by the state legislature, every sixth year. The clause referred to, respecting the elections of representatives, empowers the general legislature to regulate the elections of senators also, "except as to the places of chusing senators."[17]-There is, therefore, but little more security in the elections than in those of representatives:-Fourteen senators make a quorum for business, and a majority of the senators present give the vote of the senate, except in giving judgment upon an impeachment, or in making treaties, or in expelling a member, when two thirds of the senators present agree.-The members of the legislature are not excluded from being elected to any military offices, or any civil offices, except those created, or the emoluments of which shall be increased by themselves: two-thirds of the members present, of either house, may expel a member at pleasure.-The senate is an independent branch of the legislature, a court for trying impeachments, and also a part of the executive, having a negative in the making of all treaties, and in appointing almost all officers.

The vice-president is not a very important, if not an unnecessary part of the system-he may be a part of the senate at one period, and act as the supreme executive magistrate at another-The election of this officer, as well as of the president of the United States seems to be properly secured; but when we examine the powers of the president, and the forms of the executive, shall perceive that the general government, in this part, will have a strong tendency to aristocracy, or the government of the few. The executive is, in fact, the president and senate in all transactions of any importance; the president is connected with, or tied to the senate; he may always act with the senate, never can effectually counteract its views: The president can appoint no officer, civil or military, who shall not be agreeable to the senate; and the presumption is, that the will of so important a body will not be very easily controuled, and that it will exercise its powers with great address.

In the judicial department, powers ever kept distinct in well balanced governments, are no less improperly blended in the hands of the same men-in the judges of the supreme court is lodged, the law, the equity and the fact. It is not necessary to pursue the minute organical parts of the general government proposed.-There were various interests in the convention, to be reconciled, especially of large and small states; of carrying and non-carrying states:[18] and of states more and states less democratic-vast laboured attention were by the convention bestowed on the organization of the parts of the constitution offered; still it is acknowledged, there are many things radically wrong in the essential parts of this constitution-but it is said, that these are the result of our situation:-On a full examination of the subject, I believe it; but what do the laborious inquiries and determinations of the convention prove? If they prove any thing, they prove that we cannot consolidate the states on proper principles: The organization of the government presented proves, that we cannot form a general government in which all power can be safely lodged; and a little attention to the parts of the one proposed will make it appear very evident, that all the powers proposed to be lodged in it, will not be then well deposited, either for the purposes of government, or the preservation of liberty. . . .

Should the general government think it politic, as some administrations (if not all) probably will, to look for a support in a system of influence, the government will take every occasion to multiply laws, and officers to execute them, considering these as so many necessary props for its own support. Should this system of policy be adopted, taxes more productive than the impost duties will, probably, be wanted to support the government, and to discharge foreign demands, without leaving any thing for the domestic creditors. The internal sources of taxation then must be called into operation, and internal tax laws and federal assessors and collectors spread over this immense country. All these circumstances considered, is it wise, prudent, or safe, to vest the powers of laying and collecting internal taxes in the general government, while imperfectly organized and inadequate; and to trust to amending it hereafter, and making it adequate to this purpose? Is it not only unsafe but absurd to lodge power in a government before it is fitted to receive it? It is confessed that this power and representation ought to go together. Why give the power first? Why give the power to the few, who, when possessed of it, may have address enough to prevent the increase of representation? Why not keep the power, and, when necessary, amend the constitution, and add to its other parts this power, and a proper increase of representation at the same time? Then men who may want the power will be under strong inducements to let in the people, by their representatives, into the government, to hold their due proportion of this power. If a proper representation be impracticable, then we shall see this power resting in the states, where it at present ought to be, and not inconsiderately given up.

When I recollect how lately congress, convention, legislatures, and people, contended in the cause of liberty, and carefully weighed the importance of taxation, I can scarcely believe we are serious in proposing to vest the powers of laying and collecting internal taxes in a government so imperfectly organized for such purposes. Should the United States be taxed by a house of representatives of two hundred members, which would be about fifteen members for Connecticut, twenty-five for Massachusetts, &c. still the middle and lower classes of people could have no great share, in fact, in taxation. I am aware it is said, that the representation proposed by the new constitution is sufficiently numerous; it may be for many purposes; but to suppose that this branch is sufficiently numerous to guard the rights of the people in the administration of the government, in which the purse and sword is placed, seems to argue that we have forgot what the true meaning of representation is. . . .

In state governments the great body of the people, the yeomanry, &c. of the country, are represented: It is true they will chuse the members of congress, and may now and then chuse a man of their own way of thinking; but it is impossible for forty, or thirty thousand people in this country, one time in ten to find a man who can possess similar feelings, views, and interests with themselves: powers to lay and collect taxes and to raise armies are of the greatest moment; for carrying them into effect, laws need not be frequently made, and the yeomanry, &c. of the country ought substantially to have a check upon the passage of these laws; this check ought to be placed in the legislatures, or at least, in the few men the common people of the country, will, probably, have in congress, in the true sense of the word, "from among themselves." It is true, the yeomanry of the country possess the lands, the weight of property, possess arms, and are too strong a body of men to be openly offended-and, therefore, it is urged, they will take care of themselves, that men who shall govern will not dare pay any disrespect to their opinions. It is easily perceived, that if they have not their proper negative upon passing laws in congress, or on the passage of laws relative to taxes and armies, they may in twenty or thirty years be by means imperceptible to them, totally deprived of that boasted weight and strength.

Letter V

. . . Thus I have examined the federal constitution as far as a few days leisure would permit. It opens to my mind a new scene; instead of seeing powers cautiously lodged in the hands of numerous legislators, and many magistrates, we see all important powers collecting in one centre, where a few men will possess them almost at discretion. And instead of checks in the formation of the government, to secure the rights of the people against the usurpation of those they appoint to govern, we are to understand the equal division of lands among our people, and the strong arm furnished them by nature and situation, are to secure them against those usurpations. If there are advantages in the equal division of our lands, and the strong and manly habits of our people, we ought to establish governments calculated to give duration to them, and not governments which never can work naturally, till that equality of property, and those free and manly habits shall be destroyed; these evidently are not the natural basis of the proposed constitution.-No man of reflection, and skilled in the science of government, can suppose these will move on harmoniously together for ages, or even for fifty years. As to the little circumstances commented upon, by some writers, with applause-as the age of a representative, of the president, &c.-they have, in my mind, no weight in the general tendency of the system.

There are, however, in my opinion, many good things in the proposed system. It is founded on elective principles, and the deposits of powers in several hands, is essentially right.-The guards against those evils we have experiences in some states in legislation are valuable indeed: but the value of every feature in this system is vastly lessened for the want of that one important feature in a free government, a representation of the people. Because we have sometimes abused democracy, I am not among those men who think a democratic branch a nuisance; which branch shall be sufficiently numerous, to admit some of the best informed men of each order in the community into the administration of government.

While the radical defects in the proposed system are not so soon discovered, some temptations to each state, and to many classes of men to adopt it, are very visible. It uses the democratic language of several of the state constitutions, particularly that of Massachusetts; the eastern states will receive advantages so far as the regulation of trade, by a bare majority, is committeed to it: Connecticut and New-Jersey will receive their share of a general impost:[19]-The middle states will receive the advantages surrounding the seat of government:-The southern states will receive protection, and have their negroes represented in the legislature, and large back countries will soon have a majority in it.-This system promises a large field of employment to military gentlemen, and gentlemen of the law; and in case the government shall be executed without convulsions, it will afford security to creditors, to the clergy, salary-men and others depending on money payments. So far as the system promises justice and reasonable advantages, in these respects, it ought to be supported by all honest men; but whenever it promises unequal and improper advantages to any particular states, or orders of men, it ought to be opposed.

I have, in the course of these letters observed, that there are many good things in the proposed constitution, and I have endeavoured to point out many important defects in it. I have admitted that we want a federal system-that we have a system presented, which, with several alterations, may be made a tolerable good one-I have admitted there is a well founded uneasiness among creditors and mercantile men. In this situation of things, you ask me what I think ought to be done? My opinion in this case is only the opinion of an individual, so far only as it corresponds with the opinions of the honest and substantial part of the community, is it entitled to consideration. Though I am fully satisfied that the state conventions ought most seriously to direct their exertions to altering and amending the system proposed before they shall adopt it-yet I have not sufficiently examined the subject, or formed an opinion, how far it will be practicable for those conventions to carry their amendments. As to the idea, that it will be in vain for those conventions to attempt amendments, it cannot be admitted; it is impossible to say whether they can or not until the attempt shall be made: and when it shall be determined, by experience, that the conventions cannot agree in amendments, it will then be an important question before the people of the United States, whether they will adopt or not the system proposed in its present form. This subject of consolidating the states is new; and because forty or fifty men have agreed in a system, to suppose the good sense of this country, an enlightened nation, must adopt it without examination, and though in a state of profound peace, without endeavouring to amend those parts they perceive are defective, dangerous to freedom, and destructive of the valuable principles of republican government-is truly humiliating. It is true there may be danger in delay; but there is danger in adopting the system in its present form; and I see the danger in either case will arise principally from the conduct and views of two very unprincipled parties in the United States-two fires, between which the honest and substantial people have long found themselves situated. One party is composed of little insurgents, men in debt, who want no law, and who want a share of the property of others; these are called levellers, Shayites, &c. The other party is composed of a few but more dangerous men, with their servile dependents; these avariciously grasp at power and property; you may discover in all the actions of these men, an evident dislike to free and equal governments, and they will go systematically to work to change, essentially, the forms of government in this country; these are called aristocrates, morrisites, &c. &c.[20] Between these two parties is the weight of the community; the men of middling property, men not in debt on the one hand, and men, on the other, content with republican government, and not aiming at immense fortunes, offices, and power. In 1786, the little insurgents, the levellers, came forth, invaded the rights of others, and attempted to establish governments according to their wills. Their movements evidently gave encouragement to the other party, which, in 1787, has taken the political field, and with its fashionable dependents, and the tongue and the pen, is endeavouring to establish in great haste, a politer kind of government. These two parties, which will probably be opposed or united as it may suit their interests and views, are really insignificant, compared with the solid, free, and independent part of the community. It is not my intention to suggest, that either of these parties, and the real friends of the proposed constitution, are the same men. The fact is, these aristocrats support and hasten the adoption of the proposed constitution, merely because they think it is a stepping stone to their favourite object. I think I am well founded in this idea; I think the general politics of these men support it, as well as the common observation among them, that the proffered plan is the best that can be got at present, it will do for a few years, and lead to something better. The sensible and judicious part of the community will carefully weigh all these circumstances; they will view the late convention as a respectable assembly of men-America probably never will see an assembly of men of a like number, more respectable. But the members of the convention met without knowing the sentiments of one man in ten thousand in these states respecting the new ground taken. Their doings are but the first attempts in the most important scene ever opened. Though each individual in the state conventions will not, probably, be so respectable as each individual in the federal convention, yet as the state conventions will probably consist of fifteen hundred or two thousand men of abilities, and versed in the science of government, collected from all parts of the community and from all orders of men, it must be acknowledged that the weight of respectability will be in them-In them will be collected the solid sense and the real political character of the country. . . .

I think the honest and substantial part of the community, will wish to see this system altered, permanency and consistency given to the constitution we shall adopt; and therefore they will be anxious to apportion the powers to the features and the organization of the government, and to see abuse in the exercise of power more effectually guarded against.

Letter VIII

. . . In England, the people have been led uniformly, and systematically by their representatives to secure their rights by compact, and to abolish innovations upon the government: They successively obtained the Magna Charta, the powers of taxation, the power to propose laws, the habeas corpus act, bill of rights, &c. they, in short, secured general and equal liberty, security to their persons and property; and, as an everlasting security and bulwark of their liberties, they fixed the democratic branch in the legislature, and jury trial in the execution of the laws, the freedom of the press, &c.

In Rome, and most other countries, the reverse of all this is true. In Greece, Rome, and wherever the civil law has been adopted, torture has been admitted. In Rome the people were subject to arbitrary confiscations, and even their lives would be arbitrarily disposed of by consuls, tribunes, dictators, masters, &c. half of the inhabitants were slaves, and the other half never knew what equal liberty was; yet in England the people have had king, lords, and commons; in Rome they had consuls, senators and tribunes: why then was the government of England so mild and favourable to the body of the people, and that of Rome an ambitious and oppressive aristocracy? Why in England have the revolutions always ended in stipulations in favour of general liberty, equal laws, and the common rights of the people, and in most other countries in favour only of a few influential men? The reasons, in my mind, are obvious: In England the people have been substantially represented in many respects; in the other countries it has not been so. Perhaps a small degree of attention to a few simple facts will illustrate this.—In England, from the oppressions of the Norman kings to the revolution of 1688, during which period of two or three hundred years, the English liberties were ascertained and established, the aristocratic part of that nation was substantially represented by a very large number of nobles, possessing similar interests and feelings with those they represented. The body of the people, about four or five millions, then mostly a frugal landed people, were represented by about five hundred representatives, taken not from the order of men who formed the aristocracy, but from the body of the people, and possessed of the same interests and feelings. De Lome,[21] speaking of the British representation, expressly founds all his reasons on this union; this similitude of interests, feelings, views and circumstances. He observes, the English have preserved their liberties, because they and their leaders or representatives have been strictly united in interests, and in contending for general liberty. Here we see a genuine balance founded in the actual state of things. The whole community, probably, not more than two-fifths more numerous than we now are, were represented by seven or eight hundred men; the barons stipulated with the common people, and the king with the whole. Had the legal distinction between lords and commons been broken down, and the people of that island been called upon to elect forty-five senators, and one hundred and twenty representatives, about the proportion we propose to establish, their whole legislature evidently would have been of the natural aristocracy, and the body of the people would not have had scarcely a single advocate; their interests would have been neglected, general and equal liberty forgot, and the balance lost; contests and conciliations, as in most other countries, would have been merely among the few, and as it might have been necessary to serve their purposes, the people at large would have been flattered or threatened, and probably not a single stipulation made in their favour.

In Rome the people were miscrable, though they had three orders, the consuls, senators and tribunes, and approved the laws, and all for want of a genuine representation. The people were too numerous to assemble, and do any thing properly themselves; the voice of a few, the dupes of artifice, was called the voice of the people. It is difficult for the people to defend themselves against the arts and intrigues of the great, but by selecting a suitable number of men fixed to their interests to represent them, and to oppose ministers and senators. And the people's all depends on the number of the men selected, and the manner of doing it. To be convinced of this, we need only attend to the reason of the case, the conduct of the British commons, and of the Roman tribunes: equal liberty prevails in England, because there was a representation of the people, in fact and reality, to establish it; equal liberty never prevailed in Rome, because there was but the shadow of a representation. There were consuls in Rome annually elected to execute the laws, several hundred senators represented the great families; the body of the people annually chose tribunes from among themselves to defend them and

to secure their rights; I think the number of tribunes annually chosen never exceeded ten. This representation, perhaps, was not pro-
portionally so numerous as the representation proposed in the new
plan; but the difference will not appear to be so great, when it shall
be recollected, that these tribunes were chosen annually; that the
great patrician families were not admitted to these offices of tribunes, and that the people of Italy who elected the tribunes were a
long while, if not always, a small people compared with the people
of the United States. What was the consequence of this trifling representation? The people of Rome always elected for their tribunes
men conspicuous for their riches, military commands, professional
popularity, &c. great commoners, between whom and the noble
families there was only the shadowy difference of legal distinction.
Among all the tribunes the people chose for several centuries, they
had scarcely five real friends to their interests. These tribunes lived,
felt and saw, not like the people, but like the great patrician families, like senators and great officers of state, to get into which it was
evident by their conduct, was their sole object. These tribunes often
talked about the rights and prerogatives of the people, and that was
all; for they never even attempted to establish equal liberty: so far
from establishing the rights of the people, they suffered the senate,
to the exclusion of the people, to engross the powers of taxation;
those excellent and almost only real weapons of defence even the
people of England possess. The tribunes obtained that the people
should be eligible to some of the great offices of state, and marry, if
they pleased, into the noble families; these were advantages in their
nature, confined to a few elevated commoners, and of trifling importance to the people at large. . . .

    We may amuse ourselves with names; but the fact is, men will
be governed by the motives and temptations that surround their situation. Political evils to be guarded against are in the human character, and not in the name of patrician or plebian. Had the people of
Italy, in the early period of the republic, selected yearly, or bienni-
ally, four or five hundred of their best informed men, emphatically
from amongst themselves, these representatives would have formed
an honest and respectable assembly, capable of combining in them
the views and exertions of the people, and their respectability would
have procured them honest and able leaders, and we should have
seen equal liberty established. . . . Equal liberty never yet found
many advocates among the great: it is a disagreeable truth, that
power perverts men's views in a greater degree, than public employments inform their understandings—they become hardened in cer-

tain maxims, and more lost to fellow feelings. Men may always be too cautious to commit alarming and glaring inequities; but they, as well as systems, are liable to be corrupted by slow degrees. . . .

SPEECH OF WILLIAM GRAYSON DURING THE VIRGINIA RATIFICATION CONVENTION

June 1788

William Grayson was a London-trained lawyer who served with distinction in the Revolutionary War. A Virginia delegate to the Confederation Congress from 1784 to 1787, he was selected as one of the state's first senators after ratification. Grayson's selection as senator was engineered by his close political ally Patrick Henry, the leader of Virginia's Antifederalists. Grayson's tenure in Congress was short; he died in 1790, the year after Congress first met.

In this speech, Grayson attempts to dispel Federalist misinformation. They had expressed fear that political upheavals could not be controlled by the weak national government brought into being by the Articles of Confederation. A stronger national government, they argued, was necessary to prevent confusion, anarchy, and war. Pointing to Shays' Rebellion as an example, the Federalists noted that the states themselves were on the brink of anarchy. Grayson finds that though troubling, the revolt was effectively "crushed" by the "federal government," an indication that the confederation was not as weak as the Federalists implied. Quick-witted Federalists would have found some fault with this statement, as the government of Massachusetts suppressed the rebellion rather than the federal government.

Federalists also wrote that a stronger government was needed to prevent foreign powers from waging war on the United States. Grayson discusses various foreign nations here, arguing that none threatened the United States. Thus, there was no immediate need to form a new government. There are grave defects in the confederation, Grayson concedes, but they could be remedied with a few simple amendments. Federalists also pointed out that if the Constitution were not adopted, the union would likely split apart. Grayson counters that the states have important incentives to remain united.

Among the unusual sentiments expressed in the speech, and one that clearly marks it as that of an elite Antifederalist, is a preference for life terms for the president and senators. Life terms would allow these officials insulation from democratic impulses, allowing them to counterbalance the House. But Grayson notes that the House is not up to the task of balancing the Senate because the "democratic branch [is] marked with the strong features of aristocracy." In the end, the new system is simply too bold for Grayson to accept. As with many of Virginia's ruling class, Grayson was reluctant to cede power to a national government where his state, though the largest of the thirteen, could not determine policy and might well be outvoted.

Mr. Chairman, I must make a few observations on this subject; and, if my arguments are desultory, I hope I shall stand justified by the bad example which has been set me, and the necessity I am under of following my opponents through all their various recesses. I do not in the smallest degree blame the conduct of the gentlemen who represented this state in the general Convention. I believe that they endeavored to do all the good to this commonwealth which was in their power, and that all the members who formed that Convention did every thing within the compass of their abilities to procure the best terms for their particular states. That they did not do more for the general good of America, is perhaps a misfortune. They are entitled, however, to our thanks and those of the people. Although I do not approve of the result of their deliberations, I do not criminate or suspect the principles on which they acted. I desire that what I may say may not be improperly applied. I make no allusions to any gentleman whatever.

I do not pretend to say that the present Confederation is not defective. Its defects have been actually experienced. But I am afraid that they cannot be removed. It has defects arising from reasons which are inseparable from the nature of such governments, and which cannot be removed but by death.[22] All such governments, that ever existed, have uniformly produced this consequence—that particular interests have been consulted, and the general good, to which all wishes ought to be directed, has been neglected. But the particular disorders of Virginia ought not to be attributed to the Confederation. I was concerned to hear the local affairs of Virginia mentioned. If these make impressions on the minds of the gentlemen, why did not the Convention provide for removing the evils of the government of Virginia? If I am right, the states, with respect to their internal affairs, are left precisely as before, except in a few instances. Of course, the judiciary, should this government be adopted, would not be improved; the state government would be in this respect nearly the same; and the Assembly may, without judge or jury, hang as many men as they may think proper to sacrifice to the good of the public.[23] Our judiciary has been certainly improved in some respects since the revolution. The proceedings of our courts are not, at least, as rapid as they were under the royal government. . . .

The adoption of this government will not meliorate our own particular system. I beg leave to consider the circumstances of the Union antecedent to the meeting of the Convention at Philadelphia. We have been told of phantoms and ideal dangers to lead us into measures which will, in my opinion, be the ruin of our country. If the existence of those dangers cannot be proved, if there be no apprehension of wars, if there be no rumors of wars, it will place the subject in a different light, and plainly evince to the world that there cannot be any reason for adopting measures which we apprehend to be ruinous and destructive.[24] When this state proposed that the general government should be improved, Massachusetts was just recovered from a rebellion which had brought the republic to the brink of destruction—from a rebellion which was crushed by that federal government which is now so much contemned and abhorred: a vote of that august body for fifteen hundred men, aided by the exertions of the state, silenced all opposition, and shortly restored the public tranquillity. Massachusetts was satisfied that these internal commotions were so happily settled, and was unwilling to risk any similar distresses by theoretic experiments. Were the Eastern States willing to enter into this measure? Were they willing to accede to the proposal of Virginia?[25] In what manner was it received? Connecticut revolted at the idea. The Eastern States, sir, were unwilling to recommend a meeting of a convention. They were well aware of the dangers of revolutions and changes. Why was every effort used, and such uncommon pains taken, to bring it about? This would have been unnecessary, had it been approved of by the people. Was Pennsylvania disposed for the reception of this project of reformation? No, sir. She was even unwilling to amend her revenue laws, so as to make the five per centum operative.[26] She was satisfied with things as they were. There was no complaint, that ever I heard of, from any other part of the Union, except Virginia. This being the case among ourselves, what dangers were there to be apprehended from foreign nations? It will be easily shown that dangers from that quarter were absolutely imaginary. Was not France friendly? Unequivocally so. She was devising new regulations of commerce for our advantage. Did she harass us with applications for her money? Is it likely that France will quarrel with us? Is it not reasonable to suppose that she will be more desirous than ever to cling, after losing the Dutch republic, to her best ally? How are the Dutch? We owe them money, it is true; and are they not willing that we should owe them more? Mr. Adams applied to them for a new loan to the poor, despised Confederation.[27] They readily granted it. The Dutch have a fellow-feeling for us. They were in the same situation with ourselves.

. . . Loans from nations are not like loans from private men. Nations lend money, and grant assistance, to one another, from views of national interest. France was willing to pluck the fairest feather out of the British crown. This was her object in aiding us. She will not quarrel with us on pecuniary considerations. Congress considered it in this point of view; for when a proposition was made to make it a debt of private persons, it was rejected without hesitation. That respectable body wisely considered, that, while we remained their debtors in so considerable degree, they would not be inattentive to our interest.

With respect to Spain, she is friendly in a high degree. I wish to know by whose interposition was the treaty with Morocco made. Was it not by that of the king of Spain? Several predatory nations disturbed us, on going into the Mediterranean: the influence of Charles III. at the Barbary court, and four thousand pounds, procured as good a treaty with Morocco as could be expected. But I acknowledge it is not of any consequence, since the Algerines and people of Tunis have not entered into similar measures. We have nothing to fear from Spain; and, were she hostile, she could never be formidable to this country. Her strength is so scattered, that she never can be dangerous to us either in peace or war.

As to Portugal, we have a treaty with her, which may be very advantageous, though it be not yet ratified.

The domestic debt is diminished by considerable sales of western lands to Cutler, Sergeant, and Company; to Simms; and to Royal, Flint, and Company. The board of treasury is authorized to sell in Europe, or any where else, the residue of those lands.

An act of Congress has passed, to adjust the public debts between the individual states and the United States.

Was our trade in a despicable situation? I shall say nothing of what did not come under my own observation. When I was in Congress, sixteen vessels had had sea letters in the East India trade, and two hundred vessels entered and cleared out, in the French West India Islands, in one year.

I must confess that public credit has suffered, and that our public creditors have been ill used. This was owing to a fault at the head-quarters—to Congress themselves,—in not apportioning the debts on the different states, and in not selling the western lands at an earlier period. If requisitions have not been complied with, it must be owing to Congress, who might have put the unpopular debts on the back lands. Commutation is abhorrent to New England ideas. Speculation is abhorrent to the Eastern States. Those inconveniences have resulted from the bad policy of Congress.

There are certain modes of governing the people which will succeed. There are others which will not. The idea of consolidation is abhorrent to the people of this country. How were the sentiments of the people before the meeting of the Convention at Philadelphia? They had only one object in view. Their ideas reached no farther than to give the general government the five per centum impost, and the regulation of trade. When it was agitated in Congress, in the committee of the whole, this was all that was asked, or was deemed necessary. Since that period, their views have extended much farther. Horrors have been greatly magnified since the rising of the Convention.

We are now told by the honorable gentleman (Governor Randolph) that we shall have wars and rumors of wars, that every calamity is to attend us, and that we shall be runied and disunited forever, unless we adopt this Constitution. Pennsylvania and Maryland are to fall upon us from the north, like the Goths and Vandals of old; the Algerines, whose flat-sided vessels never came farther than Madeira, are to fill the Chesapeake with mighty fleets, and to attack us on our front; the Indians are to invade us with numerous armies on our rear, in order to convert our cleared lands into hunting-grounds; and the Carolinians, from the south, (mounted on alligators, I presume) are to come and destroy our cornfields, and eat up our little children! These, sir, are the mighty dangers which await us if we reject—dangers which are merely imaginary, and ludicrous in the extreme! Are we to be destroyed by Maryland and Pennsylvania? What will democratic states make war for, and how long since have they imbibed a hostile spirit?

But the generality are to attack us. Will they attack us after violating their faith in the first Union? Will they not violate their faith if they do not take us into their confederacy? Have they not agreed, by the old Confederation, that the Union shall be perpetual, and that no alteration should take place without the consent of Congress, and the confirmation of the legislatures of every state? I cannot think that there is such depravity in mankind as that, after violating public faith so flagrantly, they should make war upon us, also, for not following their example.

The large states have divided the back lands among themselves, and have given as much as they thought proper to the generality. For the fear of disunion, we are told that we ought to take measures which we otherwise should not. Disunion is impossible. The Eastern States hold the fisheries, which are their cornfields, by a hair. They have a dispute with the British government about their limits at this moment. Is not a general and strong government necessary for their interest? If ever nations have inducements to peace, the Eastern States now have. New York and Pennsylvania anxiously look forward for the fur trade. How can they obtain it but by union? Can the western posts be got or retained without union? How are the little states inclined? They are not likely to disunite. Their weakness will prevent them from quarrelling. Little men are seldom fond of quarrelling among giants. Is there not a strong inducement to union, while the British are on one side and the Spaniards on the other? Thank Heaven, we have a Carthage of our own!

But we are told that if we do not embrace the present moment, we are lost forever. Is there no difference between productive states and carrying states? If we hold out, will not the tobacco trade enable us to make terms with the carrying states? Is there nothing in a similarity of laws, religion, language, and manners? Do not these, and the intercourse and intermarriage between the people of the different states, invite them in the strongest manner to union?[28]

But what would I do on the present occasion to remedy the existing defects of the present Confederation? There are two opinions prevailing in the world—the one, that mankind can only be governed by force; the other, that they are capable of freedom and good government. Under a supposition that mankind can govern themselves, I would recommend that the present Confederation should be amended. Give Congress the regulation of commerce. Infuse new strength and spirit into the state governments; for, when the component parts are strong, it will give energy to the government, although it be otherwise weak. . . .

Apportion the public debts in such a manner as to throw the unpopular ones on the back lands. Call only for requisitions for the foreign interest, and aid them by loans. Keep on so till the American character be marked with some certain features. We are yet too young to know what we are fit for. The continual migration of people from Europe and the settlement of new countries on our western frontiers are strong arguments against making new experiments now in government. When these things are removed, we can, with greater prospect of success, devise changes. We ought to consider, as Montesquieu says, whether the construction of the government be suitable to the genius and disposition of the people, as well as a variety of other circumstances.

But if this position be not true, and men can only be governed by force, then be as gentle as possible. What, then, would I do? I would not take the British monarchy for my model. We have not materials for such a government in this country, although I will be bold to say, that it is one of the governments in the world by which liberty and property are best secured.[29] But I would adopt the following government. I would have a President for life, choosing his successor at the same time; a Senate for life, with the powers of the House of Lords; and a triennial House of Representatives, with the powers of the House of Commons in England.

By having such a President, we should have more independence and energy in the executive, and not be encumbered with the expense, &c., of a court and an hereditary prince and family. By such a Senate, we should have more stability in the laws, without having an odious hereditary aristocracy. By the other branch, we should be fully and fairly represented. If, sir, we are to be consolidated at all, we ought to be fully represented, and governed with sufficient energy, according to numbers, in both houses.

I admit that coercion is necessary in every government in some degree; that it is manifestly wanting in our present government, and that the want of it has ruined many nations. But I should be glad to know what great degree of coercion is in this Constitution, more than in the old government, if the states will refuse to comply with the requisitions, and they can only be compelled by means of an army.

Suppose the people will not pay the taxes; is not the sword to be then employed? The difference is this—that, by this Constitution, the sword is employed against individuals; by the other, it is employed against the states, which is more honorable. Suppose a general resistance to pay taxes in such a state as Massachusetts; will it not be precisely the same thing as a non-compliance with requisitions?

Will this Constitution remedy the fatal inconveniences of the clashing state interests? Will not every member that goes from Virginia be actuated by state influence? So they will also from every other state. Will the liberty and property of this country be secure under such a government? What, sir, is the present Constitution? A republican government founded on the principles of monarchy, with the three estates. Is it like the model of Tacitus or Montesquieu?[30] Are there checks in it, as in the British monarchy? There is an executive fetter in some parts, [but it is] as unlimited in others as a Roman dictator. A democratic branch marked with the strong features of aristocracy, and an aristocratic branch with all the impurities and imperfections of the British House of Commons, arising from the inequality of representation and the want of responsibility. There will be plenty of Old Sarums, if the new Constitution should be adopted.[31] Do we love the British so well as to imitate their imperfections? We could not effect it more than in that particular instance. Are we not all defects and corruption founded on an inequality of representation and want of responsibility? How is the executive? Contrary to the opinion of all the best writers, blended with the legislative. We have asked for bread, and they have given us a stone. I am willing to give the government the regulation of trade. It will be serviceable in regulating trade among the states. But I believe that it will not be attended with the advantages generally expected.

As to direct taxation—give up this, and you give up every thing, as it is the highest act of sovereignty: surrender up this inestimable jewel, and you throw away a pearl richer than all your tribe. But it has been said by an honorable gentleman, (Mr. Pendleton,) as well as I recollect, that there could be no such thing as an interference between the two legislatures, either in point of direct taxation, or in any other case whatsoever. An honorable gentleman, (Mr. Mason) has replied that they might interfere in the case of a poll tax. I will go farther, and say, that the case may happen in the judiciary. Suppose a state execution and a federal execution issued against the same man and the state officer and federal officer seize him at the same moment; would they divide the man in two, as Solomon directed the child to be divided who was claimed by two women? I suppose the general government, as being paramount, would prevail. How are two legislatures to coincide, with powers transcendent, supreme, and omnipotent? for such is the definition of a legislature. There must be an external interference, not only in the collection of taxes, but in the judiciary. Was there ever such a thing in any country before? Great Britain never went so far in the stamp act. . . . I never heard of two supreme coordinate powers in one and the same country before. I cannot conceive how it can happen. It surpasses every thing that I have read of concerning other governments, or that I can conceive by the utmost exertion of my faculties.

But, sir, as a cure for every thing, the democratic branch is elected by the people. What security is there in that? As has already been [demonstrated], their number is too small. Is not a small number more easy to be corrupted than a large one? Were not the *decemviri* chosen by them?[32] Was not Caesar himself the choice of the people? Did this render these agents so chosen by the people upright? If five hundred and sixty members are corrupted in the British House of Commons, will it not be easier to corrupt ninety-one members of the new Constitution? But the British House of Commons are corrupted from the same cause that our representatives will be: I mean, from the Old

Sarums among them—from the inequality of the representation. How many are legislating in this country yearly? It is thought necessary to have fifteen hundred representatives, for the great purposes of legislation, throughout the Union, exclusive of one hundred and sixty senators, which form a proportion of about one for every fifteen hundred persons. By the present Constitution, these extensive powers are to be exercised by the small number of ninety-one persons—a proportion almost twenty times less than the other. It must be degrading indeed to think that so small a number should be equal to so many! Such a preferential distinction must presuppose the happiest selection. They must have something divine in their composition, to merit such a pre-eminence. But my greatest objection is, that it will, in its operation, be found unequal, grievous, and oppressive. If it have any efficacy at all, it must be by a faction—a faction of one part of the Union against another. I think that it has a great natural imbecility within itself, too weak for a consolidated and too strong for a confederate government. But if it be called into action by a combination of seven states, it will be terrible indeed. We need be at no loss to determine how this combination will be formed. There is a great difference of circumstances between the states. The interest of the carrying states is strikingly different from that of the productive states. I mean not to give offence to any part of America, but mankind are governed by interest. The carrying states will assuredly unite, and our situation will be then wretched indeed. Our commodities will be transported on their own terms, and every measure will have for its object their particular interest. Let ill-fated Ireland be ever present to our view. We ought to be wise enough to guard against the abuse of such a government. Republics, in fact, oppress more than monarchies. If we advert to the page of history, we shall find this disposition too often manifested in republican governments. The Romans, in ancient, and the Dutch, in modern times, oppressed their provinces in a remarkable degree.

I hope that my fears are groundless; but I believe it as I do my creed, that this government will operate as a faction of seven states to oppress the rest of the union. But it may be said that we are represented, and cannot therefore be injured. A poor representation it will be! The British would have been glad to take America into the union, like the Scotch, by giving us a small representation. The Irish might be indulged with the same favor by asking for it. Will that lessen our misfortunes? A small representation gives us a pretense to injure and destroy. But, sir, the Scotch union is introduced by an honorable gentleman as an argument in favor of adoption. Would he wish his country to be on the same foundation as Scotland? They have but forty-five members in the House of Commons, and sixteen in the House of Lords.

These go up regularly in order to be bribed. The smallness of their number puts it out of their power to carry any measure. And this unhappy nation exhibits the only instance, perhaps, in the world, where corruption becomes a virtue. I devoutly pray that this description of Scotland may not be picturesque of the Southern States, in three years from this time!

NOTES

1. This speech was delivered directly after one by James Madison, in which the future president argued that one branch of the legislature should be directly elected by citizens to inspire popular confidence in the new regime. In this speech, Gerry (Madison's future vice president) counters by saying that popularly elected legislatures don't necessarily have the confidence of the people. In so arguing, he must have been thinking about his home state of Massachusetts, where the laws had been flaunted by the Shaysites despite the popularly elected legislature.

2. The "paper money" issue was an important one during the Confederation period. It divided wealthy Americans from their less fortunate peers. At the time, the American economy was generally starved for cash. The poor and middling class felt this cash shortage acutely. Basic transactions were made difficult for them because of the shortage, which resulted from a lack of gold and silver coinage. Many advocated that paper money be issued by states to serve as cash equivalents. This paper money usually caused inflation. The wealthy fought paper emissions. Being wealthy, they possessed cash reserves regardless of their scarcity, and they understandably did not want their fortunes diminished by inflation. Gerry, who happened to be one of the nation's wealthiest men, aimed to make the emission of paper money by the new regime unlikely.

3. Gerry's view was that for the good of the state, an executive often had to take actions that were unpopular. He therefore opposed direct election of the president. Only about a fifth of the delegates advocated direct election of the president. A much more likely option was to have Congress elect the president. But Gerry opposed that, too, because he wanted to preserve the executive's independence from Congress. A third alternative that Gerry initially favored was to have the state governors select the president. When that option was rejected, he proposed the electoral college, the system that was eventually adopted.

4. A freeholder was someone who owned land. Extending the right of suffrage "beyond the freeholders" meant that these states had eliminated landholding as a qualification for voting. Mason thinks it would be problematic for the national government to reintroduce that qualification for federal elections.

5. The convention was debating "money bills," those which raise taxes. Mason's view, following British practice, is that the popular branch, the House,

should retain the power of introducing such bills. This stipulation was written into and is still a part of the Constitution. His premise that the two branches should be differently composed and should have competing powers which balance each other is evident in this argument.

6. That is, sarcastically.

7. Many thought that Gerry's suggestions—for the president to have a life term, for the position to be hereditary, for a "proper Senate" (i.e., one made up of true aristocrats), and to abolish the states—were simply sarcastic. They are not. He is stating what would need to be done to inaugurate a mixed regime on the British model. Gerry himself thinks that kind of government beneficial, but he does not think that is feasible, given America's circumstances. He does hope to approximate a mixed regime as far as American circumstances will allow. Power must be shared with the states; there can be no true aristocracy in the Senate; and the people would revolt at the institution of a king—so these are not feasible alternatives, nor are they, in a practical sense, desirable to Gerry.

8. The convention was debating who would elect the president if no candidate received a majority in the electoral college. Allowing the Senate to choose from among the top vote-getters was unacceptable to Randolph. His objection spurred the convention to give that responsibility to members of the House of Representatives, who would vote not as individuals, but as state delegations with a single vote each.

9. This comment is a response to Elbridge Gerry's suggestion that the president be chosen by a small ad hoc committee composed of members of the House and Senate. Gerry's proposal was designed to keep the president from being beholden to the legislature as a whole.

10. The Constitution allows a state to have no more than one member of the House for every *thirty* thousand inhabitants (except if a state would have fewer than thirty thousand inhabitants). The convention had agreed to that number at the urging of George Washington. Earlier, the ratio of citizens to representatives had been set at a maximum of forty thousand to one. Because Washington was the presiding officer of the convention, he rarely made substantive speeches. This was one of only two instances he spoke on substantive issues in Philadelphia. As Mason notes, although this change lessened his objection to the lack of representation in the House, it did not eliminate the objection.

11. See Robert H. Webking, "Melancton Smith and the *Letters from the Federal Farmer*," *William & Mary Quarterly*, 3d ser., 44, no. 3 (1987): 510–28.

12. These letters have not been identified.

13. Among the topics treated in Letter II was the necessity of a bill of rights.

14. As was common practice, Federal Farmer refers to the Northernmost states as the "Eastern" states. He separates these states from the "Middle" states by saying the Eastern states are highly democratic. In saying so, he is dividing Massachusetts, New Hampshire, Rhode Island, and Connecticut (the Eastern states); from New York, New Jersey, Delaware, Pennsylvania, and Maryland (the Middle states); and Virginia, North Carolina, South Carolina, and Georgia (the Southern states).

15. If ten of thirteen states claimed to be small, the three states left not claiming this status must have been Virginia, Pennsylvania, and Massachusetts. These were the three most populous states. Virginia and Pennsylvania were clearly large states in terms of territory as well, but with Maine a part of Massachusetts, it too claimed a good deal of territory.

16. In this sentence, Federal Farmer offers a succinct and plausible explanation for the Senate's extensive powers. After the Great Compromise, small states realized they were as powerful as large states only in the Senate, so they pushed for extensive powers there. For those like Federal Farmer who believed that the (hopefully democratic) House should possess powers equal to the aristocratic Senate, this result was disturbing.

17. Article I, section 4, clause 1.

18. The "carrying states" are the Northern states that were more mercantile, as opposed to the "non-carrying states" of the South that produced goods but relied on Northern ships and merchants to transport them.

19. Federal Farmer notes this because the goods entering Connecticut and New Jersey were usually cleared through New York's harbor. During the confederation period, New York was taxing these goods, and Connecticut and New Jersey were not receiving any of the revenue. The main reason the Constitution was so popular in those two states (and unpopular in New York) was that it would end that practice, with the new national government presumably sharing its revenue more equitably.

20. Aristocrats were called "Morrisites" after Pennsylvania's Robert Morris, one of the nation's most prominent merchants. As superintendant of finance, he was the architect of the nation's treasury system during the Confederation period.

21. Jean Louis De Lolme's *Constitution of England* (1775) attributed that nation's good political fortunes to a proper balance of popular and aristocratic interests, brought in part by numerous popular representation in the House of Commons.

22. Here Grayson indicates that he believes that a sovereign national government is indispensible, rather than just a stronger confederation.

23. Unlike most Antifederalists, Grayson does not fear a national court system—in fact, he seems to think that it would be an improvement on the administration of justice by the states. While most critics of the Constitution complained that the national judiciary would eclipse that of the states, Grayson believes that the national government did not go far enough in setting guidelines for the administration of justice. His assessment that the states, even his own, are very defective is highly unusual for an Antifederalist. The populist nature of justice on the state level is seemingly what Grayson objects to.

24. In this sentence, Grayson summarizes the subject of the first half of his speech: there is little reason to immediately adopt the Constitution that was formulated because the states are not threatened externally, nor is there a danger of civil war or anarchy within the states.

25. The "proposal of Virginia" to which Grayson refers was the call for a convention at Annapolis in 1786. This convention, called to amend the Articles of Confederation's commercial provisions, failed for lack of attendance but was a vital precursor to the Philadelphia convention of 1787.

26. During the Confederation period, several attempts were made to secure a steady source of revenue for the national government. All of these attempts failed. Though New York and Rhode Island were the states that actively resisted these reforms, Grayson cites Pennsylvania for obstructing this reform. The "five per centum" tax Grayson refers to was one such proposal. It would have allowed the confederation to directly tax imports at 5 percent of their value. Adoption of the 5 percent plan would have required Pennsylvania to amend its constitution, but it failed to do so.

27. John Adams had successfully negotiated a loan from the Dutch.

28. By "productive states," Grayson means the Southern states that produced agricultural goods, like tobacco, for export. The "carrying states" are the Northern states that built and operated ships for the Atlantic "carrying" trade. Antifederalists typically would point to the differences between these states to argue that they were too different to coexist under a single effective government. Grayson's view is very different. These states are natural partners, he points out. Both have an interest in maintaining the Union. This point was made to dispel the Federalist view that the states would split apart if they did not adopt the Constitution.

29. In saying "we have not the materials for such a government," Grayson is noting that the United States lacks both a royal family and a hereditary aristocracy. Britain's government cannot be copied in its entirety, therefore, but a mixed republic resembling the British model may be attempted, and it is what Grayson favors at the national level, if a national government must be formed.

30. Tacitus was Rome's foremost historian. He wrote in the early part of the second century A.D.

31. The reference to Old Sarum is to a particularly malapportioned legislative district in Britain. Grayson's claim is that the Constitution's mandate of equal representation of states in the Senate, there will be malapportionment as severe as in England.

32. The decemvirs were a commission of ten patriarchs who governed early Rome. The decemvirs were instituted to placate the plebeians, or common citizens, but ultimately failed to do so.

7

Post-ratification Views

As noted in chapter 1, the ratification debate lasted only a short time, about nine months. If one includes the time the convention met, just over a year passed from the conception of the Constitution to its legal approval. The documents in the previous chapters are from that year. After ratification, the political context changed, but the Antifederalists did not disappear. Nor did the issues they cared about. After ratification, the Antifederalists tried to convince the nation of the necessity for amendments. Initially, their hope was that a second convention would meet. After most state legislatures rejected that option, Antifederalists turned to seeking seats in the new Congress. Letters and newspaper editorials noted that the Constitution was faulty and that the public should therefore elect those who would perfect it.

The Antifederalist platform did not resonate nearly so well as the Federalists' arguments. Federalists asserted that the friends of the Constitution should be allowed to bring the new government to life. After all, the Constitution's critics might sabotage the new government to prove their points about it. Federalists also slyly drew a parallel between the Antifederalists and the Shaysites that was erroneous but to their political benefit. The Antifederalists had opposed a proposed government, while the Shaysites had opposed a government in practice. This distinction was a crucial one in Antifederalists' minds. What the Shaysites did was irresponsible; it set an anarchical precedent. Yet it was relatively easy for the Federalists to portray their opponents as not just critics of the Constitution, but critics of government itself. In the wake of Shays' Rebellion, those unwilling to abide by the dictates of government were severely stigmatized. Therefore, any association the Federalists could make between Antifederalists and Shaysites worked in favor of the Federalists. To prevent this misinformation from being believed, Antifederalists repeatedly vowed to abide by the ratified Constitution and advised their constituents to do the same.

Eventually, these Antifederalist protests were understood. The public came to realize that those who had criticized the Constitution during the ratification process would not attempt to bring the new government down. The Antifederalists, believers in giving the people a say in their governance, understood that popular ratification legitimated the Constitution. The new government had been sanctioned by those representing a majority of America's citizens. It was the law of the land, and it had to be abided by. In this new context, their thinking turned from arguing against the Constitution to helping define what the Constitution meant. The document was sufficiently openended to admit of multiple interpretations. The Antifederalists, along with some discontented Federalists led by James Madison and Thomas Jefferson, created a party with a constitutional philosophy that was very acceptable to them. This party aimed to maintain dual sovereignty and adopted James Wilson's argument that the national government possessed only enumerated powers. Even if this was not many Antifederalists' ideal, it was an arrangement they could live with because it preserved a good deal of state power. Together these groups administered the government as the majority party after 1800.

The following documents trace the trajectory of Antifederalist constitutional thought after ratification. Several of the pieces here relate how ratification itself changed matters. As a legally sanctioned document, the Antifederalists felt bound to it. Like the delegates to the New York ratifying convention, many initially hoped for a second convention. But it was not to be. In the wake of their major victory, the Federalists were reluctant to do something that could bring the whole process back to square one. As Federalists drew parallels between their opponents and Shaysites or Tories, Antifederalists (like "Truth") protested. Later, as the states prepared to hold their federal elections, political hopefuls like John Francis Mercer and Arthur Lee argued that they should be elected because of their demonstrated commitment to amendments.

While almost all Antifederalists acquiesced to the legal Constitution, there were a few exceptions. Connecticut's James Wadsworth was one. His letter to Governor Samuel Huntington resigning his judicial post was prompted by his refusal to swear allegiance to the Constitution. Such a stance was very rare, but it does show what the Antifederalists could have done, had they been so inclined. Instead of boycotting the new government or actively fighting it, they chose to affect its course from within. The documents reprinted here give some indication of the great variety of forums in which these views were made known. Professions of acquiescence to the Constitution occur in diaries, private letters, public statements, jury instructions, congressional speeches, and electioneering "advertisements." The Antifederalists' conservative Constitution-abiding views eventually allowed them to greatly affect the new government. Due to their efforts, the American government remained a federal system, one of its distinctive features to this day.

LETTER OF JOHN QUINCY ADAMS TO WILLIAM CRANCH

February 16, 1788

The United States' sixth president, John Quincy Adams, graduated from Harvard as the Constitution was being formulated in Philadelphia. The winter of 1787–1788 found him in Newburyport, Massachusetts, studying law with Theophilus Parsons. Adams was just twenty at the time. This letter, written shortly after the Massachusetts state convention ratified the document, explains his objections, but it also indicates that he has acquiesced to the result. A diary entry Adams wrote on February 7 provides an initial explanation: "upon the decision of this question I find myself on the weaker side, I think it my duty to submit without murmuring against what is not to be helped. In our Government, opposition to the acts of the majority of the people is rebellion to all intents and purposes."[1] In the following letter he provides an additional reason for disassociating himself from the Antifederalists, noting that they were a rather shabby lot in Massachusetts, men with whom he did not care to be connected.

William Cranch was Adams' cousin and lifelong friend. Forty years after this letter was written, Cranch returned it to Adams. Upon reading his own comments, Adams—then president of the United States—confided to his diary that though he had been "so sincere, so earnest, so vehement in my opinions . . . time had crumbled them to dust." In 1827, President Adams viewed his thoughts as "monumental errors" whose "best use is to teach me a lesson of humility, and of forbearance."[2]

The great Question it seems is decided, and according to your wishes. You and Freeman are both pretty confident, that I should have been converted, had I attended the debates:[3] this I will acknowledge, that had I been a member, it is probable I should have given a federal vote; not from the arguments and characters which favoured that side, but from those which appeared on the other. Not because a Dana, a King, a Parsons, a Bowdoin, a Hancock and a long train of the fathers of their Country supported the Constitution, with all the captivating charms of eloquence, and the weighty influence of conscious integrity, but because, a Willard, a Spring, a Thompson, a Bishop, and a number more who have appeared to wish nothing but a subversion of all government, were the only opposers.—The great points upon which the opposition in my mind was founded, were scarcely mentioned in convention; I must freely acknowledge, that I still lament, the want of an adequate representation of the people, and of rotation in the offices of government: the blending of the legislative and executive powers in the Senate; and the indefinite powers granted to the administrators; but I am convinced that opposition now would be attended with immediate evils, without being productive of any good effects, and you may now consider me as a strong federalist; though I should make a poor disputant in favour of that side.—The convention in New Hampshire are now in session. The appearances are against the Constitution; but the influence of abilities, of property, and of example will probably have the same effect there that they had in our convention, and a small majority may decide in imitation of Massachusetts. . . .

CIRCULAR LETTER OF THE NEW YORK CONVENTION

July 26, 1788

New York's Antifederalists hoped this document would jump-start the quest for amendments. They believed that many state legislatures would follow their lead in calling for a second constitutional convention. Besides their own state legislature, only Virginia did.

Antifederalists had outnumbered Federalists in the New York convention by a margin of two to one. During their deliberations, the conventions of New Hampshire and Virginia ratified the Constitution. Both ratifications were critical. New Hampshire was the ninth state to approve of the Constitution. Its approval satisfied the Constitution's own requirement that nine states needed to ratify it. Virginia was the largest and wealthiest state. Its ratification ensured that the Constitution would be implemented. New Yorkers, including the Antifederalists, wanted to amend the document and retain the national capital. Pursuing these goals necessitated ratification. If Federalists in the New York convention would agree to recommended amendments and a letter calling for a second convention, enough Antifederalists would join with them to endorse the Constitution. This letter was written to effect that compromise. It was written by a committee the night before New York's convention approved the Constitution by a vote of thirty to twenty-seven. That committee consisted of Federalist John Jay, who would become the nation's first chief justice, and Antifederalists John Lansing (see chapter 2) and Melancton Smith (see chapter 4). Approval of this letter was the last act of New York's ratifying convention, and it occurred on July 26, 1788. Ten days later, the letter appeared in the Poughkeepsie Country Journal. *Copies of the letter were sent to every state governor.*

Circular Letter from the Convention of the State of New-York, to the Executives of the different States, to be laid before their respective Legislatures.

SIR, We the Members of the Convention of this State, have deliberately and maturely considered the Constitution proposed for the United States.

Several articles in it appear so exceptionable to a majority of us, that nothing but the fullest confidence of obtaining a revision of them by a General Convention, and an invincible reluctance to separating from our sister States, could have prevailed upon a sufficient number to ratify it, without stipulating for previous amendments.

We all unite in opinion, that such revisions will be necessary, to recommend it to the approbation and support of a numerous body of our constituents.

We observe, that amendments have been proposed, and are anxiously desired, by several of the States as well as by this, and we think it of great importance, that effectual measures be immediately taken for calling a Convention, to meet at a period not far remote; for we are convinced, that the apprehensions and discontents which those articles occasion, cannot be removed or allayed, unless an act to provide for it be among the first that shall be passed by the new Congress.

As it is essential that an application for the purpose should be made to them by two thirds of the States, we earnestly exhort and request the Legislature of your State (or Commonwealth) to take the earliest opportunity of making it. We are persuaded, that a similar one will be made by our Legislature at their next session; and we ardently wish and desire, that the other States may concur, in adopting and promoting the measure.

It cannot be necessary to observe, that no government, however constructed, can operate well, unless it possesses the confidence and good will of the great body of the people; and as we desire nothing more than that the amendments proposed by this or other States, be submitted to the consideration and decision of a general Convention, we flatter ourselves, that motives of mutual affection and conciliation will conspire with the obvious dictates of sound policy, to induce even such of the States, as may be content with every article in the constitution, to gratify the reasonable desires of that numerous class of American citizens, who are anxious to obtain amendments of some of them.

Our amendments will manifest, that none of them originated in local views, as they are such, as if acceded to, must equally affect every State in the Union.

Our attachment to our sister States, and the confidence we repose in them, cannot be more forcibly demonstrated, than by acceding to a government, which many of us think very imperfect, and devolving the power of determining, whether that government shall be rendered perpetual in its present form, or altered agreeable to our wishes, or a minority of the States with whom we unite.

We request the favour of your Excellency to lay this letter before the Legislature of your State (or Commonwealth) and we are persuaded, that your regard for our national harmony and good government will induce you to promote a measure, which we are unanimous in thinking, very conducive to those interesting objects.

We have the honor to be, with the highest respect, Your Excellency's most obedient servants,

By the unanimous Order of the Convention,

GEO. CLINTON, President

PRIVATE LETTER OF JAMES HANNA TO THREE PENNSYLVANIA ANTIFEDERALISTS

August 15, 1788

Chapter 5 demonstrated that much of the virulent commentary against the Constitution was written by Pennsylvanians. The reason for this was plain: Federalists used questionable tactics to hastily ratify the document, simultaneously dismissing any Antifederalist input. Discontent culminated in the Carlisle riots and in the petition campaign instructing the Pennsylvania legislature not to accept the determination of the Pennsylvania con-

vention. Most virulent commentary was written in the eight months between Pennsylvania's ratification and New York's. After it was clear that the Constitution was ratified, Antifederalist opposition in Pennsylvania softened, just as it did in other states. This letter, written by one of the convention's delegates, is indicative of how Antifederalists moderated their views.

Hanna espouses the orthodox position that the Constitution must be submitted to and that choosing to do otherwise would produce anarchy. But he also instructs his colleagues not to fade away. The Antifederalists must not give up all opposition; they must simply pursue their objectives within constitutional bounds. Like the New Yorkers, Hanna hoped to continue the pressure for amendments. His efforts in this regard center on organizing a convention of Antifederalists to be held in Bucks County. The three men to whom the letter was addressed lived in the extreme southern part of the county, while Hanna lived in Newtown, the county seat. A convention was organized, meeting on August 25, which reiterated the Antifederalists' call for amendments.

The important crisis now approaching (confident I am you will think with me) demands the most serious attention of every friend of American liberty. The Constitution of the United States is now adopted by eleven states in the Union, and no doubt the other two will follow their example; for, however just the sentiments of the opposition may be, I do conceive it would be the height of madness and folly, and in fact a crime of very detrimental consequence to our country, to refuse to acquiesce in a measure received in form by so great a majority of our country; not only to ourselves individually, but to the community at large. For the worst that we can expect from a bad form of government is anarchy and confusion, with all its common train of grievances, and by an opposition in the present situation of affairs, we are sure of it. On the other hand, by a sullen and inactive conduct, it will give the promoters and warm advocates of the plan an opportunity (if any such design they have) to shackle us with those manacles that we fear may be formed under color of law, and we be led to know it is constitutional, when it is too late to extricate ourselves and posterity from a lasting bondage.

To you it is not worth while to animadvert on the plain and pointed tendency the Constitution has to this effect, and how easily it may be accomplished in power under its influence. That virtue is not the standard which has principally animated the adoption of the Constitution in this state I believe is too true. Let us, therefore, as we wish to serve our country, and show the world that those only who wished amendments were truly Federal, adopt the conduct of our fellow citizens in the back counties. Let us, as freemen, call a meeting of those citizens who wish for amendments, in a committee of the county, delegated from each township, for the purpose expressed in a copy of the [circular letter] inclosed. In promoting a scheme of this kind, I hope we shall not only have the satisfaction of seeing the minds and exertions of all who wish for amendments center in this object, which will swallow others more injurious, but that we will enjoy the supreme felicity of having assisted in snatching from slavery a once happy and worthy people.

I therefore hope you will undertake to call together your township, have delegates chosen to represent them in a committee to be held at the house of George Piper, on Monday the 21st inst. at nine o'clock in the forenoon, for the purpose of appointing delegates to represent them in the state conference, and for giving them instructions, etc.

If you should apprehend the people will not call a town meeting for the purpose, that you will, as we intend here, write or call on a few of the most respectable people of your township, to attend at the general meeting, as they intend to do at Philadelphia, if they cannot accomplish their purpose in the other way.

Your usual public spirit on occasions of this kind, I am sure, needs no spur. We shall, therefore, rest assured that we will meet a representation of the township *committed to your charge* on the day appointed.

TRUTH

Boston Gazette, September 1, 1788

"Truth" responds to a brief editorial by "Laco" in the Massachusetts Centinel. *Massachusetts Antifederalists suggested in print that Samuel Adams and Elbridge Gerry be elected to Congress. Laco responded by saying that electing them would be like electing Thomas Hutchinson or Timothy Ruggles, two prominent Massachusetts natives who had sided with the British during the Revolution. Laco felt that it was wrong to press for "the appointment of the enemies of a plan of government, to be its guardians."[4] But by comparing Adams and Gerry to Hutchinson (the last royal governor) and Ruggles, he implied that they were disloyal and perhaps even enemies of the state. Truth points out the absurdity of portraying these two revolutionary heroes as traitors simply for having qualms about the Constitution.*

The distinguished effrontery of the writers, who have lately appeared in the *Centinel*, in placing the "early" and "decided" friends of the Revolution on the same footing with two of the most execrable traitors which the state of Massachusetts has produced, has met the resentment of the honest and respectable of every denomination. To mention a Gerry and an Adams in the same page with a Ruggles and a Hutchinson, as objects of comparison, is a profanation of freedom, and an insult upon every real whig in the community. The shuffling and contemptible Laco, that—but I forbear personalities, as I detest the authors of those infamous scurrilities with which some of our modern papers are crowded—personalities, Messrs. Edes, which were execrated as long as the open enemies and lukewarm friends of the Revolution were the objects of them, by the same persons who now read them with pleasure when the firmest, wisest, and most resolute supporters of this momentous event are the subjects of their infamous and accumulated slanders. I am sometimes led to question whether this town is the same, or whether its inhabitants or their principles are the same as they were, when the first effort of American heroism disclosed itself in the expulsion of the British regiments after the horrid massacre of our citizens. Would the people then tamely have submitted to the names of Hutchinson and Adams being insolently compared, in order that the reputation of this last and steady patriot should be infamously traduced. But *they* do not now; they feel the insult, and execrate the insidious attempt—to blast the long tried virtues of this hoary patriot, bending with age, venerable with cares, but firm in courage and persevering in his integrity; whose strong marked features denote the soul within—hated for his consistency—hated for the virtues which proclaim his fame and fix his immortality. Yet Laco says he is an enemy to the Federal Constitution, and surely Laco is an "honorable man"; so are they all "honorable" who are his open or concealed enemies, who basely mean to pierce the heart of liberty with a dagger when they appear merely to aim the stroke at the character of Adams.[5]

It is very certain indeed that this sage and enlightened statesman has not "wholly" approved of the Constitution which is now the great political medium by which we are united, and under the influence of which we are to hope that our freedom will be secured and our commerce extended. But is Mr. Adams the only man who is in a similar predicament? Have the public testimonials of a Franklin, a Washington, a Jay, or a Hancock been expressive of the high approbation, of the blind idolatry with which many have affected to contemplate this fancied model of perfection—in saying it is the "greatest single effort of human wisdom?" Does the finished politician of Braintree[6] declare that it is beyond the reach of amendments? Not a character of the first rank throughout America has pretended it.

Where then is the crime of doubting its superlative excellence, when the Convention, which formed the Constitution, declared it to be the result of compromise, and by no means the object of their entire approbation. To suppose the united wisdom of America, after a long and dispassionate enquiry, cannot improve upon the labor of thirty of her citizens, however respectable, is paying a very extravagant compliment to them, at the expense of the rest. Let us be wise and temperate; but in justice to him, let the citizens of Boston respect and revere the man, whose resolution has been invincible, and whose wisdom has been only equalled by his virtue.

The following three letters each advocate the election of former Antifederalists to Congress. Two of the letters were written by prospective candidates who wished to gain office, John Francis Mercer of Maryland and Arthur Lee of Virginia. This active electioneering was a very unusual practice for the time. Societal norms generally dictated that political hopefuls not actively seek votes. Candidates were supposed to be "disinterested" in personal achievements and without substantial ambition, meaning that they should be convinced to stand for office rather than actively run for it. While many politicians worked behind the scenes to effect their own election, most scrupulously avoided campaigning. The presence of these two letters indicates how critical these Antifederalists thought the first federal elections were.

Mercer was the Marylander who briefly attended the Philadelphia convention and wrote out a list of delegates whom he thought favored a king on August 6 (see chapter 2). Maryland's election law was formulated to ensure a Federalist sweep in the first federal election. It allowed every voter to cast a ballot for each of the state's six districts regardless of which district they resided in. Since Federalists were a firm majority statewide, each of the Antifederalist candidates was defeated by a sizable margin. Mercer garnered 2,339 votes in the Third District race to Benjamin Contee's 5,476. Though he would lose his first race for the U.S. Congress (he had been a member of the Continental Congress from 1782 to 1785), Mercer became a member of the Second Congress, winning a special election necessitated by the resignation of William Pinkney. He was reelected to the Third Congress. Mercer eventually served as governor of Maryland from 1801 to 1803.

Arthur Lee also was not elected to Congress, even though he hailed from the most prominent family in the United States. His brothers were Richard Henry Lee (see chapter 3 for his letter explaining why he did not endorse the Constitution at the Philadelphia convention) and Francis Lightfoot Lee, a signer of the Declaration of Independence. Arthur Lee was trained as a medical doctor and a lawyer at the best schools in Europe. He had also been a delegate to the Continental Congress from 1781 to 1784. The returns from the race in Virginia's Seventh District have been lost, but John Page, a Federalist allied with James Madison, represented the district in the First Congress. Lee died in 1792. Both Lee's and Mercer's letters were printed privately and circulated locally.

Writing in a much more orthodox manner, "E" makes his electioneering plea on behalf of Antifederalists generally. E's views on what portions of the Constitution needed amending are familiar. The new wrinkle is the acknowledgment that "it has become the duty of good citizens to make a beginning with the Constitution as it is." It is important to note that all three of these letters take pains to show their acceptance of the Constitution and the need for pursuing amendments from within its framework. The real identity of "E" is unknown.

"E"

Boston Gazette, December 8, 1788

As the choice of federal Representatives is soon to take place, it is essentially necessary for the good of the Union, that those men be chosen who are the most likely to promote the general desire of the people at large—men who are of the persuasion that amendments to the new proposed Constitution are absolutely requisite and necessary to secure the freedom, security, and perfect confidence of every individual throughout the Union. That amendments are necessary you are requested to submit the following to the candid observation of your readers.

To the FREEMEN of MASSACHUSETTS: Friends and Countrymen! A fellow citizen, who is impressed with real anxiety at the approaching crisis in our public affairs, begs leave to address a few words to you. Whilst the enterprising and ambitious are pressing forward to the harvest of office and the emolument which they promise themselves under the new Constitution, he freely resigns all hopes of private advantage from the government, and feels no other interest than that which every citizen ought to feel in the misfortunes or prosperity of his country. He expects no benefit from the administration of public affairs but that which every individual will share in common with himself; he fears no misfortunes but those which will equally affect every member of the community. With these views and motives, which are alike interesting to every good citizen, he flatters himself he shall be heard with attention.

Liberty was the avowed object of the late glorious Revolution in search of which we waded with patience and resolution through all the horrors of a civil war; and the constitutions of the several states were framed with admirable wisdom, according to the best models, and upon the noblest principles of civil liberty. One only defect remained. The general government of the continent under the late Articles of Confederation, was too feeble to secure the safety of the people. Its defects were evident; and yet, as by a studied contrivance, they were suffered to remain, with hardly an attempt to remedy them until the public affairs of the continent had sunk into utter imbecility and ruin. The cry, at length, for a new form of continental government, became loud and universal.

A continental convention was called, the hopes of the people were raised to the highest pitch of expectation, and the sun never beheld a more glorious opportunity of establishing a happy form of government. Nothing short of the most glaring defects could have excited any shadow of opposition. But it is to be feared some selfish and artful men amongst us were but too willing to avail themselves of so favorable an opportunity of consulting the profit and power of the future governors of the continent, at the expense of the liberties of the people. Whether, however, it was the effect of accident or design, most glaring defects appear in the Constitution which they have proposed to the people. These defects have been freely stated by writers in the public papers throughout the continent, as well as in the debates of the several state conventions. Indeed many of these defects seem now to be generally acknowledged, even by those men who, there is too much reason to fear, would still wish to evade their amendment and to retain them in the system. Some of these defects are very glaring and important; others, perhaps, in the heat of contention have been exaggerated. One or two of the most considerable, I shall attempt briefly to lay before you.

The future Congress, if the new Constitution be not amended, will be vested with unlimited powers; the state governments, which have been founded on the most excellent constitutions in the world, will crumble into ruin, or dwindle into shadows; and, in their stead, an enormous, unwieldy government will be erected, which must speedily fall to pieces by its own weight, and leave us to the wretched alternative of anarchy or tyranny; whereas by a due temperature, the continental government may be clothed with all necessary powers for the management of foreign affairs, and leave the state governments in possession of such powers as will enable them to regulate our internal concerns which a continental government can never effectually reach. It is just as absurd to suppose that the general government of the whole empire can regulate the internal police of the several states, as to believe that the several states could regulate our foreign trade, and protect us in our intercourse with foreign nations. The latter we have already tried without success; the former will be found equally impracticable.

Another defect in the Federal Constitution is equally alarming. No security is provided for the rights of individuals; no bill of rights is framed nor is any privilege of freemen secured from the invasion of governors. Trust me, my fellow citizens! We shall not be more powerful or more respected abroad, for being liable to oppression at home; but on the contrary, the freest states have ever been the most powerful. Yet with us no barriers will remain against slavery, under the new continental government, if it be not amended. The state governments by the express terms of the Constitution can afford no protection to their citizens, and not even a single right is defined or stipulated, which the subject may appeal to against the will and pleasure of the moment.

These circumstances and others of a like tendency have excited great opposition, but the absolute necessity of a continental government of some sort has silenced the opposition of those, who were dissatisfied with the present Constitution, first in the Continental Convention, and afterwards in most of the conventions of the states. The wiser, if not the major, part of the Continental Convention would have produced to us a much better form of continental union, had it been in their power, but they preferred this to none; and in the different states, the wisest and best of the people have acquiesced in the scheme of adopting it in its present form, from the hope of obtaining those amendments which the Constitution itself provides for the attaining, provided two-thirds of Congress, or two-thirds of the state legislatures, shall concur in requiring them. Without such a clause of obtaining amendments, there is little doubt but a majority of the freemen of America would have spurned at the idea of subjecting themselves to the other terms of the new Constitution; with this clause of obtaining amendments, it has become the duty of good citizens to make a beginning with the Constitution as it is, confiding in the hope of obtaining all essential amendments in a constitutional mode. In this mode which is provided, it is certainly more eligible to reform the Constitution than by any violent or irregular opposition to attempt to overthrow it. We must have a continental government, or we are an undone people. At the same time we ought to preserve our liberties, if possible, so far as they may consist with our essential protection. If those two points can be attained, and this extensive continent held together, in the course of a few years, we may, at once, be the greatest and happiest people on earth.

JOHN FRANCIS MERCER: LETTER DECLARING HIS CANDIDACY FOR THE HOUSE OF REPRESENTATIVES

December 20, 1788

The organization of the new federal government has presented a very awful crisis to these States—Individual happiness and national prosperity are deeply involved in its first movements—The contrariety of opinion discovered throughout the continent with respect to its leading features—splendid expectations on one part—fears and disquietude on the other—the existing separation of two states heretofore united by the ties of blood, common interest, sufferings and success—the terms and instructions which five others have annexed to their ratifications, must satisfy every dispassionate mind, that mutual concession can alone produce that harmony and concord, without which the government will be neither happy in its operations, or of lasting duration—They must also prove, that to elect men to administer this government, who are altogether enthusiastic admirers of this constitution without any amendments, will not produce a real representation of the interests and wishes of the people, but tend to establish that violent adherence to party spirit and views, which destroys the mild influence of reason, the only true principle of republican government.

With these sentiments, I offer myself to represent the third district of this state in the new congress.

The conduct I have hitherto pursued in this state, however ineffectual it has been, still affords strong evidence that I am the decided friend to those declaratory acts and amendments, which will effectually guard the great and fundamental rights of the people.—These can admit of no delay.

I am also persuaded that several alterations in its form are highly necessary; but the government being adopted, and the necessities of the union requiring its immediate and energetic execution, all changes that might tend to retard its operations, should be gradually and cautiously effected, and the general sense of the continent previously consulted. If under these impressions I should meet your approbation, I shall hope your assistance at the ensuing election, in confidence that my conduct will so far correspond with your expectations. I am, with respect and esteem,

Your Obedient Servt
John Francis Mercer

ARTHUR LEE: LETTER TO THE FREEHOLDERS OF VIRGINIA'S SEVENTH DISTRICT

January [?], 1789

To the FREEHOLDERS of the Counties of GLOUCESTER, MIDDLE-SEX, ESSEX, KING and QUEEN, KING WILLIAM, CAROLINE, WESTMORELAND, RICHMOND, NORTHUMBERLAND, and LANCASTER:

WOODBERRY, *in Richmond County*

Gentlemen,
When I offer myself, as a Candidate to represent you in the General Congress of the United States, I think it proper to declare the Principles, which shall govern my Conduct, if I have the Honour of being elected.

In my Mind, it is the Duty of every good Man to submit to the Determination of the Majority of his Fellow-Citizens and therefore, although in my Judgment, the Constitution required Amendments, previous to its Adoption, yet I shall always think it incumbent on me to support what the Convention—after a full and fair Discussion—has adopted, until it shall be altered in the Mode which the Constitution itself points out.

For the same Reason, I shall deem it my Duty to use every Effort for obtaining those Amendments, which have been sanctioned by so great a Majority of the Convention, and by almost the unanimous Sense of the General Assembly. There is every Reason to hope, that the new Constitution—so amended as to remove the Apprehensions and secure the Confidence of the People—will promote our Interests at home, and our Responsibility abroad. But this will very much depend upon the Laws and Regulations of the first Congress, and the Train of Administration in which they place the new Government.

After twelve Years public Employment in the high and confidential Offices of Government, both at home and abroad, it may be permitted me to hope, that I, in some Measure, merit the Confidence of my Country, both as to Discernment of what is useful to the Public, and Integrity to pursue it.—Upon this Hope, and upon the Principles I have declared, I must rest the Success of my Election:—But whatever may be your Determination, Gentlemen, I shall always wish the Prosperity of the People, under the new Government, and endeavour to promote, as far as may be in my Power the particular Interests of this District.

> *I have the Honour to be, with the greatest Respect,*
> Gentlemen,
> *Your most obedient Servant,*
> ARTHUR LEE

Oaths of allegiance were important rituals to the founding generation. These oaths had been used to separate Loyalists from Patriots during the Revolutionary War. Federalists had every intention of applying similar loyalty tests under the new regime. Doing so would place the Antifederalists in a difficult position. On the one hand, it would be difficult for them to be seen changing course. Consistency is valued in politics, and swearing allegiance to the Constitution made it appear that the Antifederalists would change their tune simply to remain politically viable. If, on the other hand, they refused to swear allegiance to the Constitution, Federalists could charge their opponents with flaunting the law. Almost all Antifederalists in positions of authority who were required to take such oaths did so. "ABCD" points out that in doing so, the Antifederalist opposition would become tamed and that the Federalists "may rest easy." Though most Antifederalists accepted the Constitution as ABCD suggested they would, a very few continued to object to it in a more radical way. James Wadsworth was one of these rare figures. Connecticut law required him to swear an oath to the Constitution to retain his position as a judge. He refused, resigning his position instead. Wadsworth washed his hands of anything the new system would do, an exceedingly rare position for the Antifederalists, who gener-

ally aimed to improve the system that had been sanctioned by the states.

ABCD: FREDERICKSBURG, VIRGINIA *HERALD*

February 5, 1789

Messrs. Printers,
    Go into what company you will, the conversation is about the approaching election: some for a federal and some for an antifederal member. The federal party may rest easy, for before an antifederal member can take his seat in Congress, he will become federal, or appear so. He will be obliged to swear that he will support the constitution, as it stands: a bitter pill, but it must go down, and will set very uneasy on the stomach of a member that really goes there with a determination to alter or destroy it: and it is thought by the faculty that the amendments recommended by the state legislatures will not be an emetic powerful enough to make the swallower of this oath cast it up.

ABCD

JAMES WADSWORTH: LETTER TO GOVERNOR SAMUEL HUNTINGTON

October 15, 1789

I take this Opportunity to express my most gratefull Acknowledgements for the Honor done me by the General Assembly in May last in appointing me Judge of the Court of Common Pleas for the County of New Haven—The Confidence of the Publick, the kind Assistance of my Brethren of the Court and the Candor of my fellow Citizens are very powerfull Motives to induce me to accept the Trust—But by the new Constitution certain Qualifications are rendered necessary to the Execution of said Office which have not heretofore been required—I have made no Secret of my Sentiments touching the Constitution and its requirements and they are too well known to need any Explanation—must therefore decline taking the Oath to support the new Constitution—with the most fervent Wishes that the Rights & Privileges of Free Men may be enjoyed by the Citizens of this and the other of the United States and perpetuated to the latest Generations.

MICHAEL JENIFER STONE:
SPEECH IN THE HOUSE OF REPRESENTATIVES

February 5, 1789

The following speech helps illustrate what happened to the Antifederalists and Federalists after ratification. It was not delivered by a former Antifederalist. Michael Jenifer Stone had favored the Constitution and was elected by Marylanders to serve in the U.S. House of Representatives. But by the end of the First Congress, he and several colleagues had openly split with the other Federalists. Their contention was that the remaining Federalists were going back on their promise that the Constitution granted the national government only expressed powers. The issue under consideration in this instance was whether the national government could charter a national bank. The Constitution does not expressly authorize Congress to charter a bank. The Philadelphia convention had considered writing that power into the Constitution, but it ultimately rejected the clause. Therefore, if there were no powers but those expressed (as James Wilson had claimed—see chapter 1), the national government could not create a bank.

Some Federalists argued that the Preamble's charge to "promote the general welfare" allowed them to charter a bank, but Stone replies that if the Preamble grants powers, then the legislature is truly unlimited in its authority, exactly what the Antifederalists feared. What Stone's speech signals is a permanent break in Federalist ranks, based on two incompatible views about the Constitution. Most Federalists, led by Alexander Hamilton, hoped for an aggressive national government that would dominate the states. They proceeded to try to legislate that kind of regime into existence. Other Federalists, like Stone and James Madison, felt that they—and more important, the nation—had agreed to a government that divided sovereignty between the national government and the states. When the other Federalists acted as if the national government had any power its legislature thought necessary and proper, these "Madisonians" broke with them and joined the former Antifederalists. This division became the basis of the first party system in America. The Republican Party consisted of the former Antifederalists with "Madisonians" like Stone.

Stone addresses his speech to the Hamiltonian Federalists. His comments make him sound very much like an Antifederal-

ist, an indication that despite the change brought by the official sanctioning of the Constitution, the issue of national power was still very much alive after the Constitution was implemented. Stone's speech was printed in the Gazette of the United States *on March 26, 1791.*

Mr. Stone said: If upon questions like the present he had given pain to members he regarded, they might be assured the pain was reciprocal. Let us cherish mutual toleration. We might conceive that each pursued improper systems from the purest motives. We differ in our ideas of government and our sense of the sacredness of the written compact. We varied widely in our opinions of the direction of this government: The great lesson of experiment would show who is right; but we are influenced in our habits of thinking by our local situations, and perhaps the distinct interests of the States we represent. He observed, that upon the present occasion the opinions respecting the constitution seem to be divided by a geographical line, dividing the continent. Hence it might be inferred that other considerations mixed with the question; and it had been insinuated that it was warped by the future seat of government. But other causes may be assigned for the diversity of sentiment; the people to the eastward began earliest in favor of liberty: They pursued freedom into anarchy; starting at the precipice of confusion they are now vibrating far the other way . . . .

Never did any country more compleatly unite in any sentiment than America in this—"That Congress ought not to exercise, by implication, powers not granted by the constitution." And it is not strange—for the admission of this doctrine destroys the principle of your government at a blow—it at once breaks down every barrier which the federal constitution had raised against unlimited legislation. He said that necessity was the most plausible pretext for breaking the spirit of the social compact; but the people of this country have anticipated that pretext—They have said to the ministers of this country, "We have given you what we think competent powers; but if experience proves them inadequate, we will enlarge them—but in the mean time dare not usurp those which we have reserved."

It is agreed on all hands that the power to incorporate the subscribers to a bank is not expressly granted, and although gentlemen have agreed that it is implied—that it is an incident—that it is a means, for effectuating powers expressly granted; yet they are not agreed as to the particular power to which this is an incident. They admit that the sweeping clause in the constitution confers no additional power. But if he understood the gentlemen, several of them were of

opinion that all governments instituted for certain ends draw to them
the means of execution as of common right. This doctrine would make
our's but a short constitution. (Here he read the preamble) and then
said—Here is your constitution! Here is your bill of rights! Do these
gentlemen require any thing more respecting the powers of Congress,
than a description of the ends of government? and if of right they can
carry these into effect, will they regard the means tho they be expressly pointed out? But I would ask if there is any power under
heaven which could not be exercised within the extensive limits of
this preamble?

The convention might have stopped here—and there was no need,
according to the doctrine of the gentlemen, to point out any of the
means for the ends mentioned in the preamble. That portion of the
constitution which, by all America, has been thought so important,
according to their logic, would become a dead letter; but the preamble
in fair construction is a solemn compact, that the powers granted shall
be made use of to the ends thereby specified.

He then reprobated in pointed terms the latitude of the principles
premised. He said the end of all government is the public good—and if
the means were left to legislation, all written compacts were nugatory.
He observed, that the sober discretion of the legislature, which in the
opinions of gentlemen ought to be paramount, was the very thing intended to be curbed and restrained by our constitution.

. . . What then, said he, remains of your constitution, except its
mode of organization! . . .

. . . your constitution is turned upside down; and instead of being
a grant of particular powers, guarded by an *implied negative* to all others, it is made to *imply all powers*. But, strange to tell, America forgot
to guard it by express negative provisions. Is there any difference in effect between lodging general powers in a government, and permitting
the exercise of them by subtle constructions? He said there was a difference—In the one case, the people fairly gave up their liberty, and
stood prepared—in the other, they were unexpectedly tricked out of
their constitution.

. . . Gentlemen tell us that if we tie up the constitution too tight
it will break; if we hamper it we cannot stir; if we do not admit the
doctrine we cannot legislate at all. And with a kind of triumph they
say that implication is recognized by the constitution itself in the
clause wherein we have power to make all laws, to carry &c.[7] . . . if the
principles now advocated are right, it is the duty of the legislature of
the union to make all laws—not only those that are necessary and
proper to carry the powers of the government into effect, but all laws
which are convenient, expedient, and beneficial to the United States.

Then where is your constitution! Are we not now sitting in our sober discretion—a general government, without the semblance of restraint? Yes, said he, we have still a constitution—but where is it to be found? Is it written? No. Is it among the Archives? No. Where is it? It is found in the sober discretion of the legislature—it is registered in the brains of the majority.

ROBERT YATES: REPORT OF HIS INSTRUCTIONS TO A JURY, FROM A BIOGRAPHICAL SKETCH APPENDED TO HIS CONVENTION NOTES

1821

Robert Yates had been so disgusted by the Philadelphia convention that he walked out on it. Such disgruntled Antifederalists might not have acquiesced to the Constitution, but almost all of them did. This account of his instructions to a jury shortly after ratification shows that he not only accepted the Constitution, but he also made sure to instruct the public that they needed to accept the Constitution as well. This jury instruction was published in 1821, in a biographical sketch appended to his published convention notes (see chapter 2). Yates was one of the rare Antifederalists who found political opportunity in coming to grips with the Constitution. Federalists drafted him to oppose the nearly unbeatable "Pharaoh of New York," longtime governor George Clinton in 1788. Yates, however, lost.

His political opinions were open and unreserved—He was opposed to a consolidated national government, and friendly to a confederation of the states preserving their integrity and equality as such. Although the form of government eventually adopted, was not, in all its parts, agreeable to his views and wishes, still in all his discussions, and especially in his *judicial* capacity, he deemed it a sacred duty to inculcate entire submission to, and reverence for, that constitution—In the first charge which he delivered to a grand jury, immediately after its adoption, he used the following language: "the proposed form of government for the union has at length received the sanction of so many states as to make it the *supreme law of the land*, and it is not therefore any longer a question whether or not its provisions are such as they ought to be in all their different branches.—We, as good citizens, are bound implicitly to obey them, for the united wisdom of America has sanctioned and confirmed the act, and it would be little short of treason against the republic to hesitate in our obedience and respect to the constitution of the United States of America. Let me therefore exhort you, gentlemen, not only in your capacity as grand jurors, but in your more durable and equally respectable character as citizens, to preserve inviolate this charter of our national rights and safety, a charter second only in dignity and importance to the *declaration of our independence.* We have escaped, it is true, by the blessing of Divine Providence, from the tyranny of a *foreign* foe, but let us now be equally watchful in guarding against worse and far more dangerous enemies— *domestic broils and intestine divisions.*"

NOTES

1. *John Quincy Adams's Diary*, vol. 2, p. 357.

2. Adams Family Papers, Adams' diary entry of July 9, 1827.

3. Adams refers to his friend Nathaniel Freeman Jr., who attended the Massachusetts ratification debates with William Cranch, the recipient of this letter, and found the Federalists at them quite convincing.

4. *DHFFE*, vol. 1, p. 451.

5. The phrase "and surely Laco is an honorable man" echoes Shakespeare in *Julius Caesar*. In the play, Marc Antony eulogizes Caesar, but he uses the speech to turn public sentiment against the conspirators who slew Caesar by repeating the line "and surely Brutus is an honorable man" when it appears to the crowd that Brutus is not. Truth's barbs at Laco are less subtle than Antony's, but Antony's line was so well known that it was clear to readers that Truth was accusing Laco of treachery.

6. John Adams lived in Braintree and is the "finished politician" referred to here.

7. This is a reference to the "necessary and proper clause," Article I, section 8, clause 18.

Appendix 1:
Spurious and Satirical Materials

In politics, creativity often pays dividends. With hundreds of deadly serious essays written about the Constitution, authors who humorously skewered their opponents stood out. Since most commentaries were issued under pseudonyms, there was ample opportunity for Antifederalists to pretend to be Federalists or for Federalists to pretend to be Antifederalists. Both sides mocked their opponents while pretending to be them. Antifederalists posing as Federalists put on airs and openly admitted they disdained popular government. Federalists pretended to be unrepentent anarchists who would not abide by any government. While most readers understood these pieces as satires, others who paid only slight attention to politics were hoodwinked. Reprinted in this appendix is an example of each type of essay.

The spurious letter of James Bowdoin to James de Caledonia was written by an unknown Antifederalist. Bowdoin, the former governor of Massachusetts who had suppressed Shays' Rebellion, was known to be a Federalist. James de Caledonia was a derisive nickname for James Wilson, a Pennsylvanian who was born in Scotland. Use of the nickname immediately tipped off politically savvy readers that the piece was a satire. The letter purports to be a confidential private letter from Bowdoin. In it, he acknowledges and applauds unethical and even criminal behavior on the part of Federalists. As portrayed in the letter, the Federalists realize they would not stand a chance against the Antifederalists in an open, fair argument, so they use scurrilous tactics to make sure they will win.

The second document is a fake "Centinel" letter written by a Federalist. Centinel was the Pennsylvania Antifederalist whose writings helped define virulent Antifederalism (see chapter 5). Centinel frequently called the Federalists "well-born conspirators," and he did question the legitimacy of Pennsylvania's ratification. But he never took the position that "Centinel XV" does, that all government is unnecessary. Nor did the real Centinel ever match the Dr. Seuss–like language of Centinel XV's final paragraph. Despite their dubious connection to the true positions of those portrayed, these essays do raise serious points. The perspective of many Federalists was elitist, and this attitude deserved the public's consideration, even if raised in a satire. Antifederalists favored the rule of law, but there was good reason to wonder whether the rule of law could be ensured in a confederation.

SPURIOUS LETTER OF JAMES BOWDOIN TO JAMES DE CALEDONIA

Philadelphia Independent Gazetteer, February 27, 1788

Mr. Printer, I send you a copy of a real letter from one of the junto to the *Eastward*, to his friend in this city, that you may lay it before the public, who may from it, form some faint idea of the *juggling* carrying on by the *well born* few.

QUID[1]
February 23, 1788

Boston, February 12, 1788

To the Right Hon. James de Caledonia.

Dear Sir, I duly received yours of the 24th of January, containing very disagreeable accounts of our scheme being so ably opened up, and of the people falling off from you, &c. it made us very unhappy here; however do not despond; I am glad to find you have got your "*writing committee*," appointed, and employed: I confess what you say is just, and that there is somewhat disagreeable in writing, with the argument against you, and with able compettitors. In your two first numbers of the *Freemen and Pennsylvanian*, to be sure, you exceed yourself: But I would not advise you to continue the publication of them in the city, they will suit better for the country; ha, ha, ha: You make bold assertions; you should take care not to let it be known who the author of them is, the very name of a *lawyer* would ruin a publication in our country.[2]

Keep your committee hard at it; and fill *your weekly paper* from top to bottom: Your notion of answering your own pieces may do, if not found out. Do try by all means to regain your lost ground, leave no stone unturned; much is gained by confusing the business, and you are really a compleat *sophist*:[3] You know your reward should it succeed;

we have all agreed you shall have L.8000 per annum, with the office of Attorney General (of the union.) As to the office of Chief Justice which you wished for, it would have been yours, but, necessity obliged us to close with J—y—it was his price.[4]

I was glad to find you have stopped the publication of the debates of your convention; and that you had suited *your own* so well *to the tune*; you was very right to hold back the second volume containing the speeches of the minority, as perhaps the *real* ones might come out. But I was sorry you could not *silence the press* entirely: However as we have the P-t O—ce still at our service, you must prevent any of the newspapers which contain publications against us, getting out of your state. We have been remarkably successful in this hitherto; every newspaper against us has been stopped, even the reasons of dissent of your minority, and the information of Mr. Martin, has been scarcely heard of here; this was very fortunate, as it would certainly have ruined us in this quarter.[5] So great was the want of information here, that we made the people believe all to the southward of us, indeed that every state but our own were almost unanimous in favor of our plan. You would have laughed to have seen our newspapers on the day the final question was taken in our convention; there we published an account of the almost unanimous adoption of the constitution by the convention of North-Carolina; that the state of New-York had called a convention at a very early day, without any opposition; and the *trifling* opposition in your state had ceased; that Randolph, Mason, Lee, &c. had joined our party; and many other similar accounts.[6]

In this situation, when such a variety of circumstances concurred in our favor; although we had *juggled* in above 50 members of the convention, by the assistance of our country friends; and was so fortunate as to keep out any *Ciceros* from the opposition in the convention: Although we bought off the province of *Main* with the feather of a separate state; although we had such a number of able hands, among which were many as complete sophists as yourself; although we gained the man of the people by holding out to him the office of Vice President; although we had the influence of the town of Boston to assist us, still we would have lost the question almost two to one if we had not agreed to the amendments, which you find included in the ratification; and these not to be made by the first Congress as you proposed, but according to the 5th article, that is, by another convention.[7] This was a fatal stroke, but we could not avoid it.

You have seen with much surprise, I dare say, the great parade we made at the ratification; it cost us a considerable sum, but I am in hopes it will be of great service, these things have great effect on common minds.—You see we have the town of Boston under our discipline; I wish

I could say so of the rest of the state, indeed it is far otherwise, four fifths of the people are against us: But as you say, what need we care for the sentiments of the people, if we can only get the army a-foot.

I was happy to hear you was disarming your militia both for your own safety, and because you will want the arms for the troops; but at the same time I thought it a bold push, and might cause alarm.

I have lately received a letter from Mr. J—A—, our A—d-r at London, he is pleased with my compliment on his volume, it was, I told him of much service to us. He has endeavoured through *Bobby's* credit, to contract for the *necessaries* we wrote for; but he found it would not do: He then pledged the faith of the United States to fulfil the contracts he has made. He has also entered into other treaties for the *other articles*, which I shall be more particular about, by a safer opportunity.[8]

When these things were told to our friends here, many of them began to stare; for they consider the matter as lost since this state, which, they say, is the most important in the union, has called for amendments; the people of your state, the states of Virginia, New-York, North-Carolina, and Maryland so generally against it: to be sure, matters look blue; but I am in hopes still that our exertions will be crowned with success. You know that you or I have nothing to lose, and much to gain. Some of our milk and water friends here think we had better stop, and submit again to another convention; because, say they, we will be envolved in a civil war, if we persist; but I tell them we will not give it up while any hopes remain; as now, we are found out, we shall never be trusted in another convention; and so we shall lose every thing. But if we succeed in this plan, we shall never again be troubled with the people, never dread the event of elections; we shall enjoy our places, honors, and preferments, and leave them to our children after us. We shall be able to keep the people at a proper distance, and establish our numerous friends and relations in lucrative and substantial offices.

Present my compliments to *Bobby*, and also to *Billy* in the new big house; and tell them I congratulate them upon the prospect of all their old *continental balances* being done away; as I don't find that part of the constitution is yet discovered.[9]

You are an admirable man, the most useful in the convention; but you was rather for taking too much at one time; the *double powers* of our little sexentially elected senate; the controul over the press; the abolition of trial by jury in civil cases, and the common law proceedings; internal taxation; the pecuniary dependency of the judges, and their great powers; the standing army; the smallness of the lower house; the exclusion of rotation; and the "powers to make all laws which we may think *necessary* and *proper*." And that these *laws* and the *treaties* of the *little senate* should be the supreme law of the land, over the constitutions and laws of the several states. These would have been quite sufficient for us; with them alone we could chain down all America; we might have given up the rest to the winds: the controul over the elections; the command of the militia; the power of the senate to alter money bills; the powers of president to pardon criminals, to command in person the armies, navies, and militia, &c. and his long appointment, his right of being re-elected; omission of declarations in favor of liberty of conscience, and twenty others, which have been of great hurt to us, might have been left out. But between you and me, they will never discover some of the most exceptionable parts.[10]

I suppose you will soon hear of its adoption by *New-Hampshire*; but it will be many months before any other can come into it. Pray, inform me how Martin is going on; I hope he will be persuaded to discontinue his publications; we have sent him an offer of the office of chief justice of the federal court of his state, but I am afraid of him.[11]

We have gained much by deceiving one part of the continent, with plausible accounts from the other; pray, do not discontinue this; have you no more town or county meetings to publish? What M— says is very true; almost all of our strength lies in the trading towns; and his remark is just that they would consent to go to the devil, if they thought they could again sell as many British goods, as they formerly did.[12]

Keep up the spirits of your boys, and exert you[r]selves; I shall write you again shortly.

I am, dear sir, Your most obedient, And very humble servant,

J. B-wd-n.

SPURIOUS CENTINEL XV

Pennsylvania Mercury, February 16, 1788

Friends, Countrymen, and Fellow-Citizens! You have fought, you have bled, and you have conquered.—You have established your independence, and you ought to be free—But, behold! a set of aristocrats, demagogues, conspirators, and tyrants, have arisen up, and say you shall be governed—Is this to be endured by freemen,-men, who have lain in the open air, exposed to cold and hunger,-men who have worn out their health and constitutions in marches and counter-marches from one end of the continent to the other; and after they have attained the noble prize, for which they contended, are they to sit down tamely and be governed? What man can do as he pleases, who lives under a government?-The very end of government is to bind men down to certain rules and duties; therefore, 'tis only fit for slaves and vassals.-Every freeman ought to govern himself, and then he will be governed most to his own mind.

Thus, my friends, you see all government is tyrannical and oppressive. In the next place it is insulting: It is as much as to tell us, we know not how to take care of ourselves, and therefore should submit to be directed by others, who are appointed as guardians over so many wards. Now, of what use can our reason be to us, if after we have come (or ought to have come) to years of discretion, we are still to be led, guided, and bandied about by those who pretend to know better then we?-And, who pray are those who are to be thus led, guided, and bandied about? Why, the people!-Strange! that three millions of people should be led, guided, and bandied about by ninety or an hundred aristocratical, demagogical, tyannical conspirators!-Would it not be more according to order, propriety, and the nature of things, that the ninety or an hundred conspirators should be led, guided, and bandied about by the three millions of people?

In the third place, all government is expensive; for these ninety or an hundred conspirators will not govern us for nothing, they must be paid for it.-Think on that, my countrymen, we must not only be governed, be insulted by being governed, but we must pay these demagogues for coming from all parts of the continent, to lay their heads together how to govern us most effectually-for this, we must pay them mileage, pay them wages, fill their purses, supply their tables to keep them in idleness to riot on the fat of the land, to plot, contrive, and juggle us into good order and government. Now all this money might be saved to the public, by each man governing himself, and doing as he pleased, which by nature he has a right to do.

Oh my countrymen! my bowels yearn with affliction, when I think to what a pass we are likely to come-When I think, after all we have done and suffered for dear liberty, we must still be kept in order, and governed.-I had hoped, after our glorious struggle, this country would be an asylum for all those noble, untamed spirits, who were desirous of flying from all law, gospel, and government.-But alas! after all I have said and written, after all the inventions I have racked my brain for, and horrible descriptions I have laid before you, you are still unroused, and I have made no impression on any, except a few of those choice spirits at Carlisle.[13]-And how have these been treated by the conspirators and federalists-they have been called insurgents, rioters, and British deserters-true, many of them were deserters, and to their credit be it spoken,-they deserted from king and country, friends and relations, wives and children, to come here and be free-they expected we were to be a free people, and they have come among us to live at large, and do as they please-Think then how disappointed they must be, and how peculiarly hard their case is, either to stay here and be governed, or to return and be hanged.

Rouse then, my friends, my countrymen, my fellow-citizens!-Rouse, ye Shayites, Dayites, and Shattuckites![14]-Ye insurgents, rioters, and deserters!-Ye tories, refugees, and antifoederalists!-Rouse, and kick up a dust before it is too late!-Be not such a parcel of stupid, dunder-headed, blunder-headed, muddle-headed, puddle-headed blockheads-Such a tribe of snivelling, drivelling, sneaking, slinking, moping, poking, mumping, pitiful, pimping, pettifogging, poltrons,-such a set of nincumpoops, ninny-hammers, mushrooms, jackasses, jackanapeses, jackadandies, goosecaps, tom-noodles, yahooes, shitepokes, and p-ssab-ds-Rouse!-awaken!-rub your eyes!-Do not you see the aristocrats, monocrats, demagogues, pedagogues, gogmagogs, brobdingnags, conspirators, and foederal hobgoblins, are preparing to govern you, to enslave you, enthral you, and bemaul you.-If you submit to them, they will rob you of your liberties-they will tie you hand and foot,-they will play hob with you, play the dickens with you, and play the d-v-l with you-they will put halters round your necks, and hold your noses to the grindstone-they will purge you and bleed you, glister you and blister you, drench you and vomit you-they will tread on your toes, break your shins, dock your tails, draw your teeth, tear your hair and scratch out your eyes,-they will pull your noses, lug your ears, punch you in the guts, and kick you in the breech— ZOUNDS! will nothing rouse you!

NOTES

1. QUID has not been identified.

2. The American public had soured on lawyers already at this time. The fake Bowdoin's statement indicates that the Pennsylvanians had put together a committee of city-dwelling lawyers to write as if they were common rural folk.

3. The term "sophist" comes from ancient Greece at the time of Plato and Socrates. Sophists were teachers for hire. They were thought of negatively by many, as people who made arguments because they were paid to do so rather than out of conviction or dedication to the common good. By praising James de Caledonia as a sophist, the fake Bowdoin is saying that he is effectively convincing the public of something that is not in their interest. He is "making the

weaker argument the stronger," the same charge that was leveled against Socrates during his trial in Athens.

4. Though John Jay was appointed as the first Chief Justice, there is no evidence that this post was promised to gain his approval of the new government. On the contrary, the only one who could have promised him such a position was George Washington, a man whose scrupulously upright bearing would have prevented any such unsavory dealing.

5. Portions of the Pennsylvania minority's dissent and Luther Martin's "Genuine Information," referred to here, are printed in chapters 3 and 2, respectively.

6. These were all blatant falsehoods. At the time, the North Carolina legislature had refused to call a convention; sentiment was running high in New York against the Constitution; the petition campaign to annul the Pennsylvania convention's ratification was in full swing; and the objectors from the Philadelphia convention—Randolph, Mason and Lee—were holding firm against the document. Since news accounts written by Antifederalists were all intercepted at the post office according to this spurious account, the Federalists could get away with such misinformation.

7. Here the spurious James Bowdoin relates to James de Caledonia the pains to which Massachusetts' Federalists went to so that the Constitution could be narrowly ratified by the state convention. The "man of the people" referred to is Samuel Adams, the famed populist who had spoken out against the Constitution but eventually voted for it because his Boston constituency strongly favored it.

8. J—A— is John Adams, who had been arranging loans for the United States in Europe. "Bobby" refers to Robert Morris, one of the wealthiest men in the United States, who was superintendent of finance under the Articles of Confederation. Conditioned to think self-sufficiency was a virtue, most Americans were against the nation borrowing from other countries. Hence, word of Adams' negotiation of new loans was intended to reflect poorly on the Federalists. The final sentence implies that Adams is continuing to make financial deals with European countries, perhaps of personal benefit to these conspirators.

9. "Billy" is William Bingham, a Philadelphia merchant. He had recently moved into one of the "most luxurious and richly furnished houses in America" (*DHRC*, vol. 16, p. 242 n. 20). The "continental balances" refers to the money owed by the national government to Robert Morris and William Bingham. Like many wealthy patriots, these men had helped finance the Revolution. Though the loans had been made years before, the national government still owed them money because it could not afford to pay off its loans. The clause of the Constitution "not yet discovered" ensures these creditors that the debts were still valid, meaning that the new government would pay off the loans (Article VI, clause 1).

10. "Bowdoin" here skillfully works into his commentary a fairly comprehensive list of Antifederalist objections, presenting them as a list of items that will allow the Federalists to control American politics.

11. The reference is once again to Luther Martin, whose "Genuine Information" had just finished its run as a serialized piece.

12. The editors of the *Documentary History of the Ratification of the Constitution* speculate that M— might be George Mason.

13. A reference to the Carlisle riots, which took place in December 1787. Documents associated with the riots are contained in chapter 5.

14. Along with Daniel Shays, Luke Day, and Job Shattuck were leaders of Shays' Rebellion in Massachusetts.

Appendix 2:
Ratification Chronology

1786

September
Annapolis convention meets to promote commercial amendments; delegates meet only briefly, proposing a constitutional convention in Philadelphia in 1787.

Fall
Debt-ridden farmers in western Massachusetts disrupt foreclosure proceedings and hold county conventions to discuss their plight (Shays' Rebellion).

1787

February
Shays' Rebellion ends.

February 21
Confederation Congress calls for constitutional convention.

May 25
Constitutional convention achieves quorum and begins its business.

May 29
"Virginia Plan" introduced.

July 10
New York delegates Yates and Lansing leave Philadelphia.

July 16
Connecticut Compromise agreed to.

September 12
Committee of Style reports final draft of the Constitution.

September 17
Constitution signed by delegates at Philadelphia; transmitted to Congress.

September 28	Congress transmits Constitution to states.
October	"An Old Whig" begins his essay series, which runs through February 1788 (chapter 4).
October 5	Centinel's first letter appears in print (chapter 3).
October 18	Brutus' first essay appears in print (chapter 4).
November	The first pamphlet of "Letters from the Federal Farmer" circulates (chapter 6).
November 3	Elbridge Gerry's and George Mason's objections to the Constitution first appear in print (chapter 3).
November 8	Centinel III appears in print (chapter 5).
November 28	An Old Whig VII is issued (chapter 4).
December 6	Richard Henry Lee's letter to Edmund Randolph spelling out his objections is made public (chapter 3).
December 7	**Delaware** ratifies (30–0).
December 12	**Pennsylvania** ratifies (46–23).
December 18	**New Jersey** ratifies (39–0).
	The Pennsylvania convention's minority publishes its "Dissent" (chapter 3).
December 28	Luther Martin's first installment of "Genuine Information" is published; final installment appears February 8, 1788 (chapter 2).
December 29	**Georgia** ratifies (26–0).

1788

January 9	**Connecticut** ratifies (128–40).
January 14	Robert Yates and John Lansing's letter published (chapter 3).
January 16	Centinel XI printed (chapter 5).
January 23	"The Scourge" appears in print (chapter 5).
February 6	**Massachusetts** becomes the first state to propose recommendatory amendments as it ratifies (187–168); nine amendments proposed.
February 16	Fake "Centinel XV" printed (appendix 1).
	Republicus I printed (chapter 5).
	John Quincy Adams writes diary entry accepting the Constitution (chapter 7).
February 27	Fake letter of impostor "James Bowdoin" to James de Caledonia printed (appendix 1).
March 1	Republicus II appears in print (chapter 5).

March 24	Rhode Island holds a referendum on the Constitution. It is rejected 2,711 to 239.
April 26	**Maryland** ratifies (63–11).
May	John Francis Mercer writes to the New York and Virginia conventions (chapter 4).
	The Federal Farmer's second pamphlet circulates (chapter 6).
May 23	**South Carolina** ratifies with recommendatory amendments (149–73).
June	Melancton Smith delivers speeches in New York's state convention (chapter 4).
	William Grayson speech delivered in Virginia convention (chapter 6).
June 21	**New Hampshire becomes the ninth state to ratify** (57–47), making the Constitution the supreme law in those states that had ratified. Amendments are recommended.
June 25	**Virginia** ratifies with recommendatory amendments (89–79).
July 2	Confederation Congress passes a resolution recognizing the legality of the Constitution and organizes a committee to suggest how to implement it.
July 26	**New York** ratifies with recommendatory amendments (30–27).
July–August	North Carolina's first convention considers the Constitution (including Joseph McDowell; chapter 5).
August 2	First North Carolina convention decides not to ratify; proposes amendments.
August 5	New York convention's letter calling for a second convention printed (chapter 7).
August 15	James Hanna's letter to three fellow Bucks County Antifederalists written (chapter 7).
September 1	"Truth" appears in print (chapter 7).
September 13	Confederation Congress passes ordinance calling for first federal elections.
Fall–Winter	First federal elections held in several states.
December 8	"E" argues that those who favor amendments should be elected to Congress (chapter 7).
December 20	John Francis Mercer issues a circular letter declaring his candidacy for the House of Representatives (chapter 7).

1789

Winter	First federal elections continue.
January	Arthur Lee declares his candidacy for the House (chapter 7).
February 5	"ABCD" essay appears in print (chapter 7).
March 4	Congress scheduled to meet.
April 1	House of Representatives achieves quorum.
April 6	Quorum reached in Senate.
April 30	George Washington inaugurated president.
September 25	Congress approves twelve amendments to be sent to the states for consideration, ten of which will be ratified as the Bill of Rights.
October 2	President Washington transmits amendments to states.
October 15	James Wadsworth resigns judicial post (chapter 7).
November 21	**North Carolina**'s second convention ratifies (194–77) with proposed amendments.

1790

May 29	**Rhode Island** ratifies (34–32) with proposed amendments.

1791

February 5	Michael Jenifer Stone speech delivered in the House of Representatives (chapter 7).
December 15	**Bill of Rights ratified** by three-quarters of the states.

Appendix 3:
The Constitution
of the United States

We the People of the United States, in Order to form a more perfect Union, establish Justice, insure domestic Tranquility, provide for the common defence, promote the general Welfare, and secure the Blessings of Liberty to ourselves and our Posterity, do ordain and establish this Constitution for the United States of America.

ARTICLE I.

Section 1.

All legislative Powers herein granted shall be vested in a Congress of the United States, which shall consist of a Senate and House of Representatives.

Section 2.

Clause 1: The House of Representatives shall be composed of Members chosen every second Year by the People of the several States, and the Electors in each State shall have the Qualifications requisite for Electors of the most numerous Branch of the State Legislature.

Clause 2: No Person shall be a Representative who shall not have attained to the Age of twenty five Years, and been seven Years a Citizen of the United States, and who shall not, when elected, be an Inhabitant of that State in which he shall be chosen.

Clause 3: Representatives and direct Taxes shall be apportioned among the several States which may be included within this Union, according to their respective Numbers, which shall be determined by adding to the whole Number of free Persons, including those bound to Service for a Term of Years, and excluding Indians not taxed, three fifths of all other Persons. The actual Enumeration shall be made within three Years after the first Meeting of the Congress of the United States, and within every subsequent Term of ten Years, in such Manner as they shall by Law direct. The Number of Representatives shall not exceed one for every thirty Thousand, but each State shall have at Least one Representative; and until such enumeration shall be made, the State of New Hampshire shall be entitled to chuse three, Massachusetts eight, Rhode-Island and Providence Plantations one, Connecticut five, New-York six, New Jersey four, Pennsylvania eight, Delaware one, Maryland six, Virginia ten, North Carolina five, South Carolina five, and Georgia three.

Clause 4: When vacancies happen in the Representation from any State, the Executive Authority thereof shall issue Writs of Election to fill such Vacancies.

Clause 5: The House of Representatives shall chuse their Speaker and other Officers; and shall have the sole Power of Impeachment.

Section 3.

Clause 1: The Senate of the United States shall be composed of two Senators from each State, chosen by the Legislature thereof, for six Years; and each Senator shall have one Vote.

Clause 2: Immediately after they shall be assembled in Consequence of the first Election, they shall be divided as equally as may be into three Classes. The Seats of the Senators of the first Class shall be vacated at the Expiration of the second Year, of the second Class at the Expiration of the fourth Year, and of the third Class at the Expiration of the sixth Year, so that one third may be chosen every second Year; and if Vacancies happen by Resignation, or otherwise, during the Recess of the Legislature of any State, the Executive thereof may make temporary Appointments until the next Meeting of the Legislature, which shall then fill such Vacancies.

Clause 3: No Person shall be a Senator who shall not have attained to the Age of thirty Years, and been nine Years a Citizen of the United

States, and who shall not, when elected, be an Inhabitant of that State for which he shall be chosen.

Clause 4: The Vice President of the United States shall be President of the Senate, but shall have no Vote, unless they be equally divided.

Clause 5: The Senate shall chuse their other Officers, and also a President pro tempore, in the Absence of the Vice President, or when he shall exercise the Office of President of the United States.

Clause 6: The Senate shall have the sole Power to try all Impeachments. When sitting for that Purpose, they shall be on Oath or Affirmation. When the President of the United States is tried, the Chief Justice shall preside: And no Person shall be convicted without the Concurrence of two thirds of the Members present.

Clause 7: Judgment in Cases of Impeachment shall not extend further than to removal from Office, and disqualification to hold and enjoy any Office of honor, Trust or Profit under the United States: but the Party convicted shall nevertheless be liable and subject to Indictment, Trial, Judgment and Punishment, according to Law.

Section 4.

Clause 1: The Times, Places and Manner of holding Elections for Senators and Representatives, shall be prescribed in each State by the Legislature thereof; but the Congress may at any time by Law make or alter such Regulations, except as to the Places of chusing Senators.

Clause 2: The Congress shall assemble at least once in every Year, and such Meeting shall be on the first Monday in December, unless they shall by Law appoint a different Day.

Section 5.

Clause 1: Each House shall be the Judge of the Elections, Returns and Qualifications of its own Members, and a Majority of each shall constitute a Quorum to do Business; but a smaller Number may adjourn from day to day, and may be authorized to compel the Attendance of absent Members, in such Manner, and under such Penalties as each House may provide.

Clause 2: Each House may determine the Rules of its Proceedings, punish its Members for disorderly Behaviour, and, with the Concurrence of two thirds, expel a Member.

Clause 3: Each House shall keep a Journal of its Proceedings, and from time to time publish the same, excepting such Parts as may in their Judgment require Secrecy; and the Yeas and Nays of the Members of either House on any question shall, at the Desire of one fifth of those Present, be entered on the Journal.

Clause 4: Neither House, during the Session of Congress, shall, without the Consent of the other, adjourn for more than three days, nor to any other Place than that in which the two Houses shall be sitting.

Section 6.

Clause 1: The Senators and Representatives shall receive a Compensation for their Services, to be ascertained by Law, and paid out of the Treasury of the United States. They shall in all Cases, except Treason, Felony and Breach of the Peace, be privileged from Arrest during their Attendance at the Session of their respective Houses, and in going to and returning from the same; and for any Speech or Debate in either House, they shall not be questioned in any other Place.

Clause 2: No Senator or Representative shall, during the Time for which he was elected, be appointed to any civil Office under the Authority of the United States, which shall have been created, or the Emoluments whereof shall have been encreased during such time; and no Person holding any Office under the United States, shall be a Member of either House during his Continuance in Office.

Section 7.

Clause 1: All Bills for raising Revenue shall originate in the House of Representatives; but the Senate may propose or concur with Amendments as on other Bills.

Clause 2: Every Bill which shall have passed the House of Representatives and the Senate, shall, before it become a Law, be presented to the President of the United States; If he approve he shall sign it, but if not he shall return it, with his Objections to that House in which it shall have originated, who shall enter the Objections at large on their Journal, and proceed to reconsider it. If after such Reconsideration two thirds of that House shall agree to pass the Bill, it shall be sent, together with the Objections, to the other House, by which it shall likewise be reconsidered, and if approved by two thirds of that House, it shall become a Law. But in all such Cases the Votes of both Houses shall be determined by yeas and Nays, and the Names of the Persons voting for and against the Bill shall be entered on the Journal of each House respectively. If any Bill shall not be returned by the President within ten Days (Sundays excepted) after it shall have been presented to him, the Same shall be a Law, in like Manner as if he had signed it, unless the Congress by their Adjournment prevent its Return, in which Case it shall not be a Law.

Clause 3: Every Order, Resolution, or Vote to which the Concurrence of the Senate and House of Representatives may be necessary (except on a question of Adjournment) shall be presented to the President of the United States; and before the Same shall take Effect, shall be approved by him, or being disapproved by him, shall be repassed by two thirds of the Senate and House of Representatives, according to the Rules and Limitations prescribed in the Case of a Bill.

Section 8.

Clause 1: The Congress shall have Power To lay and collect Taxes, Duties, Imposts and Excises, to pay the Debts and provide for the common Defence and general Welfare of the United States; but all Duties, Imposts and Excises shall be uniform throughout the United States;

Clause 2: To borrow Money on the credit of the United States;

Clause 3: To regulate Commerce with foreign Nations, and among the several States, and with the Indian Tribes;

Clause 4: To establish an uniform Rule of Naturalization, and uniform Laws on the subject of Bankruptcies throughout the United States;

Clause 5: To coin Money, regulate the Value thereof, and of foreign Coin, and fix the Standard of Weights and Measures;

Clause 6: To provide for the Punishment of counterfeiting the Securities and current Coin of the United States;

Clause 7: To establish Post Offices and post Roads;

Clause 8: To promote the Progress of Science and useful Arts, by securing for limited Times to Authors and Inventors the exclusive Right to their respective Writings and Discoveries;

Clause 9: To constitute Tribunals inferior to the supreme Court;

Clause 10: To define and punish Piracies and Felonies committed on the high Seas, and Offences against the Law of Nations;

Clause 11: To declare War, grant Letters of Marque and Reprisal, and make Rules concerning Captures on Land and Water;

Clause 12: To raise and support Armies, but no Appropriation of Money to that Use shall be for a longer Term than two Years;

Clause 13: To provide and maintain a Navy;

Clause 14: To make Rules for the Government and Regulation of the land and naval Forces;

Clause 15: To provide for calling forth the Militia to execute the Laws of the Union, suppress Insurrections and repel Invasions;

Clause 16: To provide for organizing, arming, and disciplining, the Militia, and for governing such Part of them as may be employed in the Service of the United States, reserving to the States respectively, the Appointment of the Officers, and the Authority of training the Militia according to the discipline prescribed by Congress;

Clause 17: To exercise exclusive Legislation in all Cases whatsoever, over such District (not exceeding ten Miles square) as may, by Cession of particular States, and the Acceptance of Congress, become the Seat of the Government of the United States, and to exercise like Authority over all Places purchased by the Consent of the Legislature of the State in which the Same shall be, for the Erection of Forts, Magazines, Arsenals, dock-Yards, and other needful Buildings;—And

Clause 18: To make all Laws which shall be necessary and proper for carrying into Execution the foregoing Powers, and all other Powers vested by this Constitution in the Government of the United States, or in any Department or Officer thereof.

Section 9.

Clause 1: The Migration or Importation of such Persons as any of the States now existing shall think proper to admit, shall not be prohibited by the Congress prior to the Year one thousand eight hundred and eight, but a Tax or duty may be imposed on such Importation, not exceeding ten dollars for each Person.

Clause 2: The Privilege of the Writ of Habeas Corpus shall not be suspended, unless when in Cases of Rebellion or Invasion the public Safety may require it.

Clause 3: No Bill of Attainder or ex post facto Law shall be passed.

Clause 4: No Capitation, or other direct, Tax shall be laid, unless in Proportion to the Census or Enumeration herein before directed to be taken.

Clause 5: No Tax or Duty shall be laid on Articles exported from any State.

Clause 6: No Preference shall be given by any Regulation of Commerce or Revenue to the Ports of one State over those of another: nor shall Vessels bound to, or from, one State, be obliged to enter, clear, or pay Duties in another.

Clause 7: No Money shall be drawn from the Treasury, but in Consequence of Appropriations made by Law; and a regular Statement and Account of the Receipts and Expenditures of all public Money shall be published from time to time.

Clause 8: No Title of Nobility shall be granted by the United States: And no Person holding any Office of Profit or Trust under them, shall, without the Consent of the Congress, accept of any present, Emolument, Office, or Title, of any kind whatever, from any King, Prince, or foreign State.

Section 10.

Clause 1: No State shall enter into any Treaty, Alliance, or Confederation; grant Letters of Marque and Reprisal; coin Money; emit Bills of Credit; make any Thing but gold and silver Coin a Tender in Payment of Debts; pass any Bill of Attainder, ex post facto Law, or Law impairing the Obligation of Contracts, or grant any Title of Nobility.

Clause 2: No State shall, without the Consent of the Congress, lay any Imposts or Duties on Imports or Exports, except what may be absolutely necessary for executing it's inspection Laws: and the net Produce of all Duties and Imposts, laid by any State on Imports or Exports, shall be for the Use of the Treasury of the United States; and all such Laws shall be subject to the Revision and Controul of the Congress.

Clause 3: No State shall, without the Consent of Congress, lay any Duty of Tonnage, keep Troops, or Ships of War in time of Peace, enter into any Agreement or Compact with another State, or with a foreign Power, or engage in War, unless actually invaded, or in such imminent Danger as will not admit of delay.

ARTICLE II.

Section I.

Clause 1: The executive Power shall be vested in a President of the United States of America. He shall hold his Office during the Term of four Years, and, together with the Vice President, chosen for the same Term, be elected, as follows

Clause 2: Each State shall appoint, in such Manner as the Legislature thereof may direct, a Number of Electors, equal to the whole Number of Senators and Representatives to which the State may be entitled in the Congress: but no Senator or Representative, or Person holding an Office of Trust or Profit under the United States, shall be appointed an Elector.

Clause 3: The Electors shall meet in their respective States, and vote by Ballot for two Persons, of whom one at least shall not be an Inhabitant of the same State with themselves. And they shall make a List of all the Persons voted for, and of the Number of Votes for each; which List they shall sign and certify, and transmit sealed to the Seat of the Government of the United States, directed to the President of the Senate. The President of the Senate shall, in the Presence of the Senate and House of Representatives, open all the Certificates, and the Votes shall then be counted. The Person having the greatest Number of Votes shall be the President, if such Number be a Majority of the whole Number of Electors appointed; and if there be more than one who have such Majority, and have an equal Number of Votes, then the House of Representatives shall immediately chuse by Ballot one of them for President; and if no Person have a Majority, then from the five highest on the List the said House shall in like Manner chuse the President. But in chusing the President, the Votes shall be taken by States, the Representation from each State having one Vote; A quorum for this Purpose shall consist of a Member or Members from two thirds of the States, and a Majority of all the States shall be necessary to a Choice. In every Case, after the Choice of the President, the Person having the greatest Number of Votes of the Electors shall be the Vice President. But if there should remain two or more who have equal Votes, the Senate shall chuse from them by Ballot the Vice President.

Clause 4: The Congress may determine the Time of chusing the Electors, and the Day on which they shall give their Votes; which Day shall be the same throughout the United States.

Clause 5: No Person except a natural born Citizen, or a Citizen of the United States, at the time of the Adoption of this Constitution, shall be eligible to the Office of President; neither shall any Person be eligible to that Office who shall not have attained to the Age of thirty five Years, and been fourteen Years a Resident within the United States.

Clause 6: In Case of the Removal of the President from Office, or of his Death, Resignation, or Inability to discharge the Powers and Duties of the said Office, the Same shall devolve on the Vice President, and the Congress may by Law provide for the Case of Removal, Death, Resignation or Inability, both of the President and Vice President, declaring what Officer shall then act as President, and such Officer shall act accordingly, until the Disability be removed, or a President shall be elected.

Clause 7: The President shall, at stated Times, receive for his Services, a Compensation, which shall neither be encreased nor diminished during the Period for which he shall have been elected, and he shall not receive within that Period any other Emolument from the United States, or any of them.

Clause 8: Before he enter on the Execution of his Office, he shall take the following Oath or Affirmation:—"I do solemnly swear (or affirm) that I will faithfully execute the Office of President of the United States, and will to the best of my Ability, preserve, protect and defend the Constitution of the United States."

Section 2.

Clause 1: The President shall be Commander in Chief of the Army and Navy of the United States, and of the Militia of the several States, when called into the actual Service of the United States; he may require the Opinion, in writing, of the principal Officer in each of the executive Departments, upon any Subject relating to the Duties of their respective Offices, and he shall have Power to grant Reprieves and Pardons for Offences against the United States, except in Cases of Impeachment.

Clause 2: He shall have Power, by and with the Advice and Consent of the Senate, to make Treaties, provided two thirds of the Senators present concur; and he shall nominate, and by and with the Advice and Consent of the Senate, shall appoint Ambassadors, other public Ministers and Consuls, Judges of the supreme Court, and all other Officers of the United States, whose Appointments are not herein otherwise provided for, and which shall be established by Law: but the Congress may by Law vest the Appointment of such inferior Officers, as they think proper, in the President alone, in the Courts of Law, or in the Heads of Departments.

Clause 3: The President shall have Power to fill up all Vacancies that may happen during the Recess of the Senate, by granting Commissions which shall expire at the End of their next Session.

Section 3.

He shall from time to time give to the Congress Information of the State of the Union, and recommend to their Consideration such Measures as he shall judge necessary and expedient; he may, on extraordinary Occasions, convene both Houses, or either of them, and in Case of Disagreement between them, with Respect to the Time of Adjournment, he may adjourn them to such Time as he shall think proper; he shall receive Ambassadors and other public Ministers; he shall take Care that the Laws be faithfully executed, and shall Commission all the Officers of the United States.

Section 4.

The President, Vice President and all civil Officers of the United States, shall be removed from Office on Impeachment for, and Conviction of, Treason, Bribery, or other high Crimes and Misdemeanors.

ARTICLE III.

Section 1.

The judicial Power of the United States, shall be vested in one supreme Court, and in such inferior Courts as the Congress may from time to time ordain and establish. The Judges, both of the supreme and inferior Courts, shall hold their Offices during good Behaviour, and shall, at stated Times, receive for their Services, a Compensation, which shall not be diminished during their Continuance in Office.

Section 2.

Clause 1: The judicial Power shall extend to all Cases, in Law and Equity, arising under this Constitution, the Laws of the United States, and Treaties made, or which shall be made, under their Authority;—to all Cases affecting Ambassadors, other public Ministers and Consuls;—to all Cases of admiralty and maritime Jurisdiction;—to Controversies to which the United States shall be a Party;—to Controversies between two or more States;—between a State and Citizens of another State; —between Citizens of different States, —between Citizens of the same State claiming Lands under Grants of different States, and between a State, or the Citizens thereof, and foreign States, Citizens or Subjects.

Clause 2: In all Cases affecting Ambassadors, other public Ministers and Consuls, and those in which a State shall be Party, the supreme Court shall have original Jurisdiction. In all the other Cases before mentioned, the supreme Court shall have appellate Jurisdiction, both as to Law and Fact, with such Exceptions, and under such Regulations as the Congress shall make.

Clause 3: The Trial of all Crimes, except in Cases of Impeachment, shall be by Jury; and such Trial shall be held in the State where the said Crimes shall have been committed; but when not committed within any State, the Trial shall be at such Place or Places as the Congress may by Law have directed.

Section 3.

Clause 1: Treason against the United States, shall consist only in levying War against them, or in adhering to their Enemies, giving them Aid and Comfort. No Person shall be convicted of Treason unless on the

Testimony of two Witnesses to the same overt Act, or on Confession in open Court.

Clause 2: The Congress shall have Power to declare the Punishment of Treason, but no Attainder of Treason shall work Corruption of Blood, or Forfeiture except during the Life of the Person attainted.

ARTICLE IV.

Section 1.

Full Faith and Credit shall be given in each State to the public Acts, Records, and judicial Proceedings of every other State. And the Congress may by general Laws prescribe the Manner in which such Acts, Records and Proceedings shall be proved, and the Effect thereof.

Section 2.

Clause 1: The Citizens of each State shall be entitled to all Privileges and Immunities of Citizens in the several States.

Clause 2: A Person charged in any State with Treason, Felony, or other Crime, who shall flee from Justice, and be found in another State, shall on Demand of the executive Authority of the State from which he fled, be delivered up, to be removed to the State having Jurisdiction of the Crime.

Clause 3: No Person held to Service or Labour in one State, under the Laws thereof, escaping into another, shall, in Consequence of any Law or Regulation therein, be discharged from such Service or Labour, but shall be delivered up on Claim of the Party to whom such Service or Labour may be due.

Section 3.

Clause 1: New States may be admitted by the Congress into this Union; but no new State shall be formed or erected within the Jurisdiction of any other State; nor any State be formed by the Junction of two or more States, or Parts of States, without the Consent of the Legislatures of the States concerned as well as of the Congress.

Clause 2: The Congress shall have Power to dispose of and make all needful Rules and Regulations respecting the Territory or other Property belonging to the United States; and nothing in this Constitution shall be so construed as to Prejudice any Claims of the United States, or of any particular State.

Section 4.

The United States shall guarantee to every State in this Union a Republican Form of Government, and shall protect each of them against Invasion; and on Application of the Legislature, or of the Executive (when the Legislature cannot be convened) against domestic Violence.

ARTICLE V.

The Congress, whenever two thirds of both Houses shall deem it necessary, shall propose Amendments to this Constitution, or, on the Application of the Legislatures of two thirds of the several States, shall call a Convention for proposing Amendments, which, in either Case, shall be valid to all Intents and Purposes, as Part of this Constitution, when ratified by the Legislatures of three fourths of the several States, or by Conventions in three fourths thereof, as the one or the other Mode of Ratification may be proposed by the Congress; Provided that no Amendment which may be made prior to the Year One thousand eight hundred and eight shall in any Manner affect the first and fourth Clauses in the Ninth Section of the first Article; and that no State, without its Consent, shall be deprived of its equal Suffrage in the Senate.

ARTICLE VI.

Clause 1: All Debts contracted and Engagements entered into, before the Adoption of this Constitution, shall be as valid against the United States under this Constitution, as under the Confederation.

Clause 2: This Constitution, and the Laws of the United States which shall be made in Pursuance thereof; and all Treaties made, or which shall be made, under the Authority of the United States, shall be the supreme Law of the Land; and the Judges in every State shall be bound thereby, any Thing in the Constitution or Laws of any State to the Contrary notwithstanding.

Clause 3: The Senators and Representatives before mentioned, and the Members of the several State Legislatures, and all executive and judicial

Officers, both of the United States and of the several States, shall be bound by Oath or Affirmation, to support this Constitution; but no religious Test shall ever be required as a Qualification to any Office or public Trust under the United States.

ARTICLE VII.

The Ratification of the Conventions of nine States, shall be sufficient for the Establishment of this Constitution between the States so ratifying the Same.

Done in Convention by the Unanimous Consent of the States present the Seventeenth Day of September in the Year of our Lord one thousand seven hundred and Eighty seven and of the Independence of the United States of America the Twelfth. In witness whereof We have hereunto subscribed our Names,

[The document is signed by George Washington, the president of the convention and the deputies of the twelve states present.]

References

Anderson, Thornton. *Creating the Constitution*. University Park, PA: Pennsylvania State University Press, 1993.

Banning, Lance. "Republican Ideology and the Triumph of the Constitution, 1789–1793." *The William & Mary Quarterly*, 3rd ser., 31 (April 1974): 167–88.

Beccaria, Cesare. *On Crimes and Punishments*. 1763. Reprint. New York: Macmillan Publishing Company, 1963.

Beeman, Richard, Stephen Botein, and Edward C. Carter II, eds. *Beyond Confederation*. Chapel Hill: University of North Carolina Press, 1987.

Bickford, Charlene Bangs, et al., eds. *The Documentary History of the First Federal Congress, 1789–1791 (DHFFE)*. 14 vols. Baltimore: The Johns Hopkins University Press, 1972–.

Brooks, Robin. "Alexander Hamilton, Melancton Smith, and the Ratification of the Constitution in New York." *The William & Mary Quarterly*, 3rd ser., 24 (July 1967): 339–58.

Burke, Edmund. *Reflections on the Revolution in France*. 1790. Reprint. Indianapolis, IN: Hackett Publishing, 1987.

Committee on Political Parties of the American Political Science Association. "Toward a More Responsible Two-Party System." *American Political Science Review* 44 (September 1950).

Conley, Patrick T., and John P. Kaminski, eds. *The Constitution and the States*. Madison, WI: Madison House, 1988.

Cornell, Saul. "The Changing Historical Fortunes of the Anti-Federalists." *Northwestern University Law Review* 84 (Fall 1990): 39–73.

———. *The Other Founders*. Chapel Hill: University of North Carolina Press, 1999.

Dahl, Robert A. *Democracy and Its Critics*. New Haven, CT: Yale University Press, 1989.

De Lolme, Jean Louis. *The Constitution of England*. 1771. Reprint. London: Baldwin & Co, 1817.

Elkins, Stanley, and Eric McKitrick. *The Age of Federalism*. Oxford: Oxford University Press, 1993.

Elliot, Jonathan. *Debates on the Adoption of the Federal Constitution*. 5 vols. Philadelphia: J. B. Lippincott Company, 1836–1845.

Farrand, Max, ed. *The Records of the Federal Convention of 1787*. 4 vols. 1911. Reprint, New Haven, CT: Yale University Press, 1966.

Fiorina, Morris P. "The Decline of Collective Responsibility in American Politics." *Daedalus* 109 (Summer 1980): 25–45.

Fitzpatrick, John C., ed. *The Writings of George Washington*. 39 vols. Washington, D.C.: United States Government Printing Office, 1932.

Hamilton, Alexander, James Madison, and John Jay. *The Federalist*. 1787–1788. Reprint, ed. Jacob E.Cooke. Cleveland, OH: World Publishing, 1961.

Hobbes, Thomas. *Leviathan*. 1651. Reprint. London: Penguin Books, 1985.

Jensen, Merrill, et al., eds. *The Documentary History of the Ratification of the Constitution (DHRC)*. 22 vols., plus microfiche supplements. Madison, WI: The State Historical Society of Wisconsin, 1976–.

Kaminski, John P. "Political Sacrifice and Demise: John Collins and Jonathan J. Hazard, 1786–1790." *Rhode Island History* 42 (February 1976): 30–37.

Kenyon, Cecelia. "Men of Little Faith: The Anti-Federalists on the Nature of Representative Government." *The William & Mary Quarterly*, 3rd ser., 12 (January 1955): 3–43.

Libby, Orrin G. *The Geographical Distribution of the Vote of the Thirteen States on the Federal Constitution*. 1894. Reprint. New York: B. Franklin, 1969.

Lienesch, Michael. "In Defense of the Anti-federalists." *History of Political Thought* 4 (Spring 1983): 65–87.

Locke, John. *The Second Treatise on Civil Government*. 1690. Reprint. Buffalo, NY: Prometheus Books, 1986.

Main, Jackson Turner. *The Antifederalists*. Chapel Hill: University of North Carolina Press, 1961.

Montesquieu, Baron de. *The Spirit of the Laws*. 1748. Reprint. Cambridge: Cambridge University Press, 1989.

Read, James H. *Power versus Liberty*. Charlottesville: University of Virginia Press, 2000.

Siemers, David J. "'It Is Natural to Care for the Crazy Machine': The Antifederalists' Post-Ratification Acquiescence." *Studies in American Political Development* 12 (Summer 1998): 383–410.

———. *Ratifying the Republic: Antifederalists and Federalists in Constitutional Time*. Stanford, CA: Stanford University Press, 2002.

Storing, Herbert. *The Complete Antifederalist*. 7 vols. Chicago: The University of Chicago Press, 1981.

Sundquist, James L. *Constitutional Reform and Effective Government*. Washington, D.C.: Brookings, 1986.

Tocqueville, Alexis de. *Democracy in America*. 1835. Reprint, ed. Richard D. Heffner. New York: Mentor, 1956.

Warren, Mercy Otis. *History of the Rise, Progress and Termination of the American Revolution*. 1805. Reprint. Indianapolis, IN: Liberty Classics, 1988.

Webking, Robert H. "Melancton Smith and the Letters from the Federal Farmer." *The William & Mary Quarterly*, 3rd ser., 44, no. 3 (1987): 510–28.

Wilson, Woodrow. *Congressional Governmment*. 1885. Reprint. Cleveland, OH: World Publishing, 1969.

Wollstonecraft, Mary. *A Vindication of the Rights of Woman*. 1792. Reprint. London: Penguin Books, 1992.

Index

About the Author

David J. Siemers is an assistant professor of political science at the University of Wisconsin, Oshkosh. His first book, *Ratifying the Republic* (Stanford University Press, 2002), explains how the Antifederalists came to grips with the Constitution, allowing it to move from a highly divisive proposal to a consensually legitimate structure for governance. Siemers' primary research interest lies in discerning how practical politics is influenced by—and in turn alters—political theory. He is currently studying how presidents have dealt with political thought. Siemers received his Ph.D. at the University of Wisconsin, Madison and has previously taught at Bradley University, Wellesley College, and Colorado College.